Strangers to the Blood

Jean DeMartino

Copyright © 1994 by Nick DeMartino and Jean DeMartino
All rights reserved. Printed in the United States of America.
No part of this book may be used or reproduced without written consent except in the case of brief quotations.

K0 scanning, uploading, and distribution of this book via the Internet or via any other means without the permission of the author's representatives is illegal and punishable by law.
Please purchase only authorized electronic editions, and do not participate in or encourage electronic piracy of copyrighted materials. Your support of the author's rights is appreciated.
Copyright © 1994 by Nick DeMartino and Jean DeMartino All rights reserved.

edited by
Henry Greenfield

Reprinted by First Champvert Press, 9016 SW 215 Terrace, Cutler Bay, Florida 33189, greenfie@hotmail.com

ISBN 1479321524

Second Edition
2012

Preface

The story you are about to read is true. It is a love story. It is a story about devotion to principle. It is a story about dedication to duty and an abiding belief in God. It is mostly about family.

It has a happy ending. It has a sad epilogue. Like all stories you will find yourself and your family in it. The author lived the story. She was extremely sensitive and intelligent. She was devoted to children's causes and spent a great deal of her life working for the *little people* as she fondly called them. She believed in the preservation of the family unit as the bulwark of any society. She was diligent in anything she ever did but even more so when confronted with the possible destruction of her family.

The possible loss of Lenore was horrifying. It would affect not only Lenore but also her sister Linda, relatives, friends and the law. Jean DeMartino was not a lawyer but understood the system with all its uncertainties as few lawyers did.

It is said that *hell hath no fury like a woman scorned.* I believe that to be incorrect. *Hell hath no fury like a woman* [whose child or family is threatened]. Jean tackled everything head on without flinching. You may not agree with all of her ideas or even what she did. But you will respect her tenacity and strength and devotion to family.

I hope that this book will move you to take action toward exposing laws governing adoption that should be questioned closely. In the meantime you might contact your local politicians, become involved in organizations (adoption and otherwise) and help me preach the doctrine of the *best interests of the child* in any custody or adoption matter. Courts in most states follow the *best interests of a child.* Some judges do, some pit the biological parent against the adoptive parents, some favor the blood line. There are inequities on all sides of the triad but obligation to only one—the child.

These children of God have no say in their birth or adoption. They are surrendered and reclaimed like chattel or fought over like property. Why is this case more than forty years old still poignant and up to date? Little has changed. In fact, there are more miscarriages of justice against children than ever before. Many results become tragedies as these children mature.

May God direct us in our actions regarding the *little people*. Jean was a noble woman in thoughts and deeds. Unfortunately, she lived in an unstable world. Was she perfect? No! But she was ten times the person I am and ever will be. I was her hero, she once said, but I am unworthy of her praise.

Nick DeMartino

For many years, I avoided writing about this subject. My family and I were content to blend into the main stream and become anonymous. The few years of notoriety we experienced seemed enough for a lifetime. Every time our name turned up in connection with an adoption case or a similar circumstance, it triggered a response—one of fear—that perhaps our world might become uncertain once again. But, a little voice gnawed away at my sense of justice. I greeted it with panic and did all in my power to maintain namelessness. Even as I write, I do so with great trepidation but am convinced that the story must be told. Perhaps my conscience is jostled by the needs of others, or I am merely spurred on by my own selfish need *not to live in vain*. I would like to think, however, that my desire is to see in the eyes of other children what I managed to see in the eyes of my own—security, confidence, and love.

Jean DeMartino

Miami Herald 1976 — "Prominent Miami appellate lawyer Robert Orseck died Friday while vacationing in Israel with his family.

He was swimming in the Mediterranean waters off the coast of Tel Aviv when he was caught in a strong undertow and drowned.

Reached in Tel Aviv early today, his childhood friend and law partner Aaron Podhurst said Orseck was trying to help some children who had gone out too deep when he drowned.

"Orseck, 44, was considered one of Miami's outstanding appellate lawyers. 'He had more impact on civil law in Florida, just through his brilliance in appellate work, than any lawyer I've known in the past twenty years or so,' Lawyer James Dixon said."

I DEDICATE THIS BOOK TO MY FRIEND, ROBERT ORSECK, A *MENSCH* WHO DIED AS HE LIVED—HELPING THE LITTLE PEOPLE OF THIS WORLD.

LENORE

A daughter
    So different, So beautiful,
    So gentle—and yet so quick to ignite
    A flame that glows intensely for the moment and then fades away into gentleness…
    A looseness of person and spirit which
    feeds off the precision and stability of others and yet changes its shape effortlessly to fit into the happenings of life.
    A challenge,
    A frustration,
    A quiet catalyst bringing out the best in
    me,
A mother . . .

Written for Lenore as she approached her 15th Birthday

Introduction by Nick DeMartino

In 1953, I met Jean Martino who became Jean DeMartino. It was truly love at first sight. We met at freshman orientation at what was then known as College of the City of New York located in upper Manhattan. She was all that any man could ever wish for. She was beautiful, intelligent, kind, giving, loving, and generous.

After a first date, we agreed not to see anyone else and then three years later on January 21, 1956, we were married. She left school to support us. She put me through the remainder of my college years and supported me through three years of Law School and three years thereafter when I made very little as a young lawyer.

She loved me unconditionally and backed me in all that I ever did (and I did some crazy things.) When I started to become successful, she still lived in the time when we pooled our pennies for a subway token to get to work.

In her memory, I dedicate the rest of my life to helping children because that was her life's ambition. She gave of herself unselfishly and was always conscientious in anything she ever did.

Nothing worthwhile is ever successful without the help and dedication of many people. I would like to say a special thanks to my wonderful aides Barbara Coto and Cristina Borges for the time they put into typing, checking, editing, and working on this book all above and beyond the call of duty and never once complaining. Thanks to Claudia Ortega for putting all the pieces together. It couldn't have been done without her.

I could not go any further without thanking Jacob Fuchsberg for his masterful handling of our case through all the New York courts and on to the Supreme Court of the United States, and Bill Colson for his untiring and diligent efforts toward seeing our case successfully through all the courts in Florida and on to the Supreme Court of the United States. Marty McLaughlin, a *New York Daily News* writer, broke the story and followed through until it's conclusion. The Committee To Help Save Baby Lenore and especially Barry Tash, John Farro, and Lenny Chaimowitz (may he rest in peace) and the thousands of New Yorkers and Floridians whose work and prayers got us through a difficult time.

More than 100,000 people signed the petitions to help save Baby Lenore. Joseph Spencer started us on our long road. Jacob Fuchsberg was a dynamic and conscientious trial lawyer. Bill Colson handled his end as if Lenore was his child. The Committee to Help Save Baby Lenore and in particular John Farro, Barry Tash, and a host of others worked endlessly. Judge Ralph O. Cullen let us be persons in a court and recognized the best interests of a child. He did not pay lip service to that very important requirement of the law as regards the child's welfare.

Chapter I

We struggled for custody of our baby Lenore and for our day in court. Nick, my husband, and I went through all the New York courts, the Federal District Court, and to the United States Supreme Court. We then left New York for Miami where we went through all the courts in Florida. And once again to the Supreme Court of the United States.

Where do I begin? It was the week before Thanksgiving. Linda, my four-year-old, was so excited because of *Turkey Day* as she called it. She loved to have our family over for dinner. She seemed to talk about nothing else.

I also caught the holiday spirit. Traditionally, we spent Thanksgiving with my parents or Nick's. This year, it was our turn to have everyone at our home for dinner. We had much to be grateful for. We were happy and healthy. In fact, I just took Lenore, our five-month-old, for her checkup to Dr. Libo, our pediatrician. Aside from awaiting the results of a urine test, he gave her a clean bill of health.

The day began as usual. I took Linda to morning nursery school around the corner. It was quite cold for November. I remember bundling both girls and literally running with Lenore in my arms to school and back. Lenore's cheeks were like two red apples. I put her in her crib for a nap and immediately tidied up the house. I wanted time to make a Thanksgiving menu and shopping list and hoped to complete everything by lunchtime because I promised Linda that right after lunch we would go shopping for fur-lined boots. Just as I added a last item to my list, Lenore woke up, and we hustled to pick up her sister.

Linda, at age four, was particularly mature and verbal. Family members told her she was, "Four years old going on forty." Today she wrapped herself in the purchase of *Go-Go* boots and talked about them all through lunch: what color they would be, and what I thought they should look like, and whether people would know they were *Go-Go* boots. As I fed Lenore, she picked up on the excitement and gurgled and made a real mess of herself.

The phone rang. Nick usually called knowing the baby was awake. It turned out, however, to be an old friend. She, like many of my co-workers, was shocked by the announcement that I'd walk away from a substantial salary as a head hunter to stay home and raise a family. Now and then, she checked on my status and seemed continuously astounded with my contentment. I kept the conversation brief because I expected a call.

Nick has acted rather strange and edgy for the past week. I sensed a strain whenever we spoke. We argued the week before. It's strange how I have near total recall of the two-year period of courts, judges, lawyers, reporters, photographers, and emotional upheaval but can't, for the life of me, remember if we argued about in-law insults, a man who danced with me provocatively, a woman Nick paid undue attention to, or an important task he neglected.

He had worked late and came home about 9:00 p.m. that November with news planned by the devil to mock lives. The girls were asleep. I see us in the living room, me on the landing, and Nick, two steps above. He still wore his overcoat and held a plastic case in his hand. As we argued, our voices rose. Thank God both girls slept soundly. Ultimately, we screamed in chorus, neither hearing what the other said. It was then that he raised his hand, and cracked the plastic case against the wall just missing my face; I was shocked. I married Nick fifteen years ago. He was big and strong and very Italian about his masculinity, but I knew him as slow to anger and avoiding arguments at any cost. Oh, we had our differences, but Nick never became physical and was always ready for a fast make up and a, "Let's forget about it. Italians make love not war," he would say.

On the night of nightmares, I saw the blood drain from his face, and he appeared as though tears were in his eyes. "What is wrong with you?" I demanded.

"Nothing," he said, turning his back and dragging himself up the stairs. I sat on the lower step, trembling.

A short time later, Nick apologized. "I don't know what came over me," he said. "I'm caught up in a trial and guess the pressure is really getting to me. I'm so sorry, honey." He put his arms around me. We hugged, and he couldn't have been more concerned or attentive, but my mind still envisioned the crash and my heart felt the hurt. In the days to follow, his mind wandered at times, and I thought, there he goes to the courtroom again.

Today, however, I awaited his homecoming wrapped in warm thoughts about Thanksgiving. I hoped that Nick felt less pressure and that I could count on his old self again.

"Mommy, are we ready to go? Should I put my coat on? Is Lenore ready? Can we go now? I want to go for the boots, mommy, please."

Just as Linda reached the top of the stairs, I

heard the front door open, ran into the living room, and came face to face with Nick. He appeared ashen. His whole body drooped. I felt a sense of panic. Something was terribly wrong. He fell onto the couch, threw his head back, and rubbed his forehead as though he had an intense headache. I asked if he wanted some aspirin.

"I came home—because—because I need to tell you something, and it's not easy."

"Did something go wrong with the trial?"

"It's—it's—Lenore," he said almost inaudibly.

My mind raced to the visit with our pediatrician. "Oh, no, Nick. Did Dr. Libo call. What in God's name did the test show? Why didn't Libo call me?"

"Lenore is fine. It's her bio-mother—"

I sighed with relief. "Lenore's bio-mother? Is she ill? Has she died? What about her?"

"The adoption agency told me she wants Lenore back."

My ears heard. My maternal mind became deaf. A loud protest paralyzed my throat making an outburst impossible. Anything is a thousand times easier to take than our baby ripped from our home, our family, from the only mother Lenore's known. "That's impossible!" I gasped. If I grabbed my baby, where would we run, where would we hide? "They gave us a 'Baby Scarpetta' taken from a foster home—an anonymous, rejected child—and gave her to loving parents," I bellowed, "and now they ask us to return our Lenore?"

"Jean, honey, easy. Easy. The agency is not asking us to—"

"Mommy, why are you yelling?" Linda called from upstairs.

"It's okay, baby. I'm sorry." Tongue lashing the man I loved, firing at Nick whose message struck his heart just as deeply as mine, wouldn't end the white hot fear and outrage rising from my core. I breathed deeply. Lenore whimpered from my tense response through clenched teeth. "The woman signed legal documents, Nick, and gave our Lenore up voluntarily. Can someone just turn lives upside-down on a whim?"

"Mommy, is that daddy I hear?"

"Yes, Linda."

"Did you tell him about the *Go-Go* boots?"

"Yes, I did," I answered, straining to sound calm.

"Mommy, you sound funny."

"I'm okay, baby. Why don't you watch TV while you're waiting?"

"Please hurry. Daddy, are you going with us?"

I looked at my little Lenore in her playpen. She stopped munching her rubber toy just and gave us her broad, crooked smile which somehow always managed to make my heart leap. I felt the urge to pick her up and hold her close but instead turned to Nick. I felt nervous. My hands shook. My legs felt rubbery. Shivers started unexpectedly. I didn't want to hear any more but somehow knew there was more upsetting news. "Does she know that Lenore is already a part of our family?" My voice shuddered.

"Yes, she does."

"Did she realize what she was doing when she placed Lenore for adoption?"

"Yes"

"Was she pressured or intimidated by the agency?"

"No, there's no doubt, but she changed her mind."

"Changed her mind? We went to an agency to protect us from this happening. The time to change her mind was when the baby was with her foster mother during the first month, not now when Lenore's become a part of us. Maybe she just needs assurance that Lenore's with a loving family and doing fine."

"No, Jean, she wants her back."

I started to pace. It was what I did when I became nervous and upset. "This whole thing is absurd," I said angrily. "A human being can't be treated like a piece of furniture that you use and then return. She's our daughter in every sense of that word." As I spoke, my voice cracked, and I could no longer hold back. "We're the ones who walked the floors with her. We know her every whimper, and we sense her every need. We can't return her. Surely the agency must know that."

"The bio-mother," Nick continued, "called the agency. She said that she made a mistake. The agency told her that the baby was already placed for adoption so they could do nothing for her. But, she didn't stop there. The woman took the agency to court. I've called the agency's attorneys every day. Today, the judge finally made his decision. Lenore must be returned to her bio-mother."

The full realization of what Nick said finally hit me. The room spun. My stomach felt as though someone grabbed a handful of it from the inside and pulled tighter and tighter. I fell like a lump on the couch, sobbing and moaning. Nick cradled me. "Nick. Tell me it's not true."

Linda called again. I don't know exactly what she said, but I know Nick suggested something to keep her occupied upstairs for a while longer.

"Nick, how could a trial take place without us? When did you find out?"

"Mrs. Bynum from the agency called my office about 6:00 p.m. the night before the trial. She told me that the agency's Board of Directors took a vote and decided to let me know that Lenore's bio-mother petitioned the court to revoke her surrender. I was shook up, but there wasn't a hell of a lot to do or say. They assured me of competent lawyers, and the trial revolved around the surrender documents which were all obtained legally and with every consideration for the bio-mother. It was their suggestion that I not tell and worry you unnecessarily. They felt if you knew, you'd distance yourself from Lenore. God knows the stress I've felt keeping this secret. But, I did.

"As the agency anticipated, the hearing was short. Only the bio-mother and the agency were present. Since all parties agreed that the surrender was legal and without pressure, the agency attorneys assumed the ruling would be quick. However, it dragged on for weeks. I called the agency's lawyers every day. With each day that passed, I became more and more uneasy. Maybe this wasn't quite the open-and-shut case they led me to believe. In the beginning, I expected them to say the nightmare was over and everything was okay, but as time dragged on, I became edgy. The agency's lawyers were as surprised as I that the litigation took so long, but they advised not to worry. 'Think, Mr. DeMartino. How can a judge overturn a bonafide surrender to an adoption agency, a surrender, which by the young lady's own admission, was voluntary and without coercion?' Well, I called the law firm from the courthouse today. I spoke to Roy Reardon, the attorney in charge, and he said, "I've got bad news."

We both turned to Linda standing on the bottom of the stairs. "Sesame Street is over. Can we go for my boots now?"

"I don't know Linda if—"

I interrupted. "Linda, why don't you wait outside for mommy and daddy?"

"But mommy, it's cold."

"Go call on Sally Ann then, and play with her until we are ready." I put on Linda's coat and carried her to the door. She hummed as I kissed her cheek.

"Mommy, you said after lunch."

"Do as I tell you," I snapped and put her down.

"Yes, mommy," she said grudgingly and walked outside.

Nick went on. "Reardon said he believed the judge acted on emotion rather than law, not taking into consideration that his decision could throw the entire adoption process into chaos. No future adoptions could ever be secure if biological mothers get children returned by merely stating that they changed their minds. After reading the written opinion, Reardon felt that the judge acted more like a father giving his wayward daughter a second chance than a judge weighing the long term results of revoking a legal surrender."

"Oh, God, Nick, no wonder you were not yourself! How can we live through this? I won't return Lenore. We won't. You're a prominent attorney. Stop this legal disaster, this unjust, ludicrous court from taking our baby. How can we live knowing we won't be there for our baby?"

"We've got hope, Jean. The agency asked Reardon to appeal the case, and they were granted that Lenore stay with us until the higher court decides."

"She'll be with us on borrowed time? That's just great!" I got to my feet and started pacing again. "Mrs. DeMartino," I said harshly, "remember that child we gave you to love and call your own? Well, she can stay a while longer until it's decided whether she should be taken away. Go ahead, Nick, preach about doing everything within the letter of the law." I knocked a glass knickknack off the coffee table, and it smashed on the floor. Lenore cried. I took her in my arms and rocked her gently. I sang, "Mommy's going to buy you a diamond ring." She found peace quickly and the crooked smile returned as she said, "Mommy." With her rubber bunny in hand, she went back to the curious world of her playpen.

Nick held his face in his hands. "Don't try to take shortcuts in life," I began. "Do things the right way and you'll have no surprises facing your tomorrows." Nick's silence registered helplessness so I mouthed off more, "It's a nightmare! I can't believe any of this is really happening." My anger turned into tears as I fell into Nick's arms and remained for, I don't know how long. Where had we gone wrong? We went to a respected agency and waited two years for our little daughter. We brought her into our home and our hearts, holding nothing back, trusting in the mutual love that grew. All the time experiencing the false security of doing things the so-called *right way,* and now, five months after Lenore arrived, we were expected to remain silent and wait for some detached strangers to decide the fate of our family.

Nick whispered some words of comfort, but I was in another world. Suddenly, I thought of Linda outside. "Nick, Linda waited anxiously all morning to buy boots. I promised. Let's make the store now."

Nick knew I wasn't up to it, but he also knew how I felt about keeping promises, so I dressed Lenore and the four of us headed for the shoe store. We were silent all the way with the exception of Linda, who exuberantly talked about the boots. My mind went over the things I just heard. I tried to put the pieces together.

Somehow, we got boots and headed back home. I called my next door neighbor and asked if Linda could play with Mary. When she agreed, relief came over me. There was still so much I wanted to know, but I didn't want Linda to hear.

"Nick, how long will the appeal take?"

"Reardon said we'll have a decision between five and seven weeks."

"Oh, God! What are our chances?"

"They felt certain that the lower court decision will be reversed."

"Will we be asked to appear?"

"The law firm is a respected one. I believe they know what they're doing. The case will go before the appellate court which only rules on the case as presented in the lower court. No new evidence is heard. No new witnesses are called. There are five judges who hear oral arguments from the attorneys for each side, and then they make a ruling. Reardon said that this time he'd keep us appraised of all the happenings, and since I'm an attorney, I'm permitted to read the legal documents as they prepare them. Of course, Jean, their specialty is corporate law and mine is negligence. I'd be more comfortable with an experienced custody lawyer."

I started to cry. With me in his arms, Nick whispered, "You can't loose control. Care about yourself so you can care about the children. Lenore and Linda need you, and you can't snap at Linda and get rid of her. She'll sense something is wrong."

I wanted to lash back verbally for his bookish lessons to an emotional wife, but I didn't wish to be reminded not to act like my mother. I repeated again and again in my mind, *he means well*. The warmth of his arms around me and his cheek against mine, stopped my potential flare-up. I said nervously, "Nick, I wish I could go upstairs and sleep seven weeks away. How will I get through the holidays? Thanksgiving? Christmas?"

"Somehow, we'll find strength."

"But I feel so helpless waiting for impending

doom. Just waiting."

Chapter II

"Mrs. DeMartino, you will lose this baby. I know waiting will not be easy for you—" I guess he saw the horror on my face because he added, "—but there is one consolation. If you carried to full term, the baby would probably be born with brain damage."

I just stared at the doctor and was unable to speak. My mouth tasted salty from tears in the corners of my mouth. In spite of his words, I sensed his uneasiness. "Mrs. DeMartino, the first thing you said to me was that your previous doctor left you unprepared to handle what happened. Well, with that in mind, I'm telling it to you as it is."

I saw his eyes shift to avoid mine and managed to whisper, "You're right," then lowered my head and wept. I was five months pregnant. Was it my imagination or was the baby kicking? I felt totally helpless. This man, this doctor, the springboard of new life said, "Nothing to do." How easily those words rolled off his tongue.

"When your father x-rayed my uterus, he was quite enthusiastic and even told the nurse that he came upon the cause of my problem."

"I've spoken to my dad and he saw nothing. I've looked at the x-rays, and they show nothing. Go home and get some rest," he said. "Call me when you feel contractions. This is not my best day," he added. "Right now, I've got two women waiting in separate rooms, crying. One just found out that her test proved positive and that she is pregnant; the other was just told she's not pregnant."

"You will forgive me, Doctor, if I don't cry for them or you."

"As a doctor, I'm frustrated. As a person, I'm

weary. We're supposed to harden over the years, but somehow, the years make the baby business harder."

I cried more. When walked out into the waiting room, I passed all the ladies in their various stages of pregnancy and heard them compare notes about their symptoms while some children romped around playfully. I thought, *this can't be happening to me again! Why is it that they can have children and I can't?* How envious I was. If at home, I'd smash a few dishes on the kitchen floor and wait for Nick to come home and comfort me.

All the way home, the doctor's words rang in my ears, "No, Mrs. DeMartino, there is no way of telling when the baby will abort—three days or three months. But I'm fairly certain it will. Once the membrane surrounding the child breaks and the fluid is emitted, a minuscule chance exists that the baby will remain alive and continue to develop normally."

Well, I was home and feeling sorry for myself. I washed the dishes instead of breaking them. Nick called; he'd just spoken to the doctor and was coming home.

"Nick. You'll do better working. Besides, right now, I want to lie down and sleep." I seemed not to be able to make the effort to hang up the receiver and let it drop from my hand. There was a series of loud clicking noises, a distant buzz, and then nothing.

It seemed so long ago that Nick and I met as freshmen in college. We were in our early twenties when we married. Since Nick had several years of education ahead of him, we didn't attempt to start a family. When we finally felt ready, we waited hopefully but not anxiously. As we approached our tenth year together, Nick and I discovered we *two* were about to become *three*. I was a pregnant lady looking forward to the joys of motherhood.

That first pregnancy happened fast. I was hardly up from the examining table when the doctor blurted out "Yep, you're pregnant. Speak to the nurse. She'll give you all the particulars and tell you what to do." I walked out into the reception area, pamphlets and prescriptions in hand, and said to Nick softly, "You're going to be a father."

It wasn't until we got the positive test results from the doctor that I would permit myself to believe. Nick and I were so pleased that although I was in a very early stage of pregnancy, we couldn't hold back the news. We told the immediate world and did everything short of hiring the Goodyear blimp. When you've been childless for ten years and then announce a forthcoming offspring, it takes on greater importance. The word spread quickly to family and friends, and I beamed like the Cheshire Cat. I acted as though I was accomplishing something never done before. In a sense I was doing something important. A very new and distinct human being was making its entrance into our world.

Our joy, however, was short lived. I started almost immediately to have complications.

"Don't worry," the doctor said. "Many women stain in the first months." I decided to research problems relating to pregnancy. The picture painted was a dark one. It seemed as though Mother Nature had a way of discharging pregnancies that didn't start properly. The early warning signs were those which I experienced.

I faced my doctor armed with this information. He agreed that it was a very distinct possibility but said that since he had seen many women overcome early complications and go on to normal delivery, he didn't feel it necessary to caution me. I decided to take a positive approach.

Two weeks later, I miscarried. Any woman who has been through it can tell you it is not a pretty sight. The bathroom floor was covered with blood. Fortunately, Nick was home. He turned white. I had only mild pain, but the sense of loss was overwhelming. Nick rushed to the phone and called our doctor. When I awoke the next morning, I found myself in the maternity ward. I had a D&C (dilation & curettage), a scraping of the lining of the uterus to prevent further hemorrhaging or infection.

Nick waited downstairs. When he arrived bedside, he took a hard look at me and said, "You look good, you old bag."

I looked into his strong, smiling face and said, "Thanks for trying, dear. I look terrible and what is more I don't give a damn." I found myself fighting tears and turned my head into a pillow.

"Come on, hon, things look a little gray," he said softly, "but this kind of thing is not uncommon and, thank God, we can try again. In a few days, this will all be behind us and just a memory."

"Speaking about a few days," I said, sitting up in bed, "what in the world am I doing in the maternity ward and when can I go home?"

"All the nurses and crew have the necessary experience to handle female disorders."

I was still edgy, but when Nick said I would be discharged the following morning, I felt better. There were two women who shared my room. They busily chatted with each other. I wasn't in a particularly good mood; as a matter of fact, I felt rather antisocial, so I stopped any attempt they made to speak to me, but I couldn't help overhearing their conversation. The older woman appeared about forty. Her youngest of three children was fourteen and now unexpectedly, she had a new baby. She knitted a sweater for the child. The other woman, or shall I say *girl*, was nineteen. She just gave birth to her third boy. She looked like a baby herself.

Each was unhappy about the events which presented a child. I could sense that they tried to figure me out, as I caught glimpses of raised eyebrows and necks stretching to get a peek at me. Their conversation came to an abrupt halt when a woman entered the room, pen and pad in hand, and walked straight over to me. I wondered who she was.

"Do you have diaper service yet?" she queried. "No, you see . . . " "Very well, then let me tell you about ours." "No, you don't understand." "You'd be surprised how important it is to have service, even for the first few months." I said sharply, "I had a miscarriage!" "Oh," she said quietly. "I'm sorry."

The following morning, I awoke feeling a little better. It was a nice day. I was going home. The girls talked to one another. This time I included myself in their conversation. It occurred that the one thing which we all had in common but did not give voice to was disappointment. Each of us would deal with the letdown in our own way.

My doctor suggested I wait a few months before thinking about becoming pregnant again. Three months later, I returned to him and once again got a positive pregnancy report. He assured me that it was very common for a woman to have a miscarriage and then go on to a perfectly normal pregnancy. I believed him but was nonetheless apprehensive. This time, we waited before making our announcement to the family. We wanted stronger footing. So, after three months, we once again informed the world of a forthcoming blessed event. It had still been touch-and-go for the first three months, but I was taking extra vitamins, and the doctor saw me every week. As far as he was concerned, the critical period passed and things could only get better.

By the fifth month, I began to show and proudly changed into maternity clothes. Then, it happened. I started to stain: the same as in my previous pregnancy. The doctor told me to stay off my feet as much as possible. I followed his advice, but I became a "Nervous Nora." Things got better for a while, but in the beginning of my sixth month, the problem started again. That meant another visit to the doctor who once again assured me that all was well, so I put on my best "things are going to be all right" attitude and went home.

When I went to bed that evening, the pains began. They started from the back and moved to the front. I convinced myself that they would go away, but instead, they got more intense. I woke Nick. He turned on the light, took one look at me and dialed the doctor. "Don't call the doctor just yet. After all, it is the middle of the night. Let's wait a while longer and see if the pain subsides." Nick gave in under protest.

An hour later, we called the doctor who suggested I take a painkiller. I took Midol, the only medication in the house. Eventually, the pains became so strong they took my breath away. Nick told the doctor he was taking me to the hospital.

About four o'clock in the morning, there was no traffic. I tried to stay in control, but the pain became so intense that I couldn't. Nick passed as many red lights as safety would allow. It took forever. I walked into the hospital calmly, gave the attendant my name and address, and then doubled over. The attendant yelled, "This girl is in labor. Get the nurses."

They prepared for delivery and rolled me into another room where they strapped my arms and legs down. I could see just heads of the nurses who stood at the foot of the table. "What's happening?" I shouted. "Why aren't you doing something?"

"We're waiting for the doctor. He should be here shortly."

I kept yelling over and over, "I'm losing my baby." The nurse came to the head of the table and said softly but sternly, "You're doing no such thing. You're having a baby."

"It's too little. It will never survive," I said.

"Now, you don't know that, do you?"

I answered by grunting. The pains were really unbearable. She said something else when one of the nurses at the foot of the table called. I saw the shock on her face. "The baby is coming out side ways. Get one of the doctors," she shouted. "Tell him the baby's arm is hanging out and it's turning blue."

In the doorway, I saw my doctor still in his street clothes. That was the last thing I remember. The following morning found me in a bed in one of the labor rooms. It was a tiny room just big enough for the bed and a chair. The walls were white with gray speckles. As my eyes moved, the speckles formed fuzzy animals. A camel quickly became a bear and then a cat. The forms got bigger and then they'd shrink only to become another animal. I heard a noise and turned around to face Nick coming in the door. His beard was heavy; his eyes were red and sunken. His clothes looked as though he'd slept in them. I looked into his tired face and said, "Don't try to break it to me gently, Nick. I already know."

He reached for my hand and said in a somewhat shaky voice, "Jean, I love you."

"The baby—did you speak to the doctor—what did he say?"

"It was a little boy, Jean. He—he wasn't meant

to make it into our world," Nick said softly. He told me that he signed the burial certificate, and the baby was buried by the St. Vincent De Paul Society. I tried to cry, but tears wouldn't come. I watched the gray speckles on the white walls turn into large and fuzzy animals, into a zoo where parents took toddlers, into a toy store where parents bought stuffed animals for their newborn, into a crib where parents watched their child squeeze a soft, furry bunny.

As Nick got up, I said, "I don't want to go to the maternity ward. I'm not ready for it."

"I spoke to the doctor, hon. He thinks it would be best if you return home as quickly as possible."

I felt a sense of relief. My only other visitor in the labor room that day was my doctor. He looked almost as bad as Nick. He said, "I'm sorry," in a voice so low, I hardly heard him. He never expected this to happen. He was prepared for the early months, but my delivery took him totally by surprise. He stammered and was visibly shaken and upset; I focused on the fuzzy animals, on the zoo, on the toy store, on the crib.

I went home and for days lived in a fog content to just hang around and do nothing. What they say about time, however, is true. It has a way of obliterating the unhappy past and with few exceptions such as the coming of Mother's Day, the baby food samples received in the mail, and the happy photographer arriving to take a picture of my *three-month-old*. I managed to put memories behind. Nick and I decided that we certainly should be in more expert hands if we wanted to try a third time to have a family.

That brought me to the offices of my new doctors on Ocean Parkway in Brooklyn. The elderly doctor was a specialist in fertility problems. His office was staffed with skilled technicians and had a laboratory on the premises. The delivery doctor was his son and would handle our case.

My first encounter with the older doctor was a series of tests. Fertility was not our problem, as the good doctor knew, retention was! He searched and probed. He came up with nothing concrete except for the off-the-cuff comment about my having an immature O when he x-rayed my ovaries. But immature O's were soon forgotten, and neither father nor son figured out what he possibly meant by the statement.

At the end of their tests, I found myself pregnant once again. The younger doctor treated me with kid gloves and saw me weekly, prescribed Vitamin C, administered hormones (although he wasn't sure I needed them), and asked me to call at any time if anything unusual needed reporting. I was unhappy about not getting to the root of my problem but felt secure that my doctor did everything at this point. Then the staining started once again. Every day I wondered what would happen next but managed to keep my anxiety hidden. Inwardly, I panicked. In the fifth month, I resigned to the irregularities and convinced myself that worrying wouldn't help, least of all help my future offspring.

I finished breakfast with Nick; he kissed me goodbye and went off to work. I walked into our bathroom and felt a peculiar sensation. At first I thought I was hemorrhaging again, but when looking down at the water-like fluid on the floor, I knew the membrane surrounding the baby burst prematurely. I immediately called the doctor, a cab, and Nick's office and left a message.

I lay in bed going over the events of the past two years and wondered how much more pain lay ahead for Nick and me when the door opened and in he walked. "Did you manage to sleep any, honey?" he asked and sat down by the side of the bed and stroked my hair.

"A little, but I kept waking up. It all seems so unreal. How come you came home?"

"I couldn't concentrate. I thought of you all alone and what the doctor said about the baby and wanted to come home to you."

"I'm so glad you're here. Are we ever going to survive this waiting, Nick? Here I am with a big belly; people will ask questions about the pregnancy and, all the while, I'll know in my heart that there's not going to be any baby. Nick. I failed," I sobbed. "There's a little human being inside who's crying out to live, and I can't give it life."

"We've been through difficult times before. We've got to set our jaws and toughen our backs and face this thing head on, Jean, and we'll pull through."

The next three weeks were a nightmare. I remembered what Nick said about setting my jaw, but sometimes I couldn't convince myself and I'd cry. People tried to be kind and say the right things. My mom, my dad, and Nick's family sensed my moods and helped carry me through this harrowing time.

We watched the Honeymooners on TV. Somehow the antics of Jackie Gleason and Art Carney helped for a moment to forget what was to come, but then the pain started. This time I knew what to expect, and I wasted no time calling the doctor. He told me to get to the hospital as soon as possible. By the time I was in the delivery room, the pains were much stronger. My doctor arrived, and I remembered nothing else from then on—no pain—nothing. About 4:00 a.m., they told Nick to go home and get some sleep.

When I awoke the next morning, I found myself in the maternity ward of the hospital. This time in a private room, but I heard the babies crying in the nursery. I looked around. Everything seemed dreary. In my mind and in my heart, I had lost the baby three weeks ago. The previous night, I merely went through the motions. It's hard to explain, but in a way I almost felt relieved.

The phone rang. It was Nick. "I'm throwing some cold water on my face, and I'll be right down."

"Nick, what am I doing in a maternity ward and when can I go home?"

"Now, calm down, you're in a private room and the doctor thinks you should stay until you regain strength." I put the receiver back when in came the elder doctor. He took my hand and told me how brave I was and offered encouragement. I, in turn, told him that Nick and I had talked things over and were not prepared to try again.

"My son and I spent a great deal of time going over your past tests and think we narrowed your problem to incompetent O's." I could feel the anger and frustration building and wanted to tell him that he was an incompetent ass but bit my tongue and pretended that I was listening to the method he would use during pregnancy to control the problem. I finally ended the conversation by telling him that I would talk with Nick. My eyes followed him out the door. I could no longer contain my feelings. I threw off the covers, got out of bed, and headed toward the bathroom. "We now know your problem, Mrs. DeMartino," I mimicked. Well, isn't that just great. I'm supposed to jump for joy. Washing my hands, I looked into the mirror and saw a haggard old lady staring back. She was intensely angry. I said to her, "You're not licked yet. Your husband is not coming to this hospital to be greeted by an old lady. He will see his wife, a gal who knows how to set her jaw and stiffen her back and face life head-on."

I found my pocketbook in the lower drawer, removed a cosmetic case, washed myself down, combed my hair, and put on makeup. When through, I looked in the mirror again. *Now that's better, self*, I thought and got back into bed.

Two girls passed my room, stopped and turned back, and popped their heads in. One of them said her name was so and so and this was so and so, her friend! "You gave birth last night, didn't you?"

"Yes, I did." As they walked away, I could hear one say to the other, "That's the girl who lost her baby last night. I thought to cheer her up, but she looks and sounds like she is ready for a party. I can't figure that one out. She must have a heart of stone."

I tried not to let it hurt, but it did. When Nick walked in though, a look of relief on his face made my effort worthwhile. We talked for a while. I cried when I told him about the two girls at my door. He frowned and squeezed my hand. Then I told him what the doctor said. He listened carefully and said, "Let's give it more thought when we're in a better frame of mind."

I arrived home a day earlier than expected. Once again, I convinced the doctor that I would be better off at home.

Our landlady was a spry, eccentric woman in her early seventies. As we approached the stairs leading to our apartment, she popped out of her door and said, "I'm glad to see you home." I smiled and thought how nice it was of her to wait for our arrival. She then turned to Nick and said, "As the saying goes, Nick, 'Always a bridesmaid never a bride.' Well, in your case, it's always an uncle, never a father." Nick and I simultaneously turned our attention from the door to one another, each catching the quizzical expression on the face of the other, and we burst into laughter. All the way up the stairs, we leaned on one another and laughed till tears rolled down my cheeks. Nick put his finger to his lips in a gesture of silence, but each time he'd laugh all the more. He opened the door, and the two of us fell inside. Without realizing, my landlady gave us the first good laugh in weeks.

Chapter III

One evening, I had a dream in which I talked to Nick's sister, Doris. She said "Jean, I don't know how to tell you this because I don't know how you're going to take it. I'm pregnant." When I awoke, I found myself upset by even the thought of Doris being pregnant. My orderly mind told me that Nick and I should have our children first, then his brother Vincent (who was one and a half years younger) and his wife Marie, and then it would be Doris's turn.

In July, my goddaughter, Lisa, came as a little ball of pink with gold curly locks. She captured our hearts immediately. It was right about that time when Nick and I made it known that we had applied to the Spence-Chapin Adoption Agency for a baby. The family was jubilant and filled with so many questions. Actually we had applied with the agency back in February of that year, but we had so many previous disappointments that we wanted to be sure that all was going smoothly before we once again announced the arrival of a baby into the DeMartino home. My mom and dad were the only ones we confided in. We wanted to share the experience with them from the beginning and also wanted to know what the reaction would be.

I remember that when I told mom, she hugged me really close and said, "God bless you." Dad was pleased, too. They agreed that we had made a wise decision. So now everyone knew and our phone was busier than a betting parlor. Everyone asked the big question, "When?" and, of course, we didn't know. We explained that the agency would call as soon as they selected and had a child who would best fit our family. I never believed that one must have a child who fits into a family in order to love that child. Love knows no such boundaries. But I did and still do agree with the agency that basic similarities can be helpful to a family unit.

Why did we choose the Spence-Chapin Adoption Service? It came about through minor events. When the hurt of the last miscarriage started to disappear, Nick and I talked about future plans. I loved children and planned as far back as I could remember to have a sizable family. I remember when Nick and I were attending college and getting serious, we dreamed about having a family of six, four biological and two adopted. Of course, that was just talk on our part, but you can see that adoption as an approach to family came very easily to us. We both agreed we had a whole lot of love which we wanted to pass on to children and we would no longer gamble with my health or the life of an unborn child. So, we took the path left open to us.

The previous December, friends of ours who had been childless for ten years adopted a girl privately. They paid the natural mother's hospital bills and lawyers' fees and waited out the gestation period. They brought their baby home from the hospital when she was days old and shared their jubilance with us. They were really riding high. We were so thrilled and happy for them. In January, they once more adopted a child in the same manner, only this time it was a boy. It was quite unexpected, but the same doctor called them at the last minute and proposed the second adoption. They were so exalted by the first child that they wasted no time in accepting the second to bring both up much like twins. They certainly looked enough alike to be twins, although their birthdays were a month apart. Of course, they planned telling them that they were adopted and that, in fact, they were not twins. By the time I received the second call, I was ready to find out about the procedure. I heard that agency adoptions took forever, and we had done so much waiting, I was tempted, really tempted to try their approach. When I called Nick and spoke to him, he replied, "Jean, I'm as anxious as you, but I don't think we should take the 'Gray Market approach.'" (Private adoptions earned that name though they are not illegal—that's black market—hence they fall somewhere in the middle.)

I'm up against that legal mind of his, I thought. That part of him always says, "Let's not leave room for loop holes." Yet I heard how glad our friends sounded and saw so many private placements that resulted in happiness for all, that I couldn't resist pushing. Deep down, however, even I had misgivings. We had so many disappointments where children were concerned that I really didn't want to do anything chancy.

"I know you're right, Nick, but adopting a child through an agency can take forever."

"Listen, Jean," he said, "there's this fellow I've worked with who adopted two beautiful children from a New York City agency and he tells me they were thorough yet speedy. I was waiting for the right time to discuss it."

I felt just great. The next day Nick called the agency and asked them to forward an application. On February 1, 1966, we received the following letter:

Dear Mr. & Mrs. DeMartino:
Thank you for your inquiry about our services. We are enclosing a copy of our pamphlet and preliminary information form. If you are interested in pursuing your inquiry, please complete the form and return it to us as promptly as possible. After this form is returned, we shall invite you to a group meeting at the agency within the next few weeks.

Should you have any questions meanwhile, do not hesitate to get in touch with our Inquiry Department.

*Sincerely yours,
Helen Montgomery, Executive Director*

Nick and I were quick to fill in the application which concerned itself with such questions as age, education, type of employment, annual income, amount of savings, church affiliation, and so on. We mailed it immediately and every day thereafter I checked the mail waiting anxiously for a reply. Finally, two weeks later, staring me in the face was a letter from the agency. I ripped it open and read:

*Dear Mr. & Mrs. DeMartino:
We would like to invite you to a meeting on Monday, February 28 at 7:00 p.m. This meeting will be attended by couples who, like yourselves, are considering adoption through Spence-Chapin. Mrs. Natalie Evan who leads the meetings will discuss our procedures, including the situation in regard to available children. Couples present are encouraged to raise for discussion any questions that may have occurred to them in order that they may decide whether or not they wish to continue with us.*

We would appreciate your confirming this appointment by letter to the secretary of the Adoption Department. We hope that you will be able to attend.

*Sincerely yours,
Loyce W. Bynum, Supervisor, Adoption Department*

There was an enclosure which listed neighborhood parking in the area of the agency. I read the letter through a second time to reassure myself of what I'd read and then ran up the stairs and phoned Nick to tell him the great news.

"Take it easy, Jean; this is just the first step. We've got a long way to go," he said soothingly. "But I'm really pleased that we're on our way. I know you'll feel better if you respond to them immediately." I blew him a kiss, hung up the phone, and pranced through the house. I wanted to call everyone I knew to tell them, but I knew I couldn't and wouldn't want to go through any explanations right at this moment. So I managed to calm myself, find a pen and paper and write the following letter to the Secretary of the Adoption Department:

Thank you for your prompt response to our application for adoption. We are in receipt of your letter inviting us to the February 28 meeting and are looking forward to attending same.

Yours truly,
Jean DeMartino

It was mailed later that day, and I was on cloud nine; my life—our lives—seemed to be taking some direction, and I liked the direction.

Chapter IV

Two weeks later we entered the doors of the Spence-Chapin Agency to attend our first meeting. The building was a small townhouse on the east side of Manhattan which looked as though it had been owned by a large family at one time. It was in magnificent condition and quite impressive. We were directed down a marble hallway and ushered into a small room set up with rows of folding chairs. Some people had already arrived, although from the number of seats (about 50) it appeared as though there were a lot more to come. The only hint one had of this being an adoption agency was two pictures of smiling, happy babies hanging on the anteroom wall leading to the lecture room.

Nick and I seated ourselves in the middle of a row and waited for the speaker to arrive. A middle-aged woman entered the room, took a seat up front facing the group, and introduced herself as Mrs. Evan. I experienced a strange mixture of excitement, tension, and expectation. When Mrs. Evan started to speak, I hung on every word. "The Spence-Chapin Adoption Service is a licensed, private, nonsectarian, interracial child adoption agency. Our roots go back to the turn of the century when Miss Clara Spence, head mistress of Spence School, weighed the idea of placing children for adoption and to 1910 the year Mrs. Alice Chapin found an adoptive parent for an abandoned little girl whom her husband, Dr. Henry C. Chapin, brought home from Post Graduate College.

"Adoptive couples, such as many of you here this evening, are able to experience the fulfillment that comes with being parents. I must once again, however, stress that our primary concern is to help our children, and we, indeed, view all of you as prospective parents. But there are more applications than there are babies available. So we will not be placing a baby with every couple here this evening."

The questions began:

"Must we provide a separate room for the child?"
"No, but adequate sleeping arrangements should be provided." "Does it matter if the adoptive couple is in a higher or lower income bracket?"
"No, you need only have a steady income and provide for sufficient financial security."
"Are the babies kept here, at the agency, prior to adoption?" "No, our babies are kept by foster mothers who give them individual loving care."
"How old will the baby be at the time of adoption?"
"A few weeks to three years. Most babies, however, are under one year of age."
"Would it be possible to secure a baby right from the hospital?"
"Yes, we have had instances where infants were placed into adoptive homes without intervening foster care."
"If you do not place a child with us, will you tell us why?" "The reason is nearly always the same—there are not enough children available."

I looked around the room at the faces of various couples, watched as they asked questions, and wondered who among us would be lucky enough to go home with a baby.

Nick was thinking the same thing. He gave my hand a little squeeze as if to say, *This is it, honey; everything is going to be all right.* I smiled and raised my hand, "Must the parents be the same religion as the child?"

Miss Evan turned her gaze to me and said in a warm tone, "Well, New York State Law requires that where practicable, the child must be placed with a family who shares the same religion as the child's natural parents. Which reminds me: I should tell you that the bulk of our children are from Protestant parents and those of you here this evening who are of other faiths will either not be serviced or will have a very long wait."

Well, there was no pussyfooting about that answer. I managed to let out an almost inaudible *thank you* and sank into my chair. There were one or two young couples who asked questions that one would expect to hear at a cattle auction rather than at an adoption agency. Miss Evan handled them well. Frankly, they were annoying me, and the expression on Nick's face showed the same reaction.

"How much will we know about the child's background?"

"Will we know if it comes from a good family?"

"How much do we get to know about its lineage?"

Miss Evan responded, "We will give you all the pertinent information garnered. In most cases, we have just the natural mother to call upon for information. We secure pertinent information from two monthly examinations given to the baby by our pediatrician. The staff nurse and social workers keep complete records of growth and development. If a disorder is suspected, we keep the child under our care and supervision until sure the problem is eliminated prior to placement in an adoptive home."

Time ran out. My head spun with all the new information. I was anxious to move ahead and wished only to be walking out of that home with a lovely pink baby in my arms. Miss Evan said, "Now I must fill you in on the next procedural steps, that is, if you care to proceed further. We have supplied a booklet entitled *You Asked about Adoption* which covers some of your unanswered questions, but if there are still a few, please hold on to them, and feel free to ask on your next visit to our agency."

"We would like you think about everything discussed here this evening, talk it over with your spouse very carefully, and if you are desirous of continuing with us, please write to Miss Bynum, the supervisor of our Adoption Department. You will hear from our agency shortly thereafter. Thank you for coming this evening." She glanced around in an effort to catch as many eyes as she could, and then made a quick exit. There was a buzzing excitement. As we edged out, I caught another glimpse of the pictures of smiling babies and felt good. Outside, we were hit by the cold. I couldn't wait to feel the warmth of the car's heater and come back to life. We felt rather giddy. It was a great evening, and I can remember it all as if it were yesterday. It was a turning point in our lives. We both sensed it.

That night I got the best sleep in years. I arose early, saw Nick off to work, and sat down at my typewriter and wrote the following letter:

March 1, 1966

Dear Mrs. Bynum,

My husband and I attended the February 28 group meeting headed by Miss Natalie Evan of your organization. We found the meeting to be quite informative and are definitely interested in continuing our search through your agency.
It may be a bit premature to mention, but I would like to add that my husband and I, in our pre-adoption discussions, favored an older baby. We feel that parental love knows no age limits. Miss Evan's

discussions confirmed our views.

Like most parents-to-be, we are most anxious to move speedily toward our objective. This, however, is not the reason for the above decision. Should, in fact, a longer period of time be required, you would find us nonetheless anxious but certainly agreeable.

*Very truly yours,
Jean DeMartino*

    I read the letter through a second time to be absolutely certain that it stated all we wanted to say and then put it aside for Nick to read that evening. Next, I picked up the little booklet that had been given to us. It was written in question and answer form; I read,

WHAT IS CHILD ADOPTION?
Child adoption is the legal procedure through which a couple permanently assumes parental rights and responsibilities for a child whose natural parents have surrendered their rights and responsibilities.

ARE THEIR AGE AND RESIDENCE QUALIFICATIONS FOR ADOPTING PARENTS?
In general, we accept applications from couples under forty who have been married at least three years. Also, in general, the couple should reside within a commutable distance of New York City.

CAN A COUPLE WITH MEDICAL PROBLEMS ADOPT A CHILD?
It depends upon the nature and severity of the medical problems. Applications from such couples are given individual consideration.

    I read on but so many of the questions had been taken up and answered the previous evening that I decided to scan down the list until I came to one that seemed new.

IS IT ESSENTIAL THAT THE ADOPTING COUPLE BE UNABLE TO HAVE CHILDREN OF THEIR OWN?

No, however, preference is given to couples who cannot have children.

DOES THE AGENCY FEEL THAT THE CHILD SHOULD BE TOLD HE IS ADOPTED?

Yes, the relationship between the adopting parents and the child should be frank and open. In any event, the child is likely to learn from relatives or friends of the adopted family that he had been adopted.

WHO MAKES THE DECISION TO OFFER THE CHILD FOR ADOPTION?

The natural parents make it. (In most instances by the mother alone.) We consult with her and give her ample time to explore the alternatives before making her decision about the child's future.

CAN THE NATURAL MOTHER REMAIN IN TOUCH WITH THE CHILD AFTER ADOPTION?

No, separation from the child is permanent. We make certain that this is understood before the surrender is signed.

I thought as I read on that they really knew what made adoptive parents tick. They were covering all grounds, curiosity, our need to know the facts, and, of course, our fears.

DOES THE NATURAL MOTHER HAVE CONTACT WITH THE ADOPTIVE PARENTS?

No, we do not reveal the identity of the adoptive family to the natural mother nor is her identity given to the adoptive family.

WHAT IS THE PURPOSE OF AGENCY INTERVIEWS?

We want to get to know the applicants as people. We

will discuss their personal, social, community interest and activities with them, their ideas about children, anything that relates to the way a child might grow up in their home. In addition, the interviews help the couples to know what is involved in adoption and to evaluate their own wishes about adopting a child.

WHAT IS THE SUPERVISOR PERIOD?

That is the period usually about a year long, during which the agency supervises the child in placement. The supervisory year begins when the child is first placed with an adoptive family. It ends at the time of legal adoption.

WHAT IS ITS PURPOSE?

The purpose of the supervisory period is to help the parents and child become a family. We consult with the parents about any problems which may arise.

WILL THE AGENCY VISIT THE HOME DURING THE SUPERVISORY PERIOD?

Yes, the adopting family is informed in advance of every visit.

I read that one again. I had heard so many stories about agency social workers arriving at one's home unannounced in order to check the dust on cabinets with white gloves and to look at your bookshelves to see the kind of reading you do. I was relieved to see it in print. So much for old wives' tales! I read on.

MAY THE AGENCY TAKE BACK THE CHILD DURING THE SUPERVISORY PERIOD?

When a child is placed with a couple, the agency looks upon them as the child's parents. The agency has the right to take back a child and the adoptive couple has the right to return the child during the supervisory period. However, instances of this are extremely rare.

I wasn't particularly concerned by what I had just read. After all, I expected to give the agency no reason to want to remove the baby from our home, and I wouldn't be returning the child. Common sense, though, told me that a supervisory period would be good protection for the child.

IS THERE A CHARGE FOR THE ADOPTION SERVICE?

A fee is charged the adopting parents based on their ability to pay. One half of the fee is paid at the time interviews are completed, the other half, in the middle of the supervisory period. A family is not turned away because of inability to pay a fee.

HOW LONG DOES IT TAKE BEFORE A CHILD IS PLACED FOR ADOPTION?

It varies, depending upon the children available for placement. Sometimes a couple has to wait a long time for a particular child; others may have a child placed with them immediately after the adoption study is completed. The study usually takes from three to six months.

WHAT ARE THE ADVANTAGES OF ADOPTION THROUGH AN ACCREDITED AGENCY?

The natural mother is given ample time and consultation before reaching a formal decision about surrendering her child. In private placements, such decisions are frequently reached hastily under emotional pressures which can result in the natural mother attempting at some time to recover the child. The agency can help the family by sharing the experience of many adoption families in providing information regarding adoption in relation to the child, relatives, and the broader community. In private placements, this body of knowledge and experience is usually lacking. In addition to providing whatever medical and social study is indicated for the baby while he is in our charge, the agency gives the adopting couple all pertinent information. The agency has a larger group of prospective adoptive parents and children and consequently may make more appropriate placements.

THE CHANCES OF HAPPINESS FOR ALL CONCERNED ARE INFINITELY GREATER WHEN A CHILD IS ADOPTED THROUGH AN ACCREDITED AGENCY.

I closed the pamphlet and thought, *Nick, you are so right!* If you want to take short cuts in life, then you have to be prepared to take the extra chances that go along with them. But this was too important a step in our lives for us to take chances. I thought of Nick saying, "It'll be the long way, but it will be the right way." Although I was doing very well financially and enjoyed the executive status with my firm, something was missing. Deep down I yearned for a simpler life, one with less complications and responsibilities. I was missing out on one of the most important aspects of being a woman, which is to say, being a mother.

It never hit home more poignantly than when I was given my pension plan to peruse and there in bold print I read, "to retire in the year 2000, at the age of 65." The thought was mind-boggling. I made it known right then and there that I was leaving to stay home and concentrate on starting a family. Little did I know how difficult that would be.

So here I was now, at home, getting a little restless but believing that the best was to come. When Nick, however, suggested that I help him at his office a few days a week, I jumped at the chance. Nick was quite busy and I enjoyed being a part of his business life.

It wasn't until May 5 that we received the following letter:

Dear Mr. and Mrs. DeMartino:

With regard to your interest in adoption, we are pleased to be able to offer you an appointment for an interview with one our caseworkers.
Please telephone me as soon as possible so that we may arrange a convenient time for your interview.

Very truly yours,
(Miss) Myrna M. Gulish, Secretary, Adoption Department

    I was so excited; I couldn't decide whom to call first, the agency or Nick. Then I realized it would be best to have Nick, in turn, call the agency since he would work the appointment into his schedule.
    "Calm down, honey. I'll set up an appointment and then call you back."
    What would the agency ask? This is it, Jean. Say the wrong thing and you've muffed it. I heard the water running in the kitchen, ran inside just in time to stop it from pouring onto the floor. I looked around at the half-cleaned counters, the carpet sweeper sitting in the dining room and the dust cloth on top of the stereo and realized the excitement was getting me nowhere fast.

    The meeting went well. We were ushered into a small homelike room and introduced to a caseworker. After an hour or so of questioning and general conversation, we were told that there would be many more meetings and the agency would require personal and religious references, further medical reports, and proof of our financial capability to raise a child. If everything proved favorable, we would then go on a waiting list until the child that would best fit into our family was available.

The next six months were hectic. There were visits to the agency, visits by the case worker to our home, and letters and information passed back and forth. Although we were always felt comfortable and interviewed under the most relaxed conditions, every aspect of our lives was probed: how Nick and I felt about each other's ability to be parents, and what we thought of our own childhood.

The *Home Study* as they called it was finally completed, and Nick and I were placed on the waiting list. Nine months from our first visit with the Spence-Chapin Agency, we received that much awaited call. They had a two-month-old baby girl for us. We could pick her up the following day if it was convenient. Convenient? I wanted to rush downtown that very moment. We would most assuredly be there.

I quickly told Nick that he was about to become a father, and we spent the rest of the day gathering as many babies' needs as we could think of. By the next day, we entered the same brownstone only this time about to meet our new daughter. nI a little tote, there were some essentials that the agency suggested bringing—diapers, dress, etc. As we waited, I put the tote on my lap and clung tightly to it. It gave me reassurance that what was about to take place was real and not just imaginary.

Shortly, we were called into a small, cozy room decorated in earth tones. Two comfortable love seats faced one another. The wall directly in front of us contained a large picture window which overlooked a backyard garden. No sooner had we sat down then the placement director entered.

"Before we bring the baby in, there are a few things we would like to tell you about her." We listened attentively while she told us as much as she knew about the baby's biological parents, about her physical condition, the type of formula needed, and the fact that she appeared to have an allergy to orange juice.

The baby (like all babies placed through the Spence-Chapin Agency) had been in foster care while awaiting her permanent home. Asked whether we would like to meet the foster mother, we both agreed. The placement director appeared pleased. Most foster parents liked to personally meet the permanent parents of their little charge. It permitted them to share in the joy of the moment of meeting and to give meaning to their work.

We were also informed that if we did not feel that the child was for us, it was perfectly all right to say so and the agency would search further for another child to our liking.

I blurted out, "Do people actually turn down a child you offer them?"

She answered in a solicitous manner almost as though patting me on the head and saying, *Now, now, Jean.* "We do not want any child of ours going into a home where it is not completely wanted or accepted." A few minutes later, we were greeted by a smiling foster mother carrying a little black eyed, dark-haired bundle of joy. She placed the baby in my arms. I looked into her little face, cradled her close, and said "Welcome, my little daughter." She looked at Nick and made gurgling sounds.

"She's talking to you, Nick," I said, saw tears making their way down his cheeks, and handed the baby over. He held her like a dozen fresh eggs. It was a moment of tenderness and great joy. Linda was ours.

During the months that followed, a social worker from the agency visited with us on several occasions. It was easy to see how happy the DeMartino family was. It was on one such visit that I inquired about a second child from the agency. I was assured that it was common practice and that a second time around would be much easier since the agency already knew us and saw that the baby placed with us was thriving. We would have a shorter waiting time for the second child. Nick and I speculated that would mean approximately six months instead of the nine months with Linda. Armed with that information, we decided to wait until Linda was two years old and then apply to the agency.

Linda grew more beautiful every day. She was an extremely inquisitive and verbal child and started talking at nine months. From that moment on, the house knew no silence. She loved to be read to and digested every word. She was the light of our lives. The extended family was ecstatic over her. I could hardly keep them from spoiling her. She and our niece Lisa (three months older than Linda) were inseparable.

Times were good and looking up in the DeMartino home. When Linda was two, we applied to the Spence-Chapin Agency for another baby. The routine was much the same as before except that there were fewer visits at the agency. Most of the visits took place in our home so that they could meet with Linda and see us together as a family.

Linda was excited at the prospect of a baby sister or brother. If the waiting seemed long for us, it certainly loomed as an eternity for Linda. One year passed and still no word from the agency. Doris, Nick's sister, in the meantime, gave birth to a gorgeous baby girl named Laura. The welcomed newborn only intensified Linda's desire for a baby sister. After all, her dearest cousin had a baby sister, why hadn't hers arrived yet?

Finally almost two years after applying to the agency, we once again knew the joy of a baby girl awaiting us. There is just no way to describe the excitement of receiving that call. Linda and I danced around the house. I immediately called Nick, and Linda called any and every friend she could think of to tell the good news.

On June 18, 1970, Nick, my mother, Linda, and I entered the Spence-Chapin Agency to pick up our second daughter. Given all the particulars as to Lenore's condition and background, we were once again asked if we would like to meet her foster mother whom she'd been with for the previous month. Of course we did. We were also asked if we would like to include Linda in the first meeting. We thought it a wonderful idea. Moments after, the foster mother brought in our little daughter. We all looked at her in amazement. She was approximately five pounds and very tiny. She had the cutest features and seemed unreal. Linda asked, "Mommy can I hold my sister?" The placement director nodded her head affirmatively. Linda sat on the love seat and the foster mother placed the baby in Linda's arms. It was a scene that makes memories.

"This is exactly what happened the day we adopted you, Linda. I guess you can see how much joy you brought to Daddy and me."

Linda only held Lenore for a moment, but it seemed longer. I too was anxious to cradle my new daughter in my arms. She felt almost weightless. Nick, who had been standing close, took hold of her little fingers and said, "I've been waiting my turn to hold her long enough." She seemed to get lost in Nick's arms; he was so big and she so little. He held her tenderly then bent his head and whispered, "You were a long time coming, sweetheart. But you were worth the wait."

Nick's last words made me think of my mom waiting for us downstairs which I mentioned to the placement director who said, "She's yours now. So you may take her with you and show her off to your mother." As we approached my mom, Linda grabbed Grandma's arm and pulled her toward us. "Oh, Grandma, you've got to see her. You've just got to see her. Mommy is carrying my sister Lenore."

It seemed strange to finally hear the name Lenore. We picked it out for the baby two years earlier, and now there really was a Lenore. In keeping with what seemed to become the DeMartino tradition, we had named all the girl cousins with names beginning with *L*. There were Lisa, Laura, Lori, Linda, and now Lenore. Whenever the girls asked why we decided to do this, we always told them *Love* began with an *L,* and throughout their lives, we wanted them to have a reminder.

Mom was overjoyed. Lenore was a May baby, a Taurus, just like her grandma and you could almost sense that there was something special in their meeting.

We packed into the car and headed home. On the way, we stopped for hamburgers. Lenore slept through it all, and I was learning once again, how to eat with one hand.
When we finally pulled up to our house, we found every child in the neighborhood at our doorstep. Lenore didn't know it but she had just attained star status.

We knew from our previous experience with Linda that our family would have a full house that evening. So after getting the baby settled, we set about getting things ready. As we were working, Linda checked on her sister and would give me reports. "She's still sleeping, mom." I smiled to myself and wondered if I had checked on Linda as many times when she first came home. "Mommy," Linda asked, "is she really my sister?"

"She's our daughter now, and that makes her your sister."

"But, I mean, will she be with us forever and ever?" "Yes, Linda forever and ever."

Chapter V

I nodded and watched Nick open his attache' case and pull out a booklet with a gray cover. I let it drop to the table and looked down at it.

"Would you like to speak to the attorneys representing the agency, Jean? Maybe they can fill in some of the gaps for you and help you to get through this period a little easier."

"Can you arrange that for me?"

"There is nothing to arrange. If you want to see them, you'll see them. Call Marie and ask her to come watch the children tomorrow and I'll bring you to meet Roy Reardon and his assistant Jim Wawro, the two attorneys assigned to the case. In the meantime, if you'd like more background, read that copy of the actual trial. Do you think you're ready for it?"

"I'm afraid to start. I thought when you adopted a child through an agency that you were automatically protected. Nick, did you ever think this could happen?"

"I bet there are a lot of other people out there who are unaware of the possibility of losing their child."

"It's a bad dream. Oh, Nick, it's that dream when Lenore first came home from the agency. I woke up crying in the middle of the night. Oh Nick, it was so scary. I was alone in the house with Lenore. She sat in the playpen in the dining room. I suddenly felt as though someone's eyes were upon me, and when I looked out the kitchen window, I saw a man's face pressed against it. He had a sardonic smile. I was terrified, but then a sense of relief came because I was certain he couldn't get into the house. As I reached for the phone, I heard the lock turn. He had a key! I ran to the dining room, picked Lenore up in my arms, and turned around only to find myself facing this man. It was Lenore he wanted. I started to give her to him and then woke up."

"Yes, now I remember," he said, taking me in his arms and holding me close. "I remember that you woke up screaming and recriminating yourself. You kept saying, 'I wouldn't do that. I wouldn't hand Lenore over to anyone. Why didn't I run? Why didn't I take the baby and run?' I remember, Jean, and wish that this court proceeding was a dream as well/ But it's not a dream, and we have to be strong and work our way through."

After Nick went back to court, I moved about in a trance-like state. My mind raced. Every time I passed the dining room table and saw that gray booklet staring at me, I shuddered. It was time to call Marie and fill her in. Marie was married to Nick's younger brother Vincent, and they were childless. Needless to say, she adored our girls. I did my best to explain what happened. She was as confused and upset as I. We both had a good cry. I wasn't a bit surprised when she agreed without a moment's hesitation to come the following day and tend to the girls. Marie was always there when you needed her.

It wasn't until later on in the evening, however, that I summoned up the courage to read the copy of the trial. I somehow managed to get the kids to bed early. Nick was so exhausted when he arrived home that he barely made it to bed himself. Now that the house was quiet and free from distractions, I sat down at the dining room table, picked up the text of the trial, and read as follows:

SUPREME COURT New York County Index No. 34102/70

THE STATE OF NEW YORK, ex rel. OLGA SCARPETTA,
on behalf of Baby Scarpetta, Petitioner, against
SPENCE-CHAPIN ADOPTION SERVICE,
Respondent.
Olga Scarpetta-Petitioner-Direct The Court: Gentlemen, proceed.
Olga Scarpetta, the Petitioner, called as a witness in her own behalf, being first duly sworn, testified as follows: Direct Examination by Mr. Zalk: (I assumed he was Miss Scarpetta's attorney.)
The witness stated that until today her residence is 514 East 88th Street, New York City, New York.
Q. You said until today. Are you moving?
A. Yes, today I moved to 1072 Fenwood Road, Valley Stream, New York.
Q. Miss Scarpetta, how old are you?
A. Thirty-two.
Q. And where were you born?
A. In Medellin, Colombia not far from Bogota.
Q. Are you married or single?
A. I am single.
Q. Have you ever been married?
A. No, I have not.
Q. How long have you lived in New York?
A. I arrived a year ago today.
Q. Did there come a time in 1970 when you gave birth to a child?
A. Yes, May 18.
Q. And was that a male or female child?
A. Female.
Q. And where did you give birth?
A. New York Hospital.
Q. Is the father of the child a resident of New York or Colombia?
A. Colombia.

Q. Is the father of the child married or single?
A. He is married.
Q. After the birth of the child, did you discussed with a representative of the Spence-Chapin Adoption Service the adoption of the baby?
A. After the birth of my child, I told them I would like the baby back. She said that would be impossible. I again talked to Miss Daniels and repeated that I would like my baby back. She said that the baby had already been placed, so they could not help me and would do everything to change my mind or prevent me from getting my baby back.

After that, I returned a few more times to go into my reasons for placing my baby for adoption so that it could be more clear to me whether I had made a mistake or was just experiencing an emotion of the moment. So I finally told Miss Daniels that I was seeking legal aid to regain custody of my baby.
Q. Had you signed a consent with the Spence-Chapin for the adoption of the child?
A. Yes, I had.
Q. What were the circumstances under which you signed that consent?
A. I was very sad and frightened. All the time prior to the birth of the child, I felt insecure about my ability to find a job. I had a difficult time when I got here and was very much frightened.
Q. Had your parents known of the pregnancy?
A. No, they had not.
Q. Did any member of the family know?
A. My sister knew. The baby's father called the week before the baby was born and told her that I was pregnant, and she came and stayed with me when the baby was born.
Q. Did you write to Spence-Chapin Adoption Service requesting the return of the child?

A. Yes.
Q. I ask if this is a copy of a letter that you wrote.
A. Yes.
Mr. Zalk: Your Honor, I may have inadvertently omitted that letter from our papers so I request that it be marked in evidence.
The Court: Admitted.
(I quickly thumbed through the papers and found a letter dated August 3, 1970.)

Gentlemen:
Please be advised that I hereby revoke the consent granted on or about June 1, 1970 for the adoption of my baby daughter born May 18, 1970, and I hereby request that my child be returned to me. If prompt arrangements for the return of my child are not made, it will be necessary for me to make an application to the proper court for an order directing the return of my child.
I regret any inconvenience that my action may cause the adoptive parents of my child, but I am sure that they will understand that a child should be with its natural mother.
Very truly yours, Olga Scarpetta, 514 East 88th Street New York, New York
P.S. My attorneys are Zalk, Rubel, & Perret, Esq., and I would appreciate your cooperating with them.

As I read the last paragraph, I felt my temperature rising. She regrets any inconvenience that her action caused the adoptive parents! "Is that what she honestly believed this to be? An inconvenience?" I shouted. The sound of my voice in the still night startled me. I read on.
Q. What is your educational background, Miss Scarpetta?

A. I went through high school in Caldwell, New Jersey, Mount St. John's Academy. After that, I studied at the University of Bogota for three years and at The Sorbonne in Paris, and I obtained my B.S. in Social Science from California State College. I worked for one year to a Master's in Latin-American Studies in South America.
Q. Are you presently employed, Miss Scarpetta?
A. Yes, I am.
Q. By whom?
A. International Basic Economy Corporation.
Q. Where are they located?
A. 30 Rockefeller Plaza.
Q. And what sort of work do you do?
A. I do secretarial work in the Personnel Department and besides that I have duties relating to handling of recreation and the staff.
Q. And how much do you earn?
A. Right now I earn $135 a week.
Q. Is that gross or net?
A. That is before taxes.
Q. After taxes, how much is the amount?
A. I get my check every two weeks, and it is $225.
Q. Since the birth of the baby have you returned to Colombia to discuss the matter with your parents?
A. Yes. In August I went to Colombia. My parents thought I should have my child. They agreed that the child should be with its mother.
Q. What does your father do in Colombia?
A. My father imports heavy equipment for road construction.
Q. Did you discuss with your father possible financial assistance to help take care of the child?
A. Yes, he agreed.
Mr. Reardon: I object to conversations with the father.
The Court: Sustained.

Q. Do you have any independent resources of your own, Miss?
A. Yes, I do. In savings, about $20,000.
Q. Have you made any arrangements for help to take care of the child in the event you regain custody?
A. Yes, I have.
Q. What arrangements?
A. The lady who took care of us when we were young has agreed to come to New York. She has everything ready. She is just waiting. And also my parents will spend more time with me. The reason why I moved to a new apartment is two of my aunts and two of my cousins would also help with the child.
Q. What sort of an apartment are you moving into?
A. It has one bedroom and a living room and a dining area. It is a garden apartment.
Q. And do your aunt and cousin live in the vicinity?
A. Yes. My aunt lives around the corner, and my cousin lives one block away. I am moving there next week.

    That last statement made me very nervous. I went over her testimony again and on the first page, it stared at me. Her answer to the very first question was "Today, I moved to 1072 Fenwood Road, Valley Stream, New York." TODAY! Yet now she says, *moving in a week.*

Q. Will you tell his honor the reasons why you want custody of the child?
A. I think the best place for a child is with its natural mother unless the mother has some shortcomings which make it impossible, but I would do a very good job of raising my child.
Q. Why then did you consent to give the child for adoption?
A. I was ashamed and thought of my being an unwed

mother. I planned to marry the baby's father. When I told him that I was pregnant, he told me that he was married. Therefore, we could not get married. I was very much ashamed. I did not know what to do. That is why I decided to leave home without telling my parents. I was afraid of hurting them. I had no intention of giving my child up for adoption. I came here and couldn't get a job. When I did find a job, the salary was very low, and I felt guilty toward my child. I was denying her something by not giving her a home with a father and mother, and I just felt very guilty and very confused about the whole thing.

Q. What changed since that time to make you feel you can now take care of the child?

A. I realized that placing the child for adoption is not the best solution. I thought at the time that by giving the baby up for adoption, I was just putting her away from all the problems she would have. I realized that is not the case. The only thing I was really doing was closing my eyes.

Mr. Zalk: I have nothing further.

The Court: You may cross-examine.

Cross-examination by Mr. Reardon: (The attorney for the Spence-Chapin Adoption Agency)

Q. Miss Scarpetta, is this a copy of the surrender and your affidavit which you signed at the time you surrendered the baby to the Spence-Chapin Adoption Service?

A. Yes.

Mr. Reardon: I offer this in evidence. This is the formal surrender in accordance with the Welfare Law which is required of the natural parent.

The Court: Admitted as one Exhibit.

RESPONDENT'S EXHIBIT A - PETITIONER'S SURRENDER, RELIGIOUS PREFERENCE, AND

MARITAL STATUS AFFIDAVITS
New York, June 1, 1970
THIS CERTIFIES THAT OLGA SCARPETTA, the undersigned, residing in the County of New York, State of New York, is the Mother of the female child "Female" Scarpetta born in the New York Hospital in the Borough of Manhattan County of New York, City of New York, State of New York, on the 18th day of May 1970, and alone have the authority to surrender and commit guardianship of the person and the custody of the said child to an authorized agency, said child is now wholly or partially maintained by The Spence-Chapin Adoption Service.

     Finding that I am unable to provide a suitable home for said child and feeling that the welfare of the child will be promoted by its adoption or by its being placed in foster care. The undersigned, after due consideration, does hereby voluntarily, unconditionally, and absolutely surrender, transfer, and commit said child to the custody, control, care and management of The Spence-Chapin Adoption Service, a duly authorized agency, with the understanding that said child may be adopted by such person or persons as said agency in its discretion may select, or that the child may be placed by said agency in its discretion in foster care. The undersigned does hereby agree and pledge not to interfere with the custody, control, care, or management of said child in any way or encourage or allow anyone to do so.

     The undersigned does hereby expressly authorize and empower The Spence-Chapin Adoption Service in its discretion to consent to the adoption of said child without notice to the undersigned and in all respects and in the same manner as if the undersigned personally gave such consent at the time of adoption.
Witness

/s/ Gloria L. Daniels /s/ Olga Scarpetta (L.S.) State of New York

County of New York ss:

On this lst day of June A.D. 1970 before me personally appeared OLGA SCARPETTA to me personally known and known by me to be the individual described in and who executed the above surrender of the child "FEMALE" SCARPETTA and who acknowledged to me that she executed the foregoing instrument as her act and deed by her own free will for the purpose therein mentioned.

/s/ Grace G. Nickerson, Notary Public, State of New York No. 31-8141800 Qualified in New York County Commission Expires March 30, 1973

(Mr. Reardon continued with his cross-examination.)

Q. Miss Scarpetta, are you a citizen of the United States?

A. No, I am not.

Q. Your mother and father still live in Colombia?

A. Yes, they do.

Q. How old are they?

A. My father is seventy and my mother is sixty-eight.

Q. Following your graduation from California Poly Tech you returned to Colombia and worked?

A. Yes, I did.

Q. And you lived with your family at that time?

A. Yes, I did.

Q. During the summer of 1969, as I understand, you became pregnant, is that correct?

A. Yes.

Q. Unwed mothers are not received well in Colombia, are they?

A. I don't think they are received very well anywhere.

Q. Based on your pregnancy, you decided to come to New York, is that right?

A. Yes.

Q. At that time, did you ask the New York Hospital for suggestions of an adoption agency to place your child?

A. No, I didn't. All unwed mothers go through the Social Services Department of the New York Hospital, and the social worker asked me what I had planned to do with the child, and I said I had no idea. She asked me if I considered adoption and I said no but didn't know sufficient about adoption. So she suggested that I speak with Spence-Chapin where they could give me a better orientation if I would want to give my child up for adoption. At her suggestion, I got the appointment at Spence-Chapin.

Q. Before you came to New York, was it your intention to have your baby and take your baby back to Colombia?

A. When I first came to New York, I was so upset that the baby's father was married, something I had not dreamed possible. I thought we were going to marry. I came to New York mostly to think things out, see what the situation would be, and find myself. At that moment I felt myself completely going. My moral standards had fallen.

Q. Were you concerned about your parents and their health, the shock of your being pregnant?

A. I did not want to hurt them. They were very good to me and didn't deserve to be hurt.

Q. The natural father of your baby is a resident of Colombia. Has he a family of his own?

A. Yes.

Q. Are you still meeting since you came to New York?

A. He came once in December and then returned in April. He was here sometime in July, also.

Q. After the baby was born?

A. After the baby was born.

Q. Is it so that after your first meeting with Spence-Chapin, you had a series of discussions with various people—with Miss Daniels to be precise?
A. Yes.
Q. Yet, at the time you signed that surrender, you were convinced that the best for your baby was to have the child placed for adoption?
A. I realize I did not do the right thing.
Q. At the time you signed the surrender, though, you believed you were doing what was best for your child?
A. Yes, I did.
Q. You wanted the child to be raised in a home where she could have a father, a mother, and perhaps other children, isn't that so?
A. Yes.
Q. Being familiar with social work and social services, you are familiar with social problems and know what occurs with children who don't have the benefit of a mother and father and a natural home life; aren't you?
A. Yes.
Q. In April of 1970, before the baby was born, the natural father came to New York and visited with you, didn't he?
A. Yes.
Q. At that time, he was opposed to your plan for adoption, wasn't he?
A. Yes.
Q. He stressed that he would legally take the baby rather than have the child adopted, isn't that so?
A. Yes.
Q. And you discussed this with Spence-Chapin, didn't you?
A. Yes, I did.
Q. You read the surrender when you signed it?
A. Yes, I did.
Q. And you read the affidavits when you signed them?

A. Yes, I did.

Q. When the baby was born, she was not immediately surrendered to Spence-Chapin, was she?

A. No.

Q. Was she born on May 18?

A. That is right.

Q. And on May 18, your sister was in New York City with you, wasn't she?

A. Yes, she was.

Q. She came to New York because the natural father, having found out about the possibility of adoption, told her in South America what your plans were, isn't that so?

A. Yes.

Q. She came to New York to help you, isn't that so?

A. Yes, she wanted to speak with me.

Q. After the baby was born and within a week or so, the baby was brought by you and your sister Leah to Spence-Chapin, is that right?

A. That is right.

Q. For boarding care, wasn't she?

A. Yes.

Q. You understood Spence-Chapin would place the child for boarding care, isn't that right?

A. Yes.

Q. Within a short time afterward, you communicated with Spence-Chapin, did you not?

A. That same day, I was given an appointment to go back to Spence-Chapin.

Q. Before you went to that appointment, did you communicate with anyone in Spence-Chapin concerning the possibility of surrendering your child finally for adoption?

A. No.

Q. At the time you signed the child out for boarding care, do you recall executing any documents or

approving that arrangement in some way or other?
A. I was very confused then.
Q. The day came when you finally signed the surrender of the baby, isn't that so?
A. Yes. After the baby had been placed with Spence-Chapin for boarding care, I asked to see my baby twice and my petition was denied. They didn't think it was good for me. By the end of two weeks, I didn't know who she was. I was confused. I had also been told and learned that if the child was to be placed for adoption, the child should be as young as possible so that it would easily adjust to the parents. I was feeling very guilty about not being able to give anything to my child and decided to sign the papers.

(Once again, I found myself questioning what she said. If the child was just in boarding care, then certainly she had the right to see her. She could not only have insisted on seeing her but could have removed the child from their care if so desired. Somehow it didn't make sense.)

Q. Under those circumstances you signed the surrender that I showed you earlier in the day?
A. Yes.
Q. And your sister Leah was there that day, wasn't she?
A. Yes.
Q. Someone explained to you and your sister the step you were taking?
A. It had been explained.
Q. Did you know what you were doing?
A. I knew what I was doing, yes.
Q. In terms of Spence-Chapin, you made inquiries and satisfied yourself it was a good agency, had you not?
A. I had been told that it was a good agency.
Q. The lady who will take care of your baby part time, how old is she?

A. Sixty-five.

Q. And these various relatives that live in the same area are aware you are here today to get the return of your baby?

A. They knew last week.

Q. Did you ask them to testify for you and to indicate to the court the support they intend to give in rearing this child?

A. No, I did not ask them.

The Court: How soon after taking the baby to the Spence-Chapin Agency did you indicate that you wished to revoke your consent?

The Witness: Less than a month after I left the baby there.

The Court: Did the father live in the same town where your parents live?

The Witness: No.

The Court: Is he employed by your father?

The Witness: No. He is not.

The Court: How big a town is it?

The Witness: More than two and a half million.

Q. Is it still not possible for you to take the baby back to Bogota?

A. Yes, it is.

Q. You are not suggesting that is part of your plan?

A. I have no plan because I like New York. I'd like to stay. I was brought up here and find I get along better with the people in the United States than I do at home. I have more friends here and feel more at home. I have been thinking about giving up my citizenship. I want to be very sure before I do this.

Mr. Reardon: I have no further questions, Your Honor.

The Court: Do you have any other witnesses?

Mr. Zalk: No, Your Honor.

Mr. Reardon: I have several witnesses.

(Now it was the agency's turn to present its case. Even though I found it upsetting, I knew I had to read on.) Gloria Laverne Daniels, residing at 1230 Croes Avenue, Bronx, New York, called as a witness on behalf of the respondent, being first duly sworn, testified as follows:

Direct examination by Mr. Reardon:

Q. Miss Daniels, what is your profession?

A. I am a caseworker with the Spence-Chapin Adoption Service.

Q. How long have you been with Spence-Chapin?

A. I began working with Spence on November 3, 1969.

Q. Do you have any formal education?

A. In August of 1968 I graduated from Tennessee State University, in Nashville, with a Bachelor of Arts Degree in History. I am presently enrolled in Fordham University in the School of Social Services.

Q. Will you tell us, please, what contacts you had with Miss Scarpetta?

A. I first met Miss Scarpetta on the 21st of January. Following that I saw her approximately thirteen times. (The 21st of January? My heart skipped a beat. That was our wedding anniversary. It was an unexpected coincidence that startled me like something falling out of your closet in the dark of the night. What I did find strange, however, was Miss Scarpetta returning for so many visits even though indicating no plans for placing her child up for adoption.)

Q. And where did these visits take place?

A. In an interview room at the agency.

Q. Do you recall what Miss Scarpetta's plans were for her coming child when she first came to Spence-Chapin?

A. She planned for the adoption of the child.

Q. Tell us basically what she said.

A. She left Colombia, South America, and withdrew her savings of $5,000 to come to New York and have her child without anyone finding out.

Q. Did she tell you about her family problems?

A. She indicated that she was third of four girls and came from an upper middle-class family in Colombia. She said the stigma attached to unwed mothers was prohibitive. The father of the child was married and had two children and could not divorce his wife to marry Miss Scarpetta.

Q. Did she, at any time, discuss keeping her child and returning to Colombia?

A. We discussed that option as well as others. She said it would be impossible for her to take the child home because her family wouldn't approve and would feel resentment if she brought the child home.

Q. What did she plan to do?

A. To work a while and then return home without her family finding out about her child.

Q. Do you recall when the natural father found out about Miss Scarpetta's plan for placing the child for adoption?

A. Yes, I do. She said that once the father found out about the pregnancy, he offered to pay for an abortion. Miss Scarpetta refused and decided to give the baby up for adoption. He was resentful and offered to take the child. She refused. She didn't want him to have the child. He then told her sister, one of the sisters.

Mr. Zalk: I object to this conversation.

The Court: Sustained.

(Although abortions were illegal in New York and most probably in Bogota as well, I was not so naive as to believe that they were not taking place. I found it difficult to reconcile in my mind, however, that a man who would at first seek to abort a child would then be desirous of taking that child back to his wife and family who apparently knew nothing of her existence. What I made of all of this, however, was that a tug of war existed even before little Lenore was born. The only thing that had changed was the opponent.)

Q. Is this a conversation with Miss Scarpetta you are telling us about?

A. She told me that the father asked for the child. She told me that he offered to take the child. She told me that he told her sister about the child.

Q. Did Miss Scarpetta say why the father shouldn't have the child?

A. Yes. She said that he hadn't taken good care of his own children. It would be impossible to take the child to his wife because she didn't know about Miss Scarpetta. She wanted her child to have two parents, love, and a family.

(Once again something about bothered me, so I reread. "She said that he hadn't taken good care of his own children." If she didn't know he was a married man, how could she possibly know what kind of a father he was? The more I read, the more disillusioned I became.)

Q. Did you talk to her after the baby was born?

A. During that visit, we reviewed everything from previous meetings with Miss Scarpetta and her sister present and made arrangements for the baby to be admitted into the agency the following day.

Q. Did you explain what was to happen in the event the baby was surrendered to the Spence-Chapin Adoption Service to Miss Scarpetta and to her sister?

A. Yes, I did.

Q. Before the surrender was signed?

A. Yes.

Q. Did they understand?

A. From my observation, yes.

Q. Did Miss Scarpetta wish to sign a surrender of the

baby with Spence-Chapin?
A. Yes.
Q. About how long after the baby was born?
A. Around May 29, we had an appointment for the signing of the surrender.
Q. Will you tell us what was said when she came in to sign the surrender?
A. Well, she read and started crying and seemed upset, and we decided to wait a little longer. She would be ready, she said, the following Monday. Her mind would be made up, and she made an appointment for June 1, 1970. She came on the 1st.
Q. Was her sister in the agency that day?
A. I believe, downstairs.
Q. Then, on Monday, Miss Scarpetta signed the surrender?
A. Yes, she did.
Q. Did she read it in your presence?
A. She did.
Q. Did she understand what she was doing?
A. She said *yes*.
Q. At the time Miss Scarpetta signed the surrender, was she calm?
A. Well, she cried, but it is normal when a mother signs a surrender. She was not as upset as the previous week.
Q. After the baby was tendered, did Miss Scarpetta come to discuss the return of the baby?
A. Yes, but it didn't happen that easy. The agency received a call from Miss Veolitz, the lady that referred Miss Scarpetta to our agency, about the 23rd of June. Miss Veolitz advised Miss Scarpetta to contact her case worker, and she called me the following day to talk. I made an appointment to see her.
Q. Tell us what was said that day.
A. At the June 29 meeting, we talked about all of the

things discussed the past few months. I asked her if she understood that the surrender was a final legal document. She said *yes*. I asked her if she felt forced into signing the surrender. She said, "No, it was my decision." She just changed her mind. She wanted her baby back because she loved her. (As I read those words, my heart sank. What was I experiencing—pity for her? Fear for me? Guilt? I don't know, I only know the words cut into me like a knife.)

Mr. Reardon: I have no further questions.

Cross Examination by Mr. Zalk:

Q. Miss Daniels, the call from Miss Veolitz was on June 23?

A. Yes.

Q. And the purpose of the meeting that eventually took place on June 29 was to discuss the return of the child to Miss Scarpetta, is that right?

A. No, it was to discuss whatever she wanted to talk to me about. When Miss Veolitz called on the 23rd, I did not speak to Miss Scarpetta.

The Court: But did you know on the 23rd that her interest wasn't in putting the child up for adoption any more?

The Witness: Yes, I did.

Mr. Zalk: I have nothing further.

LOYCE BYNUM, residing at 1270 Fifth Avenue, New York City, New York, called as a witness in behalf of the respondent, being first duly sworn, testified as follows:

Direct Examination by Mr. Reardon:

Q. Mrs. Bynum, will you tell us what your position is with Spence-Chapin?

A. I am the Associate Executive Director of Spence-Chapin.

Q. Tell us what Spence-Chapin does.

A. Basically, we are a nonprofit adoption agency. We receive children from their natural parents and take steps to place them in suitable homes with steps to assure that the placements will be successful.

Q. Does the agency have any religious affiliation?

A. We are a nonsectarian adoption service.

Q. Did you participate in considerations leading to a refusal to honor the surrender of the baby in this case?

A. Yes. I participated in the decision to uphold the surrender and retain custody of the child.

Q. Will you tell the court, please, what factors entered into Spence-Chapin's judgment to do what was in the best interest of the child?

A. First, Miss Scarpetta was a mature thirty-one-year-old adult who freely and voluntarily signed the surrender without coercion or force by her own admission. She could have placed the child in long term foster care until such time as she might assume the care of the child herself. She could have told her parents about the child which I understand she plans to do at this time, or she could have asked for their help in supporting the child. She could have given the child to her sister in Colombia or cousins in New York for them to raise, or she could have worked out some arrangement with the alleged father whom she still sees. Instead, she signed the surrender for the placement of the child in adoption.

Q. Did her financial condition in any way enter into her judgment?

A. Miss Scarpetta was under no financial pressure. She suggested the child be brought up in a home with two parents which she thought was in the best interests of a child. This she decided despite all the options available to her.

Q. Has this child been placed?

A. Yes, in a fine adoptive home where the couple

adopted a child previously and the child's future is extremely bright.

Q. Is there any investigation of adoptive couples?

A. We make a thorough investigation. We get to know the people as well as possible. We visit their home. We see them in individual interviews. We see them in joint interviews. We gather reference material. We have medical reports. We go into lives to determine responsible adoptive couples.

Q. After the child is placed, is there any supervisory period?

A. We have a post placement supervision during which we visit the family periodically to satisfy ourselves that they are happy with the child and that the child is happy in the home.

Q. Is Spence-Chapin satisfied with the placement of this baby?

A. The adoption is highly satisfactory. Spence-Chapin is highly satisfied with the placement.

Mr. Reardon: I have no further questions.

Cross Examination by Mr. Zalk:

Q. Mrs. Bynum, how long has Miss Scarpetta's baby been in the home?

A. About a month, I believe, after the surrender.

Q. You referred to options that Miss Scarpetta had. Did you discuss them personally with her?

A. I did not. The caseworker, Miss Daniels, did.

Q. Did you ever have personal discussions with Miss Scarpetta?

A. No, I did not.

Q. I would like to read something to you, Mrs. Bynum. "So important is the status of a natural parent that in planning the best interests of a child, it may counterbalance, even outweigh the superior material and cultural advantages which may be afforded by the adoptive parents, provided of course, that the parent is fit, competent and able to maintain, support, and educate such a child, for experience teaches that it is mother love that is one factor which will endure after other claims and material advantages and emotional attachments may have proven transient." Do you agree with that quotation, Mrs. Bynum?

A. From my experience with adoptions, I must disagree.

Q. If I were to tell you that this quotation is from Mr. Justice Botein, presiding justice of the appellate division in New York, would that change your opinion?

A. No. I think that adoptive parents do have the love and it is not transient.

Q. Don't you think it is better for a child to be with the natural parent?

A. If a natural mother in good faith surrenders her child and the child is placed in an adoptive home where the parents invest their love and attention and hopes and dreams, then I think that the child should remain in that home because it will just play havoc in the lives of children if surrenders are overturned when natural mothers decide to rescind.

Q. In your experience, can you tell us how many times natural mothers ask to revoke a surrender?

A. I couldn't tell accurately, but the times are rather rare.

Q. Would it be 1 percent or 5 or 10 percent?

A. Well, not more than 1 percent, I believe.

Mr. Zalk: I have nothing further.

Redirect examination by Mr. Reardon:

Q. Mrs. Bynum, in that 1 percent where natural mothers come to Spence-Chapin, there are cases, are there not, where Spence-Chapin will rescind the surrender?

A. Yes, if the child has not been placed. For instance,

if the child is in one of the foster homes, pending adoption, and the natural mother has a good plan for that child, we have rescinded the surrender voluntarily.

Mr. Reardon: Thank you, Mrs. Bynum.

The Court: Mrs. Bynum, did you know at the time you placed this child for adoption that the mother sought to revoke her adoption consent?

The Witness: She had not sought to do so, sir, when we placed the child. We would never have done so if she had.

Mr. Zalk: I have nothing further.

Mr. Reardon: Your Honor, may I recall Miss Daniels for one question?

The Court: Yes.

GLORIA LAVERNE DANIELS having previously been sworn, was recalled and testified further as follows:

Direct Examination by Mr. Reardon:

Q. Miss Daniels, prior to August 3, 1970, did Miss Scarpetta ever tell you that she wanted to rescind the surrender which she signed on June 1 of 1970?

A. Yes, she did.

Q. When?

A. On the afternoon of June 29, 1970.

Mr. Reardon: Thank you.

Cross Examination by Mr. Zalk:

Q. Between June 29, 1970, and August 3, 1970, had you spoken to Miss Scarpetta on the telephone?

A. Yes. Three times, I believe.

Q. What was the substance of those conversations?

A. Long conversations about the surrender of the baby and the writ.

Mr. Zalk: That is all.

Redirect examination by Mr. Reardon:

Q. Do you know when the baby was placed with the adoptive family?

A. The baby was placed on the 16th of June, I think.

The Court: She doesn't know.

Mr. Reardon: She doesn't know. I am going to get somebody who does. (Witness excused.)

DOROTHY PERKINS MONTAGUE, residing at 453 6th Street, Brooklyn, New York, called as a witness in behalf of the respondent, being first duly sworn, testified as follows:

Direct Examination by Mr. Reardon:

Q. Are you familiar with the placement of Miss Scarpetta's baby?

A. Yes, I am. I was the supervisor of the worker who placed the child with the adoptive family.

Q. Will you tell us the date the baby was given to the adoptive couple?

A. One month after its birth the child was placed for adoption. June 18, 1970.

The Court: Did you inform the adoptive parents of the possibility that they may not keep the child; that there was a possibility of a legal action?

The Witness: Based on our long experience and the occasions that this has arisen, we discussed this thoroughly and decided it was not in the best interests of the family to inform them although I do believe they will be informed if it is necessary. I could go into the reasons further.

The Court: No. (Witness excused)

The Court: Do you have any other witnesses?

Mr. Reardon: No other witnesses.

(So that was it. I had read the entire text of the trial. The only thing left to read was the judge's decision. Obviously, I knew what he decided but felt compelled to know how and why he reached his decision. I hoped it might clear up some confusion.)

SUPREME COURT: NEW YORK COUNTY

SPECIAL TERM: PART XII The State of New York, ex rel.
OLGA SCARPETTA, on behalf of
BABY SCARPETTA,   Index No.
34102/1970 Petitioner,
-against
SPENCE-CHAPIN ADOPTION SERVICE, Respondent.

ASCIONE, J.:

Petitioner is an unwed mother who came to this country from South America for the prime purpose of having her child delivered here secretly, refusing a proffered abortion, and without the knowledge of her parents or sisters as to her pregnancy.

Upon contacting the hospital in New York County, she was referred to the Respondent, Spence-Chapin Adoption Service. After quite a few conferences with the Respondent, she agreed to give up the expected child for adoption.

The child was born on May 18, 1970, and the Petitioner voluntarily surrendered her to the Respondent, first by authorizing the child's placement in a foster home for boarding care on May 22, 1970, when she physically delivered the child to Respondent, and on June 1, by executing a surrender form with a present consent to any future adoption.

The infant was then placed in a foster home on June 18, with a view toward subsequent adoption. The petitioner repented her actions and, since June 23, has consistently tried to reclaim her baby, but the respondent has refused to return the child, indicating that it would resist her attempts to do so. There is no evidence that the prospective adoptive parents were notified.

The petitioner is thirty-two years of age, from a well-to-do family, having studied in universities here and abroad. She is employed in New York City with a take-home pay of more than a hundred dollars weekly. Further, she has informed all the members of her family of her plight and will now have the assistance and help of her family. An old and trusted family employee will come to this country to care for the child while the petitioner is at work.

She alleges that during the period prior to and at the time she surrendered the child, she was despondent, confused, and ashamed. She had not confided the moral lapse to her parents fearful that she would break their hearts. Children, regardless of age and sophistry, do not realize that parents' hearts do not break easily. They are cut quite often but do heal.

The issue here is not whether the petitioner can rescind the surrender of her child, but whether the child's best interests are served by its return to its natural mother. (Social Service Law 383; Peo. ex rel. Roe v. Edwards, 31 A D 2d 64, aff'd 23 Ny 2d 925) rather than with prospective adoptive parents (both of whom are professional people with another adopted child.)

Much has been said of motherly love. ". . . a fullness of love for the child; a totality of dedication to it, and all-embracing consecration that knows no wavering, no swerving. This is a mother's gift, for which, society holds, a child may well count all the world well lost." (Peo. ex. re. Gramert v. Free Synagogue, etc., 194 Misc. 332, 344.)

The court is aware of the excellently performed task of the Respondent, Spence-Chapin Adoption Service, in their matching ability and their sincere efforts to find suitable and compatible homes for the adoptees, but it does appear that they acted in undue haste in the placement of the one month old child in this instance. The mother had indicated her revocation quite timely and consistently.

In other cases, the lack of timeliness or consistency had been a detrimental factor for the mother. (Peo. ex rel. Roe v Edwards, 31 A D 2d 64, aff'd 23 N.Y. 2d 925; Peo. ex rel Poe V. New York Foundling Hospital, 33 A D 2d 83.) The record in this case sufficiently shows that the petitioner has adequately stabilized her own relationships and has become stable enough in her own mind to warrant the return of the child to her. It appears that the petitioner is motivated solely by her concern for the well being of her child. It appears that petitioner is fit, competent, and able to duly maintain, support, and educate the child.

This court suggests that if Respondent desires to appeal, it do so as expeditiously as possible in order not to increase the sorrows of the prospective adoptive parents, who had the infant through this five-month period when the infant is so ingratiating with recognitions, smiles, and chuckles. In all probability, if they knew that the mother wanted the child, they would have voluntarily returned the baby.

After considering all the facts, the court is of the opinion that the child should be forthwith returned to petitioner, its natural mother.
Settle judgment.
Dated, November 16, 1970.
J.S.C.

I turned over the documents and walked slowly upstairs to our bedroom. I sat on the bed. My eyes became accustomed to the dark, and it was then that I saw Nick lying on the bedspread fully clothed.
"I thought you were sleeping," I said.
"I was thinking. Did you get through the text of the trial?"

"Yes, I did." Trouble and sleep fight like cats and dogs.

Chapter VI

Despair is a horrible feeling. I sat in the outer waiting room of the law offices of Simpson, Thatcher, and Bartlett waiting for Mr. Reardon. I held onto Nick's hand tightly. Fear held me in its grip. I thought just another dream, and I would awaken shortly.

Nick and I had been waiting only a minute or two then ushered into Reardon's office. It was a large room with huge glass windows which overlooked the tip of Manhattan. Reardon, who resembled a young looking Rudy Vali, got up quickly from his huge desk, introduced himself, and shook our hands. He seemed to have a rather impersonal look which didn't set too well with me. I was pleased, however, to see pictures of his children prominently displayed around the office.

He and Nick immediately began to exchange legal ideas, and Nick spoke to Reardon on my behalf. I wanted to speak for myself but had a difficult time keeping my emotions in check. Just as I was about to say something, the door opened and a tall, thin, young man with bushy hair and a studious look entered the room.

"This is Mr. James Wawro, my assistant," said Reardon.

Young Wawro took our hands and said to me, "I'm real sorry this happened, Mrs. DeMartino." Then he looked to the floor and took a seat against the wall. His presence somehow comforted me. He was obviously shy, but I picked up good vibrations.

I turned my attention to Mr. Reardon and finally said, "I spent the entire night trying to figure out how this whole thing could possibly have come to pass, and I still don't understand any of it, but what I'd like to know is where we fit into all of it?"

"Well, Spence-Chapin is prepared to take this case as far as it has to go, but we are of the opinion that it will go no further than the next court. Nick tells me you read the decision, Mrs. DeMartino; if so, then you will agree that it was based upon emotion rather than prudence. After all, with all due respect, this case goes beyond just you and the baby. It has social significance. If the courts let natural mothers arbitrarily overturn bonafide surrenders to adoption agencies, the result would create an air of uncertainty and possibly disrupt the entire adoption process. The Appellate Court will, I'm sure, see it in that light and reverse the lower court's decision."

"According to what Nick tells me, it will take six to seven weeks for the case to be heard, and we will not be asked to appear in court."

"That's correct. The Appellate Court merely reviews the lower court trial and the decision made by the judge of that court. They hear arguments from attorneys for both sides as to why the decision should remain or be reversed and then come to their conclusion. I really think this court will be more concerned with the legalities of this case."

"Which means you are of the opinion that Lenore will ultimately remain with us?"

"Yes."

"And if the opposite should happen and the court upholds the lower court's decision and once again rules that Lenore has to be turned over to her natural mother, will there be any conditions accompanying that turnover?"

"I don't think I understand."

"Well, will there be a supervisory period? Will a social worker follow up to see to it that Lenore is doing well and that Miss Scarpetta has adjusted to the role of motherhood?"

"Jean, we could always appeal to a higher court, but as I explained, this court merely goes by what was said under oath in the lower court."

"So the answer is no! That's just great," I shouted feeling my blood pressure rise. "Do you know how much investigation was done in our lives before we were considered acceptable parents? Yet you tell me Lenore can be turned over to someone who is a virtual stranger at this point in her life and that there will be no followup. I must admit, Mr. Reardon, that I felt a surge of pity for this girl when I finished reading the text of the trial, but right now what I feel is anger, and I don't now whether it's her or you or the courts. Do you realize that the only thing that anyone knows about Miss Scarpetta is what she has chosen to tell? She could have said she was a nuclear physicist or the tooth fairy. Isn't some kind of proof of her statements or her stability necessary?

"The fact is that she turned over a little human being to the custody of someone else; now she tells the court simply, 'I made a mistake I'm sorry. Time out. Give her back to me. I'm sorry for any *inconvenience* I've caused others. I'm fit because I just told you so and will never waver again because I just told you so. Although I haven't seen my child since birth or even cared enough to name her, I want her back because I now realize I love her!"

"Now, Mrs. DeMartino, I know this is hard on you, and believe me, I wish there were two Lenores. I met and questioned the young lady, and her answers seemed honest and straightforward and she seemed a lovely girl."

I jumped up from my chair, placed both hands on Reardon's desk, and looked him squarely in the face. "Is that so?" I said. "Well, let me tell you something about this 'honest young lady' that you speak about. Her opening statement at the trial was that she moved that very day to a new address near her relatives, yet in the trial she states that she will be moving in a week. How does that strike you?" I didn't wait for an answer. I backed away from his desk and continued shouting at him as I paced up and down the office. I could feel Reardon's eyes following. "Then she testified that she didn't know the natural father was married and that she was crushed by this newfound knowledge, but Miss Daniels relates that Miss Scarpetta didn't let him have the child, because she didn't like the way he brought up his children. Well, if she didn't know of his marriage, how could she possibly have known his children, or more especially, how they were brought up? She further testified that she has $20,000 in the bank to call upon in need, yet at one point, she stated that she gave up the baby because she felt financially insecure. So much for this 'honest' young lady's testimony given under oath."

    I returned to my seat, sat on the edge of it, and once more leaned over Reardon's desk. "Permit me to remind you," I continued, "that this is a thirty-two-year-old woman we are talking about, not a thirteen-year-old child although she certainly is being treated like a child. Maybe that's it! Maybe she projects the maturity of a teenager. The judge did everything but pat her physically on the head. But then I wasn't there, so perhaps he even did that. This poor thirty-two-year-old, according to the judge, had not confided her moral lapse to her parents," I said sarcastically, "so she ran away from home. Now all is forgiven. Mama and Daddy know; the judge has given her the baby, and they can all go home and live happily ever after. Or can they? It now turns out that Miss Scarpetta wants to stay in the States because she 'gets along better with the people in the United States.' I wonder if having an

American baby would make her stay easier? She's even thinking of giving up her Colombian citizenship, but she wants to be very sure. When is this girl sure of anything? At one point she felt sure that the baby would be better off in a family environment and that it should be placed with its adoptive parents as early as possible, and now that all that has taken place, she is equally sure that she wants Baby Scarpetta back."

I searched Mr. Reardon's face for some reaction, but he merely maintained that same cool, aloof expression. I looked at Wawro whose eyes fixed on the floor. He shuffled his feet nervously. I fell back in my chair wearily. There was a moment before I once again picked myself up and leaned forward on Reardon's desk only this time I spoke softly. "You said, Mr. Reardon, that you wished there were two babies, one for me and one for Miss Scarpetta. Well, in effect, there were two babies. There was Baby Scarpetta who came into this world with an uncertain future. She was placed in limbo, in a cocoon-like stage by her natural mother until she emerged—as does a beautiful butterfly—into Lenore DeMartino. Baby Scarpetta was but no longer is! She is now Lenore, my daughter, who is caught in this web which was not of her making—poor sweet little—" I couldn't finish. My voice cracked, and I just sat there and sobbed.

Mr. Reardon came to life for the first time. "Mrs. DeMartino," he said "you've got to believe that I am on your side and will do everything in my power to make things right again for you and your family. I would like to tell you that it will take less time and that you can be guaranteed a proper verdict, but you know I can't do that. I'm trying very hard to be encouraging, but I don't think you want me to lie."

"No, Mr. Reardon, I don't want you to lie."

How many times had Nick and I driven from

the city to our home via the Belt Parkway and used time together to share our thoughts and to plan our tomorrows? Today we were silent. What was there to say? We had to somehow try to get through the holidays and pray that in six weeks our lives would be normal again. We decided that we still wouldn't let anyone other than Doris, Bud, Vinnie and Marie know about our predicament. We felt that it would be harder to pretend that all was right with the world if we told the rest of the family and put a damper on happy times. Besides, they would probably want to know how something like this could happen; we still hadn't figured that out in our minds.

I was attempting to protect my family from hurt. Wasn't that what Miss Scarpetta was attempting to do? I found the comparison unsettling. Later that evening I shared these feelings with Nick and tried to explain my confused and conflicting feelings. "Do you suppose," I asked, "that Olga Scarpetta went through a kind of inner turmoil that you and I are experiencing now?"

Nick replied, "No matter how much introspection any of us does now, there can be no winners, only losers. If Miss Scarpetta gets custody of Lenore, she will have to live with the hurt that her actions inflicted upon others and will have to wrestle with her conscience in the years to come. On the other hand, if the agency prevails, we, too, will have to explain to a grown-up Lenore why we backed the agency and kept her from going to her natural mother."

Nick was right, yet the very thought of giving up Lenore was unbearable to me. The more I thought, the more painful it became.

Nick made me promise that I would stick to my normal routine as much as possible. So the following day I forced myself to attend a nursery school board meeting at the Lutheran Church around the corner. I had just become Chairman of the Board and was supposed to lead the meeting but was having trouble concentrating on the issues. Rev. Anderson, sensing something was wrong, picked up the slack and did most of the talking. I sat in the room, asking myself what I was doing there. I had Lenore on my lap, and Linda was upstairs in the nursery room with other children. One of the mothers had her two children, and they began to squabble. In almost hushed tones she began to reprimand them and said to the older one, "You are lucky enough to have a sister to play with and love so you must always try to be nice to her." That did it for me. The tears poured down my face. I quickly excused myself from the meeting and entered Rev. Anderson's office, Lenore in hand, and cried and cried.

Rev. Anderson came in shortly thereafter and asked if I wanted to tell him about it. Did I? I poured my heart out. I could tell he was astonished. Once he digested everything, he put his arms around me and comforted me. "I know you and Nick well enough to know what this is doing to you and how concerned you must be for Lenore's future. I will remember you all in my prayers, and I am here for you if I can help in some way." I left the church feeling somewhat peaceful. The following morning Nancy, one of the young ladies who was a member of the Nursery Board, stood in my doorway. She had a son the same age as my Linda. She had been very friendly, but this was her first visit to my home.

"I heard you weren't feeling well at yesterday's meeting, so I came to find out how you are," she said.

We chatted about the nursery while I got coffee on the table. Lenore was in her infant seat at the foot of the kitchen table.

"She's darling," Nancy said. "I love little girls. In fact, I just love children," she said, straightening up. "You seem so happy with your girls."

"Yes, I am."

"I thought about adopting, you know. After I had Billy, I tried to have more children, but I couldn't conceive. When I finally did, I had trouble maintaining the pregnancy."

"Oh, I'm sorry," I heard myself say.

"To be honest, that's really why I stopped by this morning. I've seen how happy you and your family are, and I know so little about adoption. People have so many different versions. I just thought maybe you wouldn't mind telling me something more about it."

I looked at this young girl, her searching eyes staring into mine. What do I tell you, Nancy, I thought? I wanted to shout out at the top of my lungs, DON'T DO IT. THEY WANT LENORE BACK. THEY ARE TRYING TO TAKE HER FROM OUR FAMILY! All the while Lenore sat in her little infant seat, looking up at us; the frown across her little brow made it appear as though she was trying to figure out what was going on. Nancy put her head in her hand and cried softly. I looked at her tall body shaking uncontrollably, and knew right then and there what I had to do. I thought of Rev. Anderson putting his arms around me and comforting me. I put my arm around her and said, "Now, it can't be all that bad. Why don't you start from the beginning?"

Poor Nancy bared her soul. She told me about all her disappointments and how anxious she was to have more children. I calmed her down as best I could, and when she left, she had a handful of pamphlets and information about adoption in her hand. She left smiling.

I shut the door behind me, leaned against it,

and wondered whether I had done the right thing. Perhaps I should have warned her, but then mine seemed like such an isolated case. What if the courts were to set everything right, where then would that leave Nancy? Once again I was thoroughly confused. But when I thought of how sullen Nancy was when she first arrived and how happy she was when she left, I just knew that I had done the right thing. As a matter of fact, I too found myself feeling hopeful.

I looked down at my little six-month-old angel, and we exchanged smiles. Could it really be only five months that she was with us? She was so little and scrawny when we first brought her home that her diapers just hung. Linda said she looked like a skinny chicken. Well, you couldn't call her that now! She had filled out beautifully. Her cherubic face attracted all that saw her. She had a winning smile and was a bundle of love. With her by my side, I decided to sit down and write the following letter to the adoption agency:

Dear Mrs. Bynum:
For reasons known to us both, I felt compelled to write this note to you. For two days now I have lived with the idea of impending tragedy. My first reaction was anger and the need to lash out at someone or something. I found it to be a good emotional release but was quick to realize that it served no useful end.

At this point my heart is saddened but not bitter. Placing the blame on someone's doorstep for this emotional upheaval that we are all going through is of no import. In fact, in order for this to make any sense at all, I must believe that all those involved in these circumstances acted in a manner which they believed to be reasonable.

The fact remains, however, that on June 18, 1970, my husband and I brought into our home our daughter, Lenore DeMartino, sister of Linda DeMartino, granddaughter, a niece, the cousin to many. Five months may seem like a short period, but to us it's a lifetime, the lifetime of our daughter, Lenore.

We all love her dearly and the prospect of losing her is not an easy one. My husband and I have tried after many soul-searching hours to view objectively the ultimate well being of Lenore over any personal needs we might have. We hold steadfast to our belief that Lenore will have a richer, fuller, and happier life in a home where so many have already proven their great love for her. We are secure in the knowledge that you of the Spence-Chapin Agency have evidently reached that same conclusion.

I pray to God to help us all.

Yours truly,
Jean DeMartino

The next days moved slowly; Thanksgiving came and went. Somehow I managed to keep my composure. The hardest moments were when people spoke of Lenore's future, such as a friend who gave me a snowsuit that her child had out grown but that Lenore would probably fit into the next year.

Then there were mom and pop. They adored her. Every time one of them picked Lenore up in their arms my heart would sink. Mom and dad only lived a few minutes away. Dad had just retired. Mom, who was a few years younger, planned on working until retirement age. Although dad was ready to stop working, he found being home without mom difficult. He was the kind of man who had been wrapped up in his work and who hadn't taken time to develop hobbies. Now, aside from being on in years, he was also not well. He was having more and more difficulty seeing and suffered from Parkinson's disease which caused his hands to shake to the point where he couldn't even write his name. But every afternoon, rain or shine, he would stop by the house to see the children. He and Lenore seemed to share that special something that occurs between the very young and the very old, a point when life goes full circle and the beginning and end join as one.

It was on one such afternoon when I sat watching dad and Lenore together that I felt almost as though I could view life through dad's eyes. I was so moved by them that I wrote my feelings down:

There's uneasiness in my breast. My hands snap. My fingers tap. There's sweat upon my brow. What is the here and now?
I cry for yesterday when life's veil was like a window shade open on high. Now almost closed, it causes me, on bended knee, to peek out at life. I tire easily!
Acceptance is the key. Perhaps I should lie back and patiently watch life close its gap unto its natural end, but till then, what? Pretend? Yes, suppose I cannot catch up with my yesterdays, and so I must take pause and view the scheme of things. Can it be? New life has brought new hope for me?

As I watched Lenore and dad together and thought of what this turn of events could mean to him, I panicked. I had to force myself to put such thoughts out of my mind.

In the interim, Mrs. Bynum from Spence-Chapin called to find out how the family was doing. Just hearing her voice broke the composure I had built for myself, and I cried so much I could hardly speak. She asked me to keep in touch with Mrs. Montague, the supervisor in charge of our adoption proceedings. I assured her I would.

Christmas approached; Linda was so excited

about having a sister to share Christmas with that she burst with all sorts of questions. She wanted to know whether Santa would mind if she opened her sister's presents for her, since she was too little to do it for herself. And could she make two stockings to hang up—one for her and one for Lenore? Would I buy them matching nightgowns for Christmas Eve? And could we tell Santa what she and Lenore wanted for Christmas?

I had to be strong for Linda if for no one else, and since I had no intention of robbing her of the joy of Christmas, I made arrangements with my sister-in-law Doris and her girls to visit Santa in a downtown department store.

The magic of seeing Christmas through the eyes of children helped me to forget for the moment the uncertainty, which lay ahead. On our way home, Doris and I were gabbing in the front while Linda and Lisa sat in the back with their sisters who were nestled in car seats. Their holiday mood carried through to the car and so they sang Christmas carols—a little off-key and making up some of the words which they didn't know. Our holiday mood, however, came to an abrupt end when Doris and I both became aware at the same time that the girls were singing, "We have sisters. We both have sisters." I looked over to Doris and saw a tear rolling down her face and could no longer hold back the tears from pouring out of mine.

Christmas came and went and along with it went a lot of joy and a lot of tears. The weather turned cold. I was home alone one day, once again feeling really sorry for myself, when I picked up the New York Daily Newspaper. On the front page was a picture of a young lady near collapse being held up by her distraught husband. Her child, who had been left in a carriage outside a store while she shopped had been kidnaped. Mayor Lindsey had every man on the force search for the infant. The deep sense of loss came over me as well. What will we do if we lose Lenore? I thought. How will we ever be able to deal with it? At least the newspaper story had a happy ending. The child was found the following day. I wished that I too could experience the relief that the mother must be experiencing.

Marie and Doris called often and comforted me as best they could. They also did their best to keep me as busy as possible. Their love and support meant a great deal.

I started to get restless, though; the waiting was hard. Probably the hardest part was not being able to take any action on my own behalf. The agency's attorneys had drawn up the legal papers. This time Nick was abreast of all the procedures and given copies of the formal papers. Time drew near, and I felt shaky. I read and reread the original trial papers in any effort to project myself objectively into the place of one of the judges, but, of course, it was impossible. I read Judge Ascione's decision so many times that I could have repeated it verbatim. Finally, I could bear it no longer, and so I drafted a letter to Judge Ascione.

Your Honor:

I write to you not as one who disrespects or disregards the laws and decisions of our land but as one who stands in awe of them. I write to you not as one who would question the sincerity and judgment of its officers, but as one who holds in highest esteem those men whose grave responsibility is to administer justice and equality.

I write to you because I have long been a silent party in an action over which you presided and which now is in the hands of the Appellate Division. I write to give voice to those unfortunate individuals who may follow in my footsteps. I write because I am an adoptive mother whose family is being threatened by separation and heartache.

I have been told that the court's decision as to custody in cases such as mine, rests upon two factors—the voluntary surrender of the child by the biological mother and the welfare of the child in question.

As to the latter, I suppose we could discuss the benefits afforded a child who grows up living in a loving family unit, but I prefer instead to talk about love—mother love. Let us analyze the differences between a biological mother and an adoptive mother. The one big basic difference is that one brings her child home from the hospital and the other brings her child home from an agency. It appears to me that the differences end there and the similarities begin. A very precious bonding begins between mother and child. It is both strong and delicate at the same time. It is that sensitive balance of worry and joy, of work and play, of caring and sharing which creates an invisible umbilical cord upon which mother and child are nurtured, one from the other. Love is that special something, which gives the mother the ferocity of a lion and the gentleness of a lamb and which imparts to her child a sense of well being.

Even in its earliest stages, I am hard pressed to understand how the destruction of all this could ever be attributed to the well being of any child. When a biological mother requests the rescission of her surrender do we discount the fact that she carried for a long period of time the burden of this life? Do we discount the pain of delivery and the joy of new life? Obviously these facts can NEVER BE DISCOUNTED.

They are very real happenings worthy of respect and compassion, but they must take their rightful place among the memories of the past, for it is the present which deserves our consideration and the present consists of a viable little human being whose best interest should remain paramount.

If you will permit me to call upon my personal experience, I can tell you that on three occasions I carried life within me. On two of these three occasions, I too carried the responsibility of life and felt the pain of birth, but not the joy of new life. My children arrived in this world prematurely and saw their end before they were even granted a beginning. God and nature are kind so that time does cure wounds, leaving only its scars behind. Our laws are also generous in that they provide for adoption so that women like myself can share the experience of new life and motherhood. With all that has taken place in my past, I hold steadfast to the belief that I started to become a mother the day I came home with my first child from the adoption agency.

Please don't think that I am unsympathetic to the mother who gives up her child. On the contrary, I am most sympathetic and can, to a certain extent, relate to her. But I believe that a woman who voluntarily surrenders her child forfeits those considerations that are ordinarily granted to a natural mother. Which brings to the next point in question and that is voluntary surrender.

When we refer to bonafide adoption agencies such as the Spence-Chapin Adoption Service, we are referring to respected institutions which perform a much-needed service for the community. We are confident that these institutions are of the caliber to deal gently and ethically with women who are in the throes of surrendering their children. I have been told that it is the policy of adoption agencies to counsel said mothers not only in the path of adoption, but to open other avenues of approach for them. That the agencies spend a great deal of time in terms of interviews, in advising said prospective mothers of the seriousness of the steps they are about to take and of the finality of surrender. Apart from finding a loving home for the child placed in their care, the aforementioned is the heaviest burden of the agency.

If the courts, in turn, tell our agencies that they are not to take the surrender signature by the biological mother seriously, then how are they in good faith going to serve those children who are left with them and in the final analysis the community? Shall we tell the agency that a woman who changed her mind one month after she signed the surrender has merely come to the realization that she is a mother and loves her child? Would that then make her a better mother and more deserving of the return of her child than the woman who changed her mind say five months after surrendering her child but not quite as good a mother as one who say changed her mind after two weeks from the date of surrender? What then will be the guidelines used by our institutions? Is the child to remain in limbo, unwanted and unloved, or is she to be passed on to some unsuspecting family only to be wrenched from their lives at some later date? Are we saying in effect that the biological mother is to receive all considerations, the child, secondary consideration, and the adoptive parents no consideration?

Let us carry this thought still further beyond the doors of the adoption agencies and into the homes of adoptive families. It appears as though the law affords them no rights, but what about our moral obligation to such a family?

Our family consists of a father, mother and two

girls; the oldest girl who is adopted is four years old. The youngest is seven months. They brought great joy to our lives, and we have been told by many that we wear our happiness and bond of great love for one another on our faces for all to see. Needless to say, my husband and I are distraught by the prospect of losing our daughter. But let's put aside my feelings and those of my husband's. Can we also put aside the feelings of the grandparents? A man and woman who are aged and whose wounds no longer heal easily? Can we put aside the feelings of a godfather who is a Marine in the service of his country? Shall we tell him that the laws of the land for which he is prepared to fight are the very laws which might take away his goddaughter? The list goes on and can certainly be more lengthy. However, the most important consideration, I left for last. What do we tell the remaining adopted child? What do we tell little Linda? Shall we tell her that her sister is going to have to live with another lady, but she is not to worry because the law states that since she was officially adopted that her biological mother cannot remove her from our home? Shall we tell her in years to come that her sister's mother realized a short period after surrendering her that she loved her and wanted her back? Shall we tell our little four-year-old that we are sure her biological mother loved her as much as to change her mind too, but that perhaps she took just a little too long to come to that conclusion?

    Is not the traumatic impact that an event such as this might have on this adopted child, who is also a ward of the court, a concern of the court? Or are we only to consider the plight of the biological mother whose only response for all the pain she may cause to so many is that she is sorry for any inconvenience and whose only defense is that she was upset at the time she signed the surrender? If we permit the biological mothers of the children who are surrendered to bonafide agencies to take lightly this surrender, if the courts sanction their actions, then are we not permitting one individual to play havoc with the lives and emotions of many?

Despite all the hurt that may await my family, we would gladly suffer these "slings and arrows" and more, if we could believe in our hearts that in the final analysis our children would benefit. But we see only despair and confusion ahead for them.

Why have I chosen to write all this to you now? You have already made your decision in this case. I write because I believe that you, as an officer of our courts, must by virtue of your position be a thinking human being. I write this letter because I believe that the silent principles have been silent too long. I write to you because I have a need to be heard—to speak for myself and my family and most of all for my daughter Lenore. I write because it is better to "light one candle than to curse the darkness." And I write with the hopes that my letter might brighten the path of those who follow. With all that in mind, I respectfully submit this letter to you.

Yours Truly,
Jean DeMartino

When Nick came home, I asked him to read it. He took forever. When finished, he just put it on the table. I couldn't stand it anymore.

"Well, what do you think?" I asked.

He hesitated. "I understand why you felt you had to write, but why don't you sit on it a while before you mail it. After all, it's getting close to the time that the Appellate Division will—"

"Okay Nick, I won't send it."

"Jean, I think we ought to hire a private

detective to investigate Olga Scarpetta. Maybe we can do it on our own, what the court should have done to begin with and—"

"Why don't we wait till after the hearing? Perhaps we'll have a clearer view."

It's strange how we had both succeeded in stopping the other's plan. Each of us in his own way felt as though we had to do something, and yet we were afraid to make a move or a sound until the danger passed.

Chapter VII

Nick called from the courthouse. "What's the matter Nick?" I asked anxiously. Nick had checked with the agency's attorneys, and they agreed that if he wanted to hear the case, he could sit in the rear of the courtroom and pretend he was a law student taking notes.

"Jean, I think Olga's here with her attorney."

"Oh no," I moaned. I could feel my stomach drop to the floor. "That's not fair, Nick. Again the judges have only her to relate to. You and I have to remain in the shadows. It's not fair, I tell you."

"There's nothing we can do about that. Her presence here may not mean a damn thing. These are judges who are interested in the law and the right and wrong of things, so just calm down. I've got to go now. Looks like things are about to start."

When I hung up, my head spun. Lenore was in her playpen with her toys. I looked at her little chubby face and listened to the happy sounds she made. The ringing phone interrupted my anxiety. It was Marie. She called to keep my mind occupied. When I finally hung up, I felt calm. What was I getting upset about? Today was the day that all our troubles would be over. The waiting had been the hardest part, now a higher court, five judges listened to both sides again. Surely they would see that the lower court's decision left loose ends. After all, the agency attorneys were right. This was a social problem as well as an individual one and all would certainly be taken into consideration.

Having convinced myself of this, I pushed all negative thoughts out of my mind and busied myself around the house.

Dinnertime arrived and I still hadn't heard from Nick. I just put hamburgers into a frying pan when I heard the key in the door. I flew to the front door and met Nick head on. Once again his face had that ashen color. He made an attempt to smile, but when his eyes caught mine, his lip quivered. "Jean, its no use—"

I said angrily, "Could you look into the hearts and heads of the five Judges and know what they are thinking?"

"I'm trying to tell you," he said.

"I don't want to hear it," I screamed at him. "You made it a certainty, and I'm not going to accept that. I'm going to hang on to hope."

"Jean, do you want to hang on to false hope? You want the facts so you can adjust to them, right? We don't stand a chance," he shouted.

I looked at Nick's face and saw the agony. I sank into the nearest chair and said, "All right, Nick, tell me about it."

"There were only four of the five judges present and as you know each side had an allotted amount of time to speak. The agency's attorneys, Reardon, appeared to make an honest attempt to reach the Judges, but as he spoke, the judges interrupted to ask questions. Now, Jean, that, in itself, is not unusual, but as the questions continued, I realized that they asked in a jeering and sarcastic manner. I thought it was my imagination, at first, but toward the end, I wanted to get up and shout, "What the hell is going on here?" I bit my tongue, however, and waited for Scarpetta's attorney, Zalk, to take the podium thinking to myself that if they handled him in the same manner, there would still be hope. What happened next was so unbelievable that I'm still in a state of shock. Zalk put his papers on the podium, opened them, and was about to make his presentation, when one of the judges said solicitously, "Mr. Zalk, I imagine you have a lot to do back at your office."

"Why, yes I do," he replied.

"Why don't you take care of it then? Quit while you're ahead," the judge said. "Can you believe? Those were his exact words. 'Quit while you're ahead.' I don't know what held me back from running up there and telling them all to go to hell. For the first time I felt personally disgraced by my profession. I looked over to Zalk who beamed. The woman with him threw her arms around him and kept saying *thank you*. It was Olga.

"I spoke to Reardon after the hearing," Nick continued, "He was really shook up. All he could say was, 'I'm sorry. I really tried my best.' He asked me to tell you how sorry he was and to assure you that the agency was prepared to take the case as high as the courts would permit in an effort to have the ruling overturned."

"What other appeals do the courts permit?"

"What Reardon meant was that if this court comes down with a unanimous decision, and it sure looks as though it will, then the only way the agency can get to the highest state court is if the Court of Appeals, itself, gives the agency permission to be heard. In other words, where you have a split decision, you have the right to be heard by the state's highest court, but in the case of unanimous decisions, it is the higher court which has the right to decide whether or not it will take the case."

"Terrific," I said sarcastically, "Is that all the good news you've got?"

"No, there's more, and I don't know how to soften what I'm about to say, Jean, but I think you also need to know that a unanimous decision would mean that Lenore would have to be turned over at that point. The agency could attempt to continue its legal battle but without Lenore. The only way it could be avoided is if the agency moves swiftly and gets one of the judges from the higher court to sign what we call a stay of execution which would permit Lenore to stay with us until such time as the higher court decides whether it will hear the case."

I threw myself into Nick's arms. "Isn't there anything we can do?" I asked.

"Nothing much," he said softly, "except hope and pray that the decision is not unanimous. I know this is difficult; it is difficult for all of us, but I felt you needed to know where we stand."

I pulled myself away from his arms. "It's all very simple. If the agency gets a five-nothing ruling against them, we lose Lenore. Unless, of course, they get a stay of execution. If the agency does get the stay of execution, but the high court decides not to hear the case, we lose Lenore. If the higher court decides to hear the case but decides against the agency, we lose Lenore. Am I right?" I asked hysterically.

"What we need right now are a few minor miracles."

"What if we manage to survive all this, and the high court rules in favor of the agency, would that be the end of it? Would Lenore finally stay with us?"

"Reardon and I both agree that the best we can hope for is that the Appeals Court will send the case back to the first court for a retrial and that a stronger case will be presented by the agency."

"Nick, this uncertainty can go on forever," I sobbed.

He said put his arms around me and stroked my hair, "And remember, it gets harder for all of us with every day that passes. I wish I could tell you that everything is going to be all right, but I see very little hope." How do you sleep at night when you face the certainty that you are going to lose your daughter and that an uncertain fate awaits her? I thought about the many people who lost little ones through sickness and accidents. What pain they carried in their hearts. So many must have cried in their pillows as I cried that night.

I was grateful that Nick was an attorney and was able to explain the legal procedures so that my mind could grasp what lay ahead. But on the opposite side of the coin was the realization that his opinion was a legal one, based upon his knowledge, experience, and understanding of the law and he saw "little hope."

Nick spent no better night then me. By five o'clock the next morning, my bloodshot eyes looked into his weary face, and we both decided that it was futile to stay in bed much longer. I dragged myself downstairs and sipped coffee when Nick said, "It came like a flash this morning, Jean. There is something we can and must do." My ears perked up. I could feel my heart beating fast and my body coming alive. "We've got to go to the newspapers with our story. All night, those words, 'Quit while you're ahead' danced in my head. I could feel a furor building up. It was my good fortune to be sitting in that courtroom to hear what went on, but now the public is going to find out what goes on behind those doors. I don't really expect the public's reaction to be of any direct help to us or Lenore, but at least everyone will be informed. We won't spend the rest of our lives explaining or making excuses for ourselves. Besides, no one should be placed in the position that our family has been placed in, a woman going to sleep at night, her whole world falling apart because she dared to love. Childless couples applying to adoption agencies and opening their hearts and homes with full faith to little ones only to find that they are faced with tragedy at the mere whim of another human being and that they are left helpless and defenseless in the eyes of the law. Jean, as attorney, I was totally unaware of this possible outcome, so how about Joe Public? They have a right to know, and we've got to tell them our story."

"But Nick, then Miss Scarpetta will know who we are."

"It's either now or when the baby gets taken from us. There's little choice. Besides, Jean, we've been doing things the so-called right way and it kept our mouths shut and hands tied. If we really care about Lenore and her future, then we are going to have to shout. We are going to have to be heard in the press and the courtroom. For too long, we sat in the shadows afraid to be seen by the natural mother, afraid that our anonymity which we held so dearly would be lost. But isn't it better to lose our privacy than our daughter? You and I are going to fight. I'm going to figure a way to get us into that courtroom to plead our cause. There must be a custody lawyer somewhere who can help me figure out a way. No more sitting back and taking it on the chin. What do you think? Are you up to it, honey?"

Am I up to it? I looked at this man who had just given me renewed hope and probably loved him more at that moment than ever in my entire life. "Nick, I've never been more ready."

"I'll call Bernie Keegan, his best man when he got married was Owen Fitzgerald who writes a byline for the *Daily News*. I'll ask him to get an appointment for me." Nick dialed. Bernie was a brother attorney, and Nick was fond of him. The feeling seemed mutual. Nick said, "Bernie, this is too important to me. I can't waste time. If Fitzgerald is half the guy you say he is, then he won't mind being awakened by a stranger with a weird story at 6:00 A.M. But do me a favor, call him later and tell him I'm on the level and not a crackpot."

My mind drifted back to the week before when

in an effort to forget our problems, we had gone to the movies and seen *Tora, Tora, Tora*. When the news reached Admiral Yamamoto that the Japanese bombed Pearl Harbor, he failed to join his crew in the excitement of the moment. When one of his men asked why, he replied, "I had hoped that our ambassador would have made the declaration of war prior to our attack. Now it has taken on the appearance of a sneak attack and WHEN YOU APPRISE THE AMERICAN PUBLIC OF INJUSTICE, YOU AWAKEN A SLEEPING GIANT." When Nick got off the phone, I repeated those words to him. He looked at me quizzically. His words came back just as you were speaking to Mr. Fitzgerald. What did he say?"

"He'll call me back. He took my office and home number. I didn't expect more than that, Jean. After all, our story is pretty wild. Let's face it, all he had to go on was Bernie's name. He did say, however, that he's going to check with another reporter to see if he can get us an appointment. I'm sure he's going to check with Bernie too. In the meantime, I'm going to the office. While I'm gone, I'd like you to see if you can trace down a Mr. Joseph Spencer. He has been making inquiries about our case. Get in touch with him and find out why."

I checked the telephone book and came up with a Mr. Joseph Spencer, Esq. I waited until nine o'clock and then put through a call to his office.

"This is Mrs. DeMartino. You don't know me, but I'm the woman involved in the adoption case that you've made inquiries about."

"I'm on the board of the Adoptive Parents Committee, and we keep informed on all litigation regarding adoption."

"I see. You just answered my question, Mr. Spencer. I truthfully didn't know such a committee existed."

"Our main thrust is to enlighten our legislators about the need for newer and more realistic laws regarding adoption."

"You mean there have been other cases like mine?"

"Not exactly, Mrs. DeMartino. Yours has some unusual twists especially since there is an agency involved. But I think you'd have to agree that whether the case involves an agency or private placement, the hurts and heartaches are the same."

"I'm sure they are."

"You might be interested in knowing, Mrs. DeMartino, that I read a transcript of your original trial and the judge's decision. I never read anything more outlandish or dangerous in my life and wait anxiously to hear what the Appellate Court has to say."

"The hearing was yesterday, Mr. Spencer, but Nick and I are pretty sure of the outcome." I proceeded to fill him in on the events as best I could. When I finished, there was a long dead silence from the other end of the phone.

"Mr. Spencer?"

"I'm thinking, Mrs. DeMartino, just thinking. All may not be lost. You say that you and your husband are ready to fight?"

"Yes, Mr. Spencer, we are very ready."

"Have your husband call me. I have a few ideas to talk over with him."

"Thank God," I whispered.

"What did you say Mrs. DeMartino?"

"I said, 'thank God,' and thank you too, Mr. Spencer." He chuckled a little and said, "You've placed me in good company. I'm sure He will be on our team too, Mrs. DeMartino."

I lost no time in getting to Nick. The ray of

hope that Nick and I saw that morning shone brightly now. I paced the dining room floor. Finally, the phone rang.

"Honey, we just got ourselves a lawyer," Nick said. "Spencer and I believe that we should be able to intervene in the case. Since custody of Lenore was passed on to us by the agency, we too should have a right to be heard in court. Since I will be a party in this litigation, it's best that Spencer represents us as our attorney."

"Be my guest."

Back and forth, back and forth over the same path in the rug. I was alive again, reborn. For the first time since this awful nightmare began, we were actually doing something to help our daughter. Some of the fear and panic began to leave. But a nagging pain in the pit of my stomach still ached and refused to be still. Up and down, up and down the green rug I walked. I heard Nick telling Mr. Spencer about the proposed interview with the press. "I've got to call back today to find out if they'll talk to me." "Good," Mr. Spencer would say, "very good. Based upon what you told me Nick, we're fighting a game of time. So I think we better get our wheels in motion real fast."

At the office, Nick's secretary was a good sport and very eager to help. Mr. Spencer and Nick drafted a "Show Cause Order," directed to the Appellate Court where the decision was pending. Mary typed and I paced. Only this time with anticipation.

Nick and Mr. Spencer explained that if we could get one of the five judges to sign our order, then we would be permitted to intervene and hopefully a new trial would follow where all parties would be heard. When I recalled the options available to us yesterday, that sounded like one of those miracles we were looking for.

We literally flew to the Appellate Court. I asked the men what they thought our chances were of getting the Order signed. Nick hesitated but Mr. Spencer was confident. "They'll have to sign," he said. "I don't see that they have any choice in the matter."

We walked assuredly up the steps of the courthouse and into a marble corridor practically empty except for statues and long benches. The tall ceilings and large wooden doors leading into other rooms gave an awesome appearance. Nick and Mr. Spencer asked me to wait on a bench as they searched out one of the Judges. I sat for a while looking around and becoming fidgety. What if it didn't work out as we thought? What if they don't get one of the Judges to sign the papers? Panic gripped me again. I felt my body buckling. I tried desperately to put these thoughts out of my mind when Mr. Spencer and Nick entered the corridor from an adjacent room. They talked hurriedly, and Nick had that worried look on his face.

"Oh please, God," I heard myself say, "don't let it be false hope. Please help us. I don't think I'll be able to pick myself up after this fall." I walked toward them. Nick waved me back into my seat and talked to a tall, thin man who stood about six feet away. I heard the man say, "Yes, I'm the chief judge's secretary, and I'll tell him of your request, but I don't think it will do much good. I'm familiar with the case and can tell you that the judge felt strongly about it."

My heart sank. I felt my body tilting and heard the moans emerging while I rocked back and forth. The conversation went on, then the man turned on his heels and left. Nick and Mr. Spencer walked over. I looked up and continued to hold my belly with both hands and rock back
and forth on the bench.

Nick said, "We've run into a few snags, but

there's a good chance. The chief judge's secretary is checking to see if he'll meet with us now."

Just then the secretary returned. He walked over and said, "I'm sorry, he won't see you."

"You mean, he won't see us this morning?" Nick asked.

"He won't see you at all." I watched Nick grab him by the arm and try to move him out of earshot. It was very quiet in the corridor and I heard everything.

"What the hell kind of man is he?" Nick asked. "Can you take a look at my wife over there and see what this is doing to her and then just as calmly as you please tell me I'm dismissed? Is this the justice Americans hold so dear? Is this what it all boils down to?" Nick's voice rose a little, and I heard the secretary say, "Calm down a little please." Mr. Spencer just stood by shaking his head like a man who refused to believe what he'd heard.

"Calm down?" Nick said. His voice was louder and louder. "My wife suffered the loss of children in childbirth and now this. How much more is she expected to take? And you stroll down and tell me His Majesty refuses to see us."

"Mr. DeMartino, the agency will probably give your wife another baby, and she'll forget about all of this soon enough."

"You make me sick," Nick said.

"Mr. DeMartino, I understand what you're going through far better than you think. My wife had a miscarriage too, and we both still bear the scars of it, but they do wonderful things these days with bed rest and the like. So maybe you'll be blessed with a child of your own."

"We're not talking about another child. We're talking about this one, and there's no way that we are going to turn her over. Get it? So, do me a favor and cut this shit out. Just tell me, are you going to help us or not?"

"Okay, Mr. DeMartino, don't ask me why I'm doing this but here goes. First of all, even if you get to speak to the judge, you'd get nowhere. He's got it *in* for this agency and that's where it's at!" When I heard him say that, total frustration overcame me. Lenore's whole future lay in the balance and the court played politics. I sprawled out on the bench and wished I were dead.

"Next," he said, "You brought your Show Cause Order to the wrong place." It should be presented to Judge Ascione of the lower court where the case was originally heard, but if you plan on getting him to sign your order, you'd better do it in a hurry because a little bird told me that the decision on this case will be coming down on Tuesday."

"That's more like it! Thanks." Nick patted my shoulder and said "Come on, honey, the going got a little tough but we're still in there."

I noticed two men approaching Nick and Mr. Spencer. They each took one by the arm and said, "May we help you to the door?"

As we walked down the steps, I could hear Nick muttering every curse word he'd ever heard in his life. I think he would have put a career sailor to shame. Mr. Spencer was noticeably silent. As for me, I couldn't care less what was said or not said for that matter.

We, all three, got into the front seat of the car. Nick and Mr. Spencer threw legal jargon back and forth to one another. I just sat hunched over in a trance-like state.

"Damn it, Jean, you're no good like this," Nick shouted. "Sit up straight and stop the bullshit." He turned to Mr. Spencer. "Joe, if what the secretary said is so, the Appellate Court decision will be forthcoming Tuesday. That means we have to get to Judge Ascione today. I'll have my secretary retype the documents. Then it's on to plead our case."

Nick literally pulled me through the building to the office and threw me into a chair in the waiting room.

"Joe, you work with Mary and get this stuff retyped while I try to get an appointment with Judge Ascione. These guys usually leave early on Fridays, so we've got to work fast."

The clock on the office wall read 1:00 p.m. *How futile*, I thought, and didn't budge.

Mr. Spencer whispered, "How are we going to get Judge Ascione to see us?"

"I don't know," Nick said, "but damn, before the day is over, we'll be there."

As Spencer's words drifted out, Mary's eyes caught mine. She looked like a gal who had wished she'd gotten up in time to shut the door and keep the hurt away. I sat with my big tent-like winter coat weighing me down in the seat.

Mr. Spencer went over the papers with Mary. She retyped all the cover pages. The text remained the same.

Over and over I heard Nick dialing. I paid no attention to what he said. It didn't matter; in fact, nothing mattered. Just then Nick shouted, "I hit pay dirt; I reached a friend who is the secretary to a Brooklyn judge who is a friend of Judge Ascione. The judge will see us if we get there by 3:00."

The clock read 2:15 p.m.

"We'll be through retyping in about fifteen minutes and hightail it down there, Nick," Spencer replied.

"Some more good news, Joe. I got back to my friend on the *Daily News,* and he arranged an appointment for Sunday morning."

Mary finished typing the last letter on her machine when Nick ripped it from the typewriter. It was 2:35 p.m. Nick walked at such a fast pace that Mr. Spencer and I took running steps. My normally heavy coat felt like a ton on my shoulders. It was a cold day and my face, which was used to make up and lipstick, felt the lack of it as bitter wind slapped against my cheeks. If Judge Ascione agreed to see us, could that mean a shred of hope? I wanted so badly for hope to chase away despair.

Nick drove like a maniac as minutes ticked away. We got into some traffic on the West Side Highway. Mr. Spencer looked at his watch and said, "Three o'clock. With any luck we'll be there in ten minutes." Ten minutes later, Nick frantically made a left turn down the street to the courthouse when we heard a crash and felt a blow to the rear of our car. Through the rear view mirror, we could see a young man in a Volkswagen yelling at us. Nick had cut him off, and the other driver hit our rear fender. Nick stopped the car, jumped out, said something to the young man, got back in the car just as quickly and drove straight on. I could see through the rear view mirror that the young man followed us.

Mr. Spencer asked Nick what happened.

"I told the guy that the accident was my fault, but that I couldn't talk to him because of only a matter of minutes to get help for my daughter. I gave him my wallet and asked him to follow me. I'd square things out with him when I finished my business in the courthouse." Nick drove into the only available parking spot in front of the courthouse. We all jumped out leaving the doors wide open and ran. Spencer and I had a tough time keeping up with Nick. He yelled over his shoulder to us that he would meet us inside. Spencer said, "Jean, as long as Nick is going to find the judge, why don't you and I slow down a bit?" We slowed our pace to a walk and just as I did, I felt a tap on my shoulder. I came face to face with the young man from the Volkswagen.

"Here," he said handing me Nick's wallet. "There's nothing wrong with my car, so just forget the matter. All right? I hope everything works out for you all."

"That's kind of you," I replied fighting back tears. Spencer nudged me gently and said, "We better catch up with Nick." So we turned our heels and made our way up the court house steps. As we entered, we noticed the clock in the hallway read 3:00. We got onto a nearby elevator and asked one of its occupants if he could tell us where we could locate Judge Ascione. We rushed down the corridor to the courtroom only to find Nick running out. "He's not there; they tell me he is in his chambers."

When we finally got to the judge's chambers, we found Nick in the anteroom speaking to the judge's male secretary.
Nick said, "He's here, and he'll speak to us!" Spencer and I both let out a sigh of relief. The three of us were shown into Judge Ascione's chambers. I was feeling tired and beat.
Sitting behind a big desk was Judge Ascione, a middle-aged man with dark hair plastered down on his head, which gave him the look of the thirties. The room smelled of cologne. The judge looked more like he belonged in a cocktail lounge than in the court system. I don't know what I expected; perhaps I'd seen too many Andy Hardy films as a girl.

"I'm seeing you this afternoon because of Judge Monteleone who is a good friend of mine," he said in a very annoyed and unpolished tone. "But don't think that it's going to change anything because I've made my decision. So whatever these papers are about, don't bother to leave them. It's not going to do you any good."

I glared at him, unable to believe my eyes or ears. I could hear Nick and Mr. Spencer pleading their case and getting nowhere. I looked into this man's eyes and said almost inaudibly, "Judge, may I speak to you as a concerned mother?"

"No, Mrs. DeMartino, because you are not one," came as reply. I could feel my face flush and my heart beat quicker. "If I am not a mother," I said strongly, "then what would you call me?"

"Have you ever heard of parents going to a movie and leaving their child with a baby sitter?"

"Is that what you consider me then, a baby sitter?" I asked, my voice rising. "I respectfully submit that you don't know the meaning of the word mother. Permit me to be the one to enlighten you." I could hear my voice getting louder and higher pitched.

"A mother," I continued, "is a woman who scrubs floors to see that her children are well taken care of. A mother is not a woman who plays Ping-Pong with her child. She decides what is best for her child, not herself, and works endlessly toward that goal. I, a baby sitter? I'll tell you what, Judge; you bring that mother in here, present her with seven children, including my daughter, and ask her to pick out the child she claims is hers. Show me the same seven children, only this time, turn them over on their bellies, and I'll pick out my daughter by her buttocks." By now I shouted.

"Calm down, Jean," the judge said. I was no longer Mrs. DeMartino. "Now, listen to me," he said. "It wasn't an easy decision. It might interest you to know that I'm a godfather to an adopted child, so I really agonized. If you think I didn't lose sleep, you're mistaken. I had visions of that child turning up in an airport sink somewhere."

The thought of my Lenore left in a sink sent shivers down my spine. "What makes you so sure now that she won't?" I asked.

"Because Miss Scarpetta is a nice girl. Believe me, if you met her you'd like her."

"Because she's a nice girl? How did you make that determination, Judge? Because she looked like a nice girl or was it because she told you she's a nice girl. Do you know that she lied in your court room the very moment she opened her mouth to testify about where she lived and where she was moving?"

"Where she lives," he interrupted, "is of no importance, Jean. The fact remains that it's her child."

"Oh, I see, it's her property to do with as she sees fit, leave with a babysitter or drop in an airport sink as the mood may strike her. Perhaps you can explain why you picked an airport sink in particular?"

"Now stop it, Jean, I told you she's a nice girl, and you'll find that out if you meet with her."

"Fine. Everybody keeps telling me she's a nice girl; I believe you. But being a nice girl is not very high on my priority list for motherhood. Why don't we try responsible adult on for size? Are you convinced that she fits into that category?"

"Boy, you've really built up a lot of anger against her, haven't you?" he said.

"You have no concept of what is going on here. My anger is not directed at her. It's at you and a court system that permits this to happen. Maybe it is because Miss Scarpetta is nice that she permitted herself to get into all this difficulty from beginning to end. I don't know. But nice or not, she certainly is mixed up. That was evident through most of her testimony, and you can't be *Iffy* when you take on the responsibility of motherhood. You either do it or you don't. These are the things you should have considered when you made your decision. You had within your power the end of all this confusion and heartache, hers included. Now you're being given a second chance to get things right, and you're still closing your eyes."

"Perhaps your idea of the DeMartinos meeting with Miss Scarpetta would prove beneficial," Spencer interrupted placing himself between Ascione and me so that neither of us could see one another. "But in the meantime would you consider signing this Show Cause Order so that the DeMartinos can get a full hearing on what is best for Lenore?"

"When did you say the Appellate Court was going to announce its decision?"

"Tuesday!" he replied.

Judge Ascione picked up the papers and said almost to himself, "What can I do now? The case is before the Appellate Court. It's out of my hands."

"Judge, if you have any doubts at all, I'm pleading with you to sign those papers," Nick added quickly.

Once again the judge picked up the papers, glanced at them, and put them down. "Leave them here," he said. "I'll take them home and read over the weekend and think about signing."

As we left Ascione's chambers, I thought of the letter I almost mailed to him. What a waste that would have been!

We dragged ourselves to the elevator. All the way down, Nick and Mr. Spencer discussed the ramifications of the orders left with Ascione. The elevator door opened, and we were about to get off when Nick pushed us back.

"The papers!" Nick shouted.

"What about the papers?" asked Spencer.

"We didn't have them notarized. They are

absolutely useless as they are now."

We scurried back to Judge Ascione's office only to find it empty. We asked his secretary of his whereabouts. He informed us that he had gone for the day. When we explained to him that the papers we had given the Judge needed to be notarized, he dutifully took them off of his desk and handed them to us. "You have plenty of time to get them notarized and bring them back," he said. "I'll be here for a while."

Judge Ascione had, in fact, intended to do nothing about our plea. We nonetheless went through the motions. We searched through the courthouse for a Notary Public. My body went through the motions by rote. My brain was certainly incapable of sending any intelligent messages to my body. Nick took one look at Mr. Spencer and me and sent us on our way to the car. He would return the papers to the judge's office and meet us.

Mr. Spencer made a call to his office and then the two of us started on our way. I followed him blindly. The various doors and entrances blurred into one another. As we walked down the steps, the hall way appeared to darken. Mr. Spencer opened the door at the bottom and I followed. We found ourselves in the basement of the Supreme Court Building. I'm sure that if I weren't feeling so down that I probably would have broken into laughter. What else could go wrong? "Mr. Spencer, we had better go back and start all over again," I said.

"No, Jean, one of the doors must lead outside." We walked through a few hallways and opened a door only to find ourselves in what probably was the boiler room. Machinery made loud, grinding noises. By this time, we lost track of our turns and weren't quite sure about making it back to the original stairwell. I thought Mr. Spencer was upset about our circumstances and tried to comfort him when he blurted out, "I lost my hat. I've got to go back and find it."

We wandered through the basement to find an exit while Mr. Spencer lamented the loss of his hat. Nobody would believe this day, I thought, and now the curtain was closing on the final act—Mr. Spencer and I lost in the dungeons of the Supreme Court building. We finally made our way out of there, *sans chapeau*, and back to the car. Of course, Nick was there already.

"I've got to go back in the building and to find my hat. My wife Marta made it for me. (It was a Cossack type hat—black with gray Persian trim) and she would be upset if I lost it," Mr. Spencer said.

"Okay, Joe, you look and we'll wait here," Nick said.

Ten minutes later he returned without his hat. He was tired and hungry. None of us had eaten all day, but I couldn't eat anyway. We drove Mr. Spencer home. On the way, Nick tried to engage him in conversation, but Mr. Spencer was distraught over the loss of his hat, and could think and speak of nothing else. I was silent and physically and mentally spent. As Mr. Spencer got out of the car, he asked, "What will I tell Marta?" He didn't wait for an answer, I just absent-mindedly sputtered out after he was gone, "Why doesn't he tell her it's been a hard luck day all around. He lost his hat, and we lost our daughter."

As Nick drove off, he said, "I hope you feel better, taking out your frustration on an old man who has tried to help us. I sure am glad that he wasn't in earshot of your gratitude."

I stared out the window. I was beginning to feel detached. I wished to fall asleep. The next thing, Nick shook me violently. His face came into focus.

"You are not going to do this to yourself," he said. "You are not going to give up. Do you understand me?" he shouted. "I want you to get out of that trance right now! You are a fighter, and you are going to fight."

Nick drove to a nearby hamburger stand and bought me a hamburger and a milk shake. Just the smell of the meat made me nauseous. I heard him shout, "You've got to eat to maintain your strength!"

I put the burger and the shake down next to me.
He shoved the shake in my face and commanded me to drink. I put my lips to the straw and sipped. The sweet taste of the malt in my mouth made my stomach turn. I pulled the straw out of my mouth.

Nick started for home. All the way he preached. He never stopped talking. I didn't hear the words, only the sounds.
Finally, he parked the car in front of another Brooklyn Courthouse. "I 'm going to see Frank and thank him and Judge Monteleone for getting us in to see Judge Ascione. If police come along, just drive around the block. Do you hear me, Jean?"

I was so cold and had my big coat wrapped around me tightly, but my whole body shook uncontrollably. I watched Nick run across the big avenue and up the courthouse steps. The buses came and left. People lined up, entered the bus only for it to leave and have more people gather for the next one. I looked at their faces, wondered where they were going. They were all total strangers and yet I envied them. They went about their everyday living with no threats of disaster hanging over. I watched a black lady, who appeared to be of meager means, pick up her little snow-suited baby and hold him close as she entered the bus. I wondered if she knew how really rich she was. My thoughts race back to Lenore. Her smiling, trusting face, looking up into mine as she peered out through the crib slats this morning. How confident I felt. What a big kiss and hug I'd given her. Was that this morning? It felt like weeks had passed, and yet it was only one day.

I heard the car do or open. It was Nick jumping back into the driver's seat. "Jean, we have just begun to fight. I spoke to Frank, and thanked him for his help. We both agree that nothing will probably come of our talk with Judge Ascione, but we can still find a way. I believe that Jean."

Saturday and Sunday were hectic, but I still felt out of it most of the time. Nick broke the news as gently as possible to mom and dad and to the rest of the family. My telephone never stopped. Marie and Vinnie stayed the weekend. My mom and dad tried to be useful, but the news was so fresh to them and so confusing by this time that the poor old folks just walked around the house like two lost souls.

Doris took Linda for the weekend. That would be less confusing being away from the turmoil. She was right and I was grateful. Marie helped me take care of Lenore. I just sat on the dining room chair and rocked back and forth. Our family and friends were so concerned; they just kept calling all day long asking what they could do.

Nick did most of the talking; I did a lot of rocking!

Among our visitors that Saturday was Nick's law partner, Hal. He was upset but resigned. He held very little hope for us and in his own way thought the best help he could give was to accept the inevitable. Nick listened and fought him. He wasn't ready to resign himself to anything just yet.

I listened and just rocked.

Nick's friend, Frankie, who had gotten us to see Judge Ascione, dropped by. As a lawyer, he too was not optimistic but kept trying to think of new approaches, perhaps find some legal loophole that had not been hit upon. He and Nick threw ideas back and forth and came to dead ends by reaching the same ultimate conclusion. All the roads led nowhere.

I listened and rocked.

A business associate of Nick's came by, Barry Tash. Barry was born argumentative. He was a short, feisty fellow with furrowed brows and a frown. He was an intense man driven by love of family and loyalty to Nick among the few he considered friends. He bounded into our house, his face as red as a beet, shouting almost before he entered, "They can't do this. Who the hell do they think they are?"

"Wait a second, Barry," Nick said. "Look at her rocking. What do you think you're going to accomplish by carrying on?" he shouted then put his face very close and said in angrily, "He's got to throw shit against the wall. Do you understand, Jean? Shit! And hope something sticks."

I just rocked. Nick told Barry that he had managed to get an appointment with the *New York Daily News*. "Good, good" Barry shouted. "In the meantime, I'm going home to call Lenny. He works with a TV station. I'll have him call you. Tell him your story," he shouted.

Lenny had one adopted girl and one biological son. We had gotten into a lengthy discussion on adoption with him and his wife one evening at Barry's home and shared experiences and emotions. Lenny was a sensitive human being, and we thoroughly enjoyed being with him and his wife.

The following day, Sunday, Nick made his visit to the *New York Daily News* and came home jubilant. "Honey, they didn't believe me at first but listened. When I told them that I had all the documents to prove what I said, they decided that if what I said was substantiated, it was certainly newsworthy and they'd print it. I spoke to a guy named Marty McLaughlin. He seemed rather detached and disinterested at first. 'Come now, Mr. DeMartino, he said.' Are you telling me that our courts overturned a legally binding release given to an adoption agency because the birth mother simply said she made a mistake?" He looked at me in a funny way. "In Limbo is where that places future adoptive kids, not so?"

"In Limbo," I said.

"And the court came to its decision without even meeting you or your wife or even telling you about the trial?"

"The agency told us about the trial taking place the evening before and advised us not to be concerned and me not to inform my wife and upset her, but I was never given legal notification about the trial." Again he gave me a look as though carrots grew in my ears. I finally said, "Mr. McLaughlin, do me a favor. Don't believe a word I tell you. Just read this copy of the original trial, then tell me what you think. I broke down a little, Jean, and my voice cracked. McLaughlin said, 'Mr. DeMartino, you better get ready to take acupuncture because you're going to become news.'"

"Oh, Nick, do you really think it will help?" I asked.

"I'm not sure how, Jean. I wish I could tell you that our troubles would be over once our story hits the news stands, but I can't. I've got this gut feeling that the public must be informed and that Barry is right: we've got to try everything and hope something sticks."

"While you were gone, Mr. Spencer called," I said. "I told him you were at the newspaper office. He thinks we ought to try to see Miss Scarpetta. He feels that there is the possibility that if she meets us and realizes that Lenore is with a loving family and well taken care of that she might follow her original plan with peace of mind and call a halt to the litigation."

"Jean, I don't see that as happening, do you?"

"I suppose we should try, Nick."

Nick tried to get her phone number, but was unsuccessful. "She must not have had her telephone installed yet, " he said. "Do you want to take a chance and to her apartment?"

I was apprehensive but said *yes*.

As we approached the apartment house in Queens, where Miss Scarpetta lived, I sensed my body becoming tense. Nick parked the car, grabbed me by the hand, and directed me toward the garden apartment that bore her address. We walked inside the narrow corridor, and checked the mailboxes, but her name did not appear on any of them. Nick walked outside again to check the number of the building. He came bac and said, "Let's check the names on the apartment doors." We checked the two apartments on the first floor, walked upstairs, and checked the two apartments there, but no Scarpetta.

I felt a dull thump in my stomach, and my head tightened as though a hat was much too tight. Nick grabbed me by the arm and led me downstairs. He knocked on a door. We heard people speaking Spanish and the sound of children. Finally a man answered the door.

Nick said, "We are friends of Olga Scarpetta. We were told that she just moved to this building. Could you tell us what apartment she is in?"

"Olga Scarpetta?" he repeated in a Spanish accent. "She doesn't live here. She stayed in that apartment across the hall a long time ago for only a week."

"Oh," said Nick. "It is important that we get in touch with her. Do you know where she lives?"

"I'm sorry, I don't," he said.

I heard his answer and felt the hall spin. Nick's arms took me out into the cold air. He put me in the car and headed home. He muttered, "How do you like that? She stayed in that apartment across the hall a long time ago and then only for one week." I remembered her testimony at the trial, *Today I moved to 1072 Fenwood Road, Valley Stream, New York.* She was moving close to her relatives who were to assist her in bringing up my Lenore.

"Judge Ascione said, Nick, 'Go meet her. She's a nice girl. You'll like her.' I knew in my heart that we wouldn't find her, but I just wouldn't let myself believe. Who is she? Where is she?" I shouted on the top of my lungs. "Nick, I don't know how, but we must get to the bottom of all this. We have got to give it all we've got." I looked at Nick smiling. "What are you grinning about?" I asked.

"Welcome back," he replied. "I need you by my side. It was tough going it alone there for a while."

Chapter VIII

Pace, I did as my mind worked. I asked Nick to explain our status in an effort to make sense out of a senseless situation.

"Okay, hon, now that we know for sure that Miss Scarpetta lied under oath what can we do about it?"

"Nothing!"

"You told Judge Ascione that she lied. You heard what he said, 'Where she lives is of no importance?'"

"Yes, but shouldn't it be brought to light in a court of law?"

"So far we haven't been able to get into a court of law. But the agency has, so what we've got to do now is get together with their attorneys and plan our next move. Hopefully, the newspaper will get back to us soon. I still don't know how much good that will do, but we've got to try everything. And finally Jean, I have the feeling we should still meet with and talk to Miss Scarpetta. How do you feel about that?"

"I'll try anything, but how can we find her?"

"I'll have Spencer call her attorney to arrange a meeting. However, I think we should hire a private detective to find her."

I was about to tell him that I agreed when the phone rang. It was Lenny. I could hear Nick taking Lenny back to the very beginning on all the details. Little did I know how often Nick and I would be repeating our story. Lenny obviously reacted, and being the father of *one and one,* he particularly was sensitized what Nick related. At the end of the conversation, Nick told me Lenny said, "I hope you don't mind, but I recorded throughout our talk. Can I have your permission to let some TV people hear it?"

Nick had said, "You sure do, Len. Anything you can do will be greatly appreciated. But we don't want anyone to know what took place at the Appellate Court just yet. We still don't want to antagonize the court or be accused of unduly influencing its opinion. I know that may sound crazy, but Lenore's future hangs in the balance." Lenny understood.

Nick called Spencer and asked him to contact Miss Scarpetta's attorney for a meeting. He then called a friend who recommended a private detective that was efficient and not too costly. We were to meet with him at our home that evening.

The news of our plight was traveling fast now. Family and friends called by the score. They meant well, and it was comforting to know they cared, but we found ourselves answering the same questions over and over only to leave them as bewildered at the end of the conversation as they were in the beginning. "What did we plan to do about all this?" they kept asking. Of course we had no idea but just as long as the bullets were fired at our feet, we intended to keep dancing. We spoke to the detective and told him everything which wasn't much, and he set about tracing down Miss Scarpetta.

Nick and I didn't get much sleep that night and were up Monday morning at 5:00 a.m. We sat in our dining room when the doorbell rang. It was Lenny. He had been up most of the night going over the tape he'd made. There were questions he wanted answered. I can't tell you how touched I was to see Lenny—dark circles under his eyes—standing on my doorstep at that time of the morning.

"Phyllis will be here as soon as she gets the children off to school." He went on to say, "Don't worry about a thing, Jean. She plans to stay the day and take care of any cooking or cleaning you might have to do." Then he turned to Nick, started asking questions and wrote with a fury.

At about 9:00 a.m., the immediate world merged upon the house. Phyllis walked in, apron in hand, followed by Bunny (Bernice) Barry's wife who announced, "I'm here with Phyllis for operation Cleanup. Then Barry arrived. "Fill me in," he said. Marie arrived shortly thereafter. Friends moved in and out. Doris said she would pick up Linda at noon from the nursery and take her to play with Lisa. Everything happened quickly at this point.

Nick picked up the constantly ringing phone. I saw his face light up. "That was the *Daily News*, Jean. They want us to take a Polaroid picture and bring it down to them. We are making news!"

"Yipee!" I yelled. My emotions soared.

"Don't get your hopes up too high, Jean. This doesn't mean a thing legally."

"I know, but it's the first positive thing that happened, and I feel as though it's a break through."

Doris got in touch with her husband Bud who was an amateur photographer, brought Linda home, and took a few pictures of us. We looked exactly as we felt—cameras tell the truth! Bud delivered the pictures to the *Daily News*.

All the men left for their offices including Nick. The woman remained to give moral support and help. Most of the day, the phone rang with well wishers. I was back to my old routine, taking care of Lenore and pacing. My friends took care of everything else. I was so grateful.

That evening, we waited patiently for the "Night Owl Edition" of the *New York Daily News*. In the meantime, Dom the detective called but had nothing positive to report. Nick's law partner waited with us and once more tried to let us down gently.

"You know, Jean," he said, "they probably won't write too big an article. Sometimes they have the best intentions but the stories get bumped to the back of the paper or are pre-empted by national news."

I just wasn't ready to accept what he said. I felt in my heart that somewhere out there was a sleeping giant and that tonight we were about to give him a nudge. Finally, my brother-in-law Vinnie, who had been keeping watch at the neighborhood newsstand, arrived with five newspapers in hand. "It's on the fifth page," he shouted. We all grabbed at him for a paper. There it was in black and white:

COURT'S RULING THREATENS ADOPTION MACHINERY

> *A Brooklyn couple, the adoptive parents of an eight-month-old baby girl are fighting the unwed mother's right to reclaim the child after she legally signed the baby over for adoption. The mother won a Supreme Court decision which, if upheld, challenges all adoption machinery in the city and places in question the future of thousands of children already placed in homes by city and private agencies. A decision by the Appellate Division is expected shortly.*

It then went on to relate the details of the case. The picture that Bud had taken topped the article. Nick took me in his arms, and we both cried only this time tears of hope. Barry followed Vinnie with some newspaper copies of his own in hand. His face seemed even redder than usual. He was exhilarated. "Now the shit begins to fly."

"Barry, I adore you," I said, "but can't you change that expression to another one? After all, you might forget yourself and say it in front of the children."

"I would if I could, but when I say shit, I mean shit."

Well, that was Barry, and I thanked God for him! Of course, the following morning, New Yorkers read about our situation. My phone was constantly in hand, and an endless parade of people came through my home. Some time during the day Lenny called. "Be ready for TV cameras," he said. "My station is sending a crew as a follow up to the *New York Daily News* story."

If we put stock into what the secretary of the presiding judge of the Appellate Division said, today the court arrived at its decision. But there was no news. In the meantime, Spencer was delighted about the news coverage. As for our meeting with Miss Scarpetta, her attorney, Mr. Zalk was concerned about the news coverage. Zalk said his client doubtfully would want to meet with us. She didn't want to take off any more time from work. Besides, he personally would advise her against any such meeting. Spencer, however, kept pushing for one.

Nick's office phones were busier than our home phone. Friends, relatives, neighbors, and strangers made a steady stream of calls. Most were well wishers; some were adoptive parents panicked by what they read or heard and wanted Nick to keep them informed.

The day passed with no decision from the Appellate Court, and the evening found us sitting around the dining room table, only this time more than just conversation took place. Barry made a number of photostats of the article which appeared in the paper.

Nick composed a letter which started out: "PLEASE HELP SAVE OUR BABY" and went on to briefly explain our position. We sent the letter and article to anyone and everyone who might think of some way to come to our aid including the President of the United States. I think deep down we knew it was a futile effort, but once again it made us feel like we were doing something.

Dom the detective called. I saw Nick writing feverishly. We started by passing on her vital statistics: date of birth, family members, schools attended, and the date she arrived in the U.S. It turned out that she didn't live at either address mentioned in the text of the trial but had given her correct place of business.

The detective waited for her to leave work one evening. An elderly man met her at the elevator—probably her father. After a few blocks, they parted, and she stopped for coffee. It took her forever to eat the muffin. He then followed her to the subway station where she took a train uptown but lost her in the crowds. That was all to report. Lenny volunteered to meet the detective at Rockefeller Center the next day and help trail her, so we would find out where she lived.

I tossed and turned that night dreaming of what I would say on TV. I had eaten as little over the past few weeks and gotten such little sleep that I felt near collapse. Yet, I had to get in front of the cameras and appear alert and look neat so that I wouldn't come off to the public as a Kook. Our initial meeting with the TV crew was unsettling to say the least. They did a job done a thousand times before. I'm sure sad stories—murder, mayhem, and injustices were all in a day's work. But our tragedy was new to us, and we found it difficult to adjust to what was happening. We were offered a brief "Hello" and then the crew moved in equipment and checked outlets and talked to one another as though they saw me for the first time. "Do you always dress like that around the house?" a man asked. His eyes moved from my shoes to my skirt and blouse and then met mine.

I said, "Mr. Smith, what I do normally at this hour of the morning bears no resemblance to what I'm doing now. As a matter of fact, my home has not been normal for weeks. These good people who you see have come to help me get through the necessary routine. As for me, I pace and read legal documents, pray and stand in front of TV cameras, and would stand on my head if I thought it would help my daughter."

He looked straight into my eyes then said, "Mrs. DeMartino, why don't you tell me the story from the beginning so I get a feel for what happened?"

Once again we told our story. Mr. Smith got it on camera and took background shots around the baby. He asked if he could interview Linda with Lenore in their room. I was a little apprehensive. There had been times when Lenore, as sweet and as outgoing as she was, would take an immediate dislike to someone. I hoped and prayed that this would not be the case. And it wasn't. Linda and Lenore came through with flying colors. Linda spoke freely to the reporter. She read her *Manners* book to Lenore and hugged and kissed her. Lenore, in turn, gave the interviewer a big smile and seemed quite content with the goings-on. I was pleased with the outcome but none-the-less upset. I had always been such a private person, and here I opened my home and my heart aches for the world to scrutinize. I experienced a conflict of emotions. I wanted the media to report our plight and yet resented them for invasions of our privacy. The crew packed up and moved out their equipment. The interviewer said his goodbyes. I thanked him for being considerate and for being gentle with the children and tried to explain the conflict I felt.

"Don't fret, Mrs. DeMartino. Off the record though, it sure would seem a waste to break up those two sisters. Good luck in your fight."

Outside our door sat the *Daily News*, Wednesday, January 27, 1971. I looked over Nick's shoulder and saw a picture of Judge Ascione staring at me. The Caption read "ORDER TO RETURN TOT DECIDED BY MOTHER LOVE." Evidently, Mr. McLaughlin, who wrote the original story, followed up with an interview. It read as follows:

Supreme Court Judge Alfred M. Ascione defended yesterday his decision ordering the eight-month-old Lenore DeMartino be returned to her natural mother despite a legal surrender signed by the mother. He cited mother love as the determining factor.

Judge Ascione said that the adoption agency in the case, Spence-Chapin Adoption Service, "Used undue haste in placing the child" with Mr. and Mrs. DeMartino of Bay Ridge, Brooklyn. He pointed out that the baby's natural mother, Olga Scarpetta, told the agency that she wanted her baby back only two weeks after the child was placed with the DeMartinos.

"It was a difficult decision to make," said the judge. "But in the end, mother love took precedence over the adoptive parents."

Ascione felt that the Spence-Chapin Agency should have taken the infant back when Miss Scarpetta said she wanted to rescind the legal order of surrender. In the judge's opinion, the legal Surrender Order that Miss Scarpetta admits signing freely was not binding because she changed her mind so soon.

Miss Scarpetta signed the Order on June 1 and informed the agency that she wanted her baby back on June 30. The DeMartinos took Lenore home on June 18 when the baby was a month old.

The judge's decision is being appealed. A decision by the Appellate Division is expected shortly. If upheld, the entire adoption machinery in the city will be in question. Arthur Friedman, president of the 900 member Adoptive Parents Committee, attacked the court decision by saying that adoptive parents are "Always second class citizens with little or no standing whatsoever. The right of a biological mother," he explained, "is considered the primary factor even above the rights and welfare of a child. When a child is placed in an adoptive home," he went on, "and the parents advised that the child was legally surrendered, it is unconscionable to force the adoptive parents to withhold their love for fear that they could still have the child taken away."

After a child is placed in an adoptive home, it takes from six months to more than a year before the adoption becomes final. "The Adoptive Parents Committee," Friedman said, "is presently seeking help from state legislation to prevent cases like the DeMartinos from happening."

So now there it was for all the world to see. He based his decision on mother love. That day became more chaotic than the last. Phones rang, friends called, reporters called, TV cameras and crews from other stations arrived and set up their cameras. Nick and I told the same story over and over. Nick didn't hold up as well as I did in front of a camera. It seemed strange that he, a trial attorney and an extrovert who loved an audience, could react so poorly. Of course, I know now what I didn't know then, that I thought we were accomplishing something. Nick, on the other hand, lived with the knowledge that underneath the hooting and hollering, there was nothing, nothing to hang his hat on. The hoopla was a simple exercise in futility. As the brain surgeon might go through the motions and know the agony of not being able to save his own child, so Nick went through the motions and knew all the while that legally he wasn't making a dent.

In the meantime, Lenny worked to help the detective locate Miss Scarpetta's residence. The first night Len and Dom followed her from work on the Uptown train, but Lenny, who was closest, did not realize she was about to get off and when he tried to make his way through the crowd to follow her, the door closed in his face. The second night, however, they followed, as we anticipated, to an uptown apartment house where she more than likely lived. She finally emerged as a person and not just a threat. To our surprise and dismay the Appellate Court had not yet made public its decision. We wondered whether the publicity affected them. But we all, including Mr. Reardon, the attorney for Spence-Chapin, still held little hope for anything but a unanimous decision against us. So Reardon prepared the legal documents for *certiorari,* permission to be heard in a higher court. Nick kept in close contact with Reardon.

The house was quiet now, and I was lying down when the phone rang. It was one of the TV interviewers who had been to our home that morning. I was still groggy when I answered the phone. At first I couldn't place him. "Yes, Bill Aylward, how are you?"

"I wondered whether you had any word about the court's decision."

"We did have some indication that it was to be made public this past Tuesday, but your guess is as good as mine. However, it really doesn't matter. We're not expecting a verdict in our favor. As a matter of fact, anything better than a unanimous decision against us will be a welcomed surprise."

I explained what happened at the hearing and how Miss Scarpetta's attorney, Mr. Zalk, never spoke, but was just told to quit while he was ahead. Suddenly I realized what I had done. I was speaking not to just a concerned person, but a TV news reporter. I panicked. "Please," I said, "Don't make that information public. Let's just wait for the decision and hope for the best."

"Okay Mrs. DeMartino, I won't report it, but under one condition. You must promise to call me the minute the court reveals its decision."

"I promise someone will call as soon as we know anything." I had every intention of keeping that promise, but it became impossible. Twenty minutes later, a call came from the same reporter.

"Mrs. DeMartino, I don't want to upset you any more than necessary, but I called Mr. Zalk and asked directly if he did not have to speak on his client's behalf and if he was told to quit while he was ahead and, little lady, he confirmed your story. Boy, would I love to let the public know!"

"Please, mister—" My voice trailed off.

"Don't worry. I just wanted you to know that I followed up. Mum's the word for now. But Mrs. DeMartino, I think you're going to see a lot of me. I want to be there when those rocks get overturned! Remember my name Bill Aylward, and don't forget to call!"

Nick had gone to the office for some files. I couldn't wait to tell him what I had done. I worried about my conversation with the reporter. Nick, as usual, was reassuring. "You told the truth so don't concern yourself anymore.

Anyway, I've got some new news to report. Spencer called. Miss Scarpetta consented to meet with us tomorrow morning at Mr. Zalk's office."

"What do you think will come of it, Nick?"

"Nothing, but we'd never forgive ourselves if we didn't try." It was Thursday, January 28. We were up bright and early. Marie was en route to our house, as usual. This was the day to come face to face with Lenore's biological mother. I don't know how to explain my feelings. Like Nick, I didn't expect our visit would change anything, and yet I did allow myself to hope. I was going to be calm, but the butterflies in my stomach belied my thoughts. What would she be like? What would she look like? The detective and Nick gave a general description that was too general. Would Nick convince her to end the legal battle? Could reassurance be what she wished? Should we bring pictures of Lenore with her family and maybe her medical reports? Would she be receptive or argumentative? I wanted so much to believe that she would put this nightmare to rest. I gathered several pictures of Lenore because I knew, if nothing else, Olga Scarpetta wanted to know about Lenore—how and what she was doing. After all, Miss Scarpetta had neither seen nor heard anything about Lenore since birth.

Nick, Joe Spencer, and I went to Mr. Zalk's office in New York. We were tense. Mr. Spencer turned on the car radio, and the quiet was interrupted by a special news bulletin: "THE APPELLATE COURT ARRIVED AT A DECISION IN THE BABY LENORE CASE. They unanimously upheld the lower court's ruling to return the baby to her natural mother."

We looked at one another. I seemed not to have any more tears. Mr. Spencer spoke first, "This may affect today's meeting, but there is the outside chance it may not. In any event, let's not bring the decision up in our conversation or discuss it at all unless, of course, they do."

I must have had a strange look on my face because Nick commented. "What's on your mind, hon?"

"I was thinking of my promise to that TV reporter. I'd let him know about the decision as soon as I got word of it."

We were led into Mr. Zalk's library/conference room by a young lady. Mr. Zalk then led us into his office. He sat behind a desk, and we were asked to take three seats in front of him. He was a tall, middle-aged man whose hair appeared to be thinning. He wore glasses, and had an average appearance. The most noticeable thing was that he spoke with an accent. There was an empty straight back chair along his side, but no Olga Scarpetta.

"Miss Scarpetta is here," he said, "but there is something I'd like to clear up before the meeting takes place. First of all, I want you to know once again that I advised her against meeting, but she nonetheless agreed to go ahead. We must insist, however, under the circumstances, that this meeting be kept in the strictest confidence and that you tell no one.

"Mr. Spencer, I ask as a fellow attorney and gentleman to agree to these conditions. It is especially important since you decided to turn this into a three-ring circus." With that, he picked up a copy of the newspaper with our picture and the original story and threw it onto his desk.

Mr. Spencer looked over to Nick and me. We nodded approval. Mr. Spencer said, "You have our word on it."

"Miss Scarpetta's parents accompanied her here, and they would like to attend this meeting too. How do you feel about that?"

I immediately objected. It was difficult enough for me to come face to face with Miss Scarpetta. The thought of confronting her elderly parents seemed too much. "I would prefer to talk to Miss Scarpetta woman to woman if you don't mind."

Nick and Mr. Spencer agreed, and Mr. Zalk returned shortly after with Miss Scarpetta who took the vacant seat next to him. This was a moment I waited for. This was the mystery woman whom I built up in my mind to be many things, and now I looked into her face and felt nothing but pity.

Mr. Zalk began, "Now there are two of you and one of her and she's here of her own free will, so give her an opportunity to be heard."

I stared, but her eyes looked past me. They never once met my gaze. Olga Scarpetta was a slightly built young lady with dark hair pulled back into a ponytail. Her eyes slanted giving a definite oriental appearance. The simple gamp-like dress appeared too big, making her seem lost and frail. She sat with her hands folded and her shoulders hunched over a little. She had the overall appearance of a straight *A* introverted student who had just been sent to the principal's office and was scared.

I heard a little voice in me say, *Jean, think Lenore, think of what is best for Lenore,* and with that in mind, I addressed her. "Miss Scarpetta, we came with the hope of convincing you that Lenore is so loved and well taken care of that you might revert to your original decision and call all this litigation to a halt."

She answered in a whisper with the trace of a slight Spanish accent, "I will not change my mind. A daughter belongs to her mother." All the while, she looked down at her folded hands. How pathetic she looked.

Mr. Zalk interjected, "Mrs. DeMartino, I believe, Mrs. Scarpetta came here with a similar object in mind. She thought you might come to the realization that a daughter belongs with her mother."

"Oh," I said almost inaudibly and slumped back in my chair. I heard Nick ask, "Miss Scarpetta, why did you say all those things on the stand that were not true. We tried to find the address you gave the court and you were not there."

"You want to know why?" she started to say.

Mr. Zalk interrupted. "Miss Scarpetta, you don't have to answer. Mr. DeMartino, we did not come to discuss addresses."

Nick became tense, so I patted his hand. "Miss Scarpetta, we love Lenore very much, and she loves us. She has a mommy, a daddy, and a sister, the things you wanted for her. Right now we are her whole world. Yes, our motives are selfish too. I cannot deny that. To lose Lenore would tear us apart, but we are truly worried about Lenore's future. At the moment she is like a flower which has been planted in fertile ground. She took root and thrives. She is growing and found a place for herself. Your suggestion is that we uproot and replant her with you. Have you considered the danger to that move?"

She continued to look down at her lap. "I want my baby," only this time she took deep breaths between each word.

I said as gently as possible, "I understand this must be very difficult, but won't you at least give some consideration to what I've just said?" She once again said "I (sigh) want (sigh) my (sigh) daughter (sigh)," all the while keeping her eyes fixed on her lap.

Mr. Spencer interjected, "Miss Scarpetta, like Mrs. DeMartino, I realize what you are going through, but I must not only reconfirm what she just told you but must be a little more blunt. I spoke to several child psychologists about this case and there is good reason to believe that if you go ahead with your plans, little Lenore will definitely suffer emotional damage. We are, after all, talking about a child, not a plant, and it is not quite as iffy as Mrs. DeMartino made it sound."

Miss Scarpetta's response remained the same and said in the same manner. I found myself becoming annoyed with her but kept my emotions in check and spoke as gently as I could. "Olga," I said, "children are a grave responsibility and a lot of hard work. Have you considered what it would be like for Lenore to go from a home with a mommy, daddy, and sister to a small apartment and watched by an aged lady who does not know the country, its customs, or its language which Lenore is accustomed to hearing? Having a child in your home can present a whole set of new problems."

Olga said, "I have been around children. I know what is involved. A baby belongs with its mother. I (sigh) want (sigh) my (sigh) baby (sigh)."

I said sharply, "I know what you want. You've repeated it enough times. We all know what you want! But have you given any thought to what Lenore wants? Didn't you ever learn how to talk in the second or third person? Is *I* the only pronoun you know? What happened to *she*? I thought it was *she* we came to discuss, and I haven't even heard you use the word once. You haven't even asked how she is. You haven't seen her for months and know nothing about her since the day she was born, and not a single question has crossed your lips. I came prepared with all sorts of information."

"Mrs. DeMartino!" I finally heard Mr. Zalk.

"That will be enough. My client didn't come here to be harassed."

It was my turn to heave a deep sigh. I fell back in my seat. "I have nothing more to say."

Mr. Zalk picked up the telephone, "I thought I told you I didn't want to be interrupted. Oh, I see. Thank you very much," he said. He leaned over and whispered in Miss Scarpetta's ear. Her face lit up. She sat up straight and said in a brisk, direct tone of voice, "That's great news."

We all knew what the news was, of course. Miss Scarpetta shot a glance over to us, and then returned to her previous hunched-over position.

"Well," Zalk said, "I guess this conversation is academic at this point. I suspect you already know the Appellate Court reached a unanimous decision in favor of my client."

"Yes we do," Mr. Spencer said, "but, please, before we call this meeting to an end, permit me to say just one last thing. Miss Scarpetta, Olga, if I may, if we had a psychiatrist examine Lenore and her family life and present his findings would it make a difference?"

"No, it would not!"

"Suppose we hired a psychiatrist of your choice?"

"It would make no difference."

"If we were to arrange and forward the psychiatrist's reports, would you at least read them?"

"No, I would not."

Mr. Spencer stammered. Mr. Zalk interrupted and said rather nervously, "Mr. Spencer, if you got a psychiatrist's report, I'm sure Miss Scarpetta would agree to read it."

Mr. Spencer rose from his chair and said, "You know, Miss Scarpetta, I'm an old man, and my children are not adopted but . . . " his voice cracked and tears rolled down his cheeks. He sobbed. Nick put his arms around the man and said, "It's all right, Joe. It's not over yet." As we walked toward the door, Nick turned to Miss Scarpetta, and said, "I want to thank you for having this meeting with us. I may have had little to say, but I did a lot of listening, and now, thanks to you, even the slightest doubts have been erased from my mind. I am convinced of what I must do. As bleak as things look, they are not ending here. Lenore will not bear your burdens. You're thirty-two, Olga, so stop acting like you're sixteen. Stand up and be counted. You made a mistake, fine. Nobody can fault you for that. But stop sidestepping the consequences. You made the mistake and you are the one who must pay, not Lenore. I will not let you pass the costs on to her—not while I'm alive—not while I can think and breathe and exist. I will fight you with the last ounce of blood in my body. You may sit there now thinking that you finally reached your goal, but you're kidding yourself. This is not the end. This is the beginning."

    We walked out of Mr. Zalk's office into a cold winter day. Nick and Joe Spencer agreed that we should immediately get Lenore out of the house. We were afraid that Zalk would take fast action to take her away from us before the agency was able to get a stay. Time was of the essence, and we needed to buy as much of it as possible.

    Poor Marie was so shook up. She said the phone hadn't stopped ringing. The news media tried to get in touch with us for hours. By the time we got home, Lenore had been safely whisked away to Doris's house. Luckily, Linda didn't mind spending as much time as she did there since she got to play with Lisa. We had prepared Linda for all this time away from home by telling her that daddy's office was being painted and that he would be doing much of his work at home and that there would be a lot of people entering the house. But it was becoming increasingly difficult to keep the realities from her. We wanted to be definite in our approach before we let Linda tackle any of this in her mind. Just the knowledge that her sister might be taken away, we felt, could be as damaging to her as the act itself. As it turned out, it was just as well that neither of them was home as the TV crews were backed up down the street waiting.

We managed to make contact with the agency attorneys. They had all the necessary legal documents available for a request for a stay and were attempting to locate the whereabouts of Justice Fuld, the Chief Justice of the Court of Appeals. As it turned out, however, he was conspicuously unavailable. All we needed was one of the six judges to sign a stay order which would leave Lenore with us just long enough to petition the Court of Appeals to hear the case. Of course, the litigation was still strictly between the agency and Miss Scarpetta. We were just going along for the ride.

Justice Charles Brietel was at his office located on 44th Street in Manhattan, and he agreed to speak to the Spence-Chapin attorneys, Friday, January 29. Nick, Mr. Spencer and I met the attorneys at Brietel's office. We remained in the outer office while the meeting took place. Mr. Brietel's secretary finally approached us.

"I know who you are," she said. "Don't worry. I've worked for the judge for a very long time. He's a kind and just man. He'll do what's right. I know to a certain extent how you feel. You see, I lost my daughter when she was a little girl. Only someone who has experienced that kind of a loss can truly understand."

I thanked her for the kind words. How nice of her to care and to lighten our burden. Suddenly, the doors flung open, and the attorneys exited wearing broad smiles. Nick and I breathed relief. The X was erased from our door for a little while longer.

We called Marie and told her that Doris could bring Lenore home. When we returned, we found a gang of reporters waiting on our doorstep. As we approached, one of them yelled out, "Did you get your stay, Mrs. DeMartino?"

"Yes, we did" I replied, "and you're welcome to share the good news, but first we want to make sure that all is well with the kids." As I entered the house, Marie carried Lenore who reached for me. I took her in my arms and pressed her close. It was at that precise moment that a photographer unexpectedly took a picture.

Nick said, "Gentlemen, please make your questions brief. You see my wife is exhausted. This ordeal is taking its toll on us, and we really need some time to be a family again."

The reporters, I must say, were cooperative. After a few questions, they left. A photographer matter-of-factly asked, "By the way, what is that medal you wear, Mrs. DeMartino?"

When I glanced down, I realized that my St. Jude medal beneath my outer clothing now hung clearly visible on my dress.

"Oh," I said, "that was given to me many years ago by a friend. It's a medal of St. Jude."

"Does he have any significance?"

"I think he's the patron of hopeless cases."

The next morning, Saturday, January 30, I picked up a copy of the *New York Daily News* and there, covering the front page, was me hugging Lenore. Out in the forefront of the picture was my medal of St. Jude. It seemed that Lenore had turned

her body in such a way as to grab onto the chain of my medal with her tiny hand and held it for all to see. The Headline read:
CLINGING TO FINAL HOPE
It went on to state:

> Mrs. DeMartino hugs her adoptive daughter, Lenore, as she hears the news that the Court of Appeals, Judge Charles D. Beetle, granted a temporary Stay Order returning the baby to her mother. The Stay allows Mrs. DeMartino and her husband Nick, of Bay Ridge Brooklyn, to keep the baby until they can make their final plea to the state's top court in March.

For me, the medal was a reminder that God was with us and that He would walk with us and be by our side every step of the way. Of course, by now our case was receiving mass media coverage. Other articles appeared not only in the *Daily News* but in the other New York papers as well. There was a big cry for new adoption laws to prevent another "DeMartino situation from ever happening." Assemblyman Joseph Pisani (R., New Rochelle) proposed an amendment to the State Social Service Law making the voluntary surrender of a child for adoption irrevocable after thirty days.

There were those who objected, however, because the proposed law gave the natural mother a right which she didn't have before. Nick explained that as long as there wasn't a final decree in our adoption, in effect, custody could always be scrutinized by the court. So, since final adoption proceedings took six months to a year, the natural mother could conceivably change her mind during that time and ask the court to return her child. The existing Social Service Law stated that a parent "shall not be entitled to the custody thereof except upon consent of the court determining that the interest of such child will be promoted thereby and that such parent is fit, competent, and able to duly maintain support and educate such child."

With the new proposed law, however, a mere change of mind within thirty days of signing the surrender would be enough to get a child returned to its natural mother. On the surface, it appeared like a fair compromise to Nick and me. Unfortunately, though, it would have no effect on our lives.

"Nick, I still can't believe that Ascione was able to twist the law to say that Lenore's well being would be promoted by returning her to her biological mother because she alone could give her mother love which he described in his decision as being "a totality of dedication, an all-embracing consecration, that knows no wavering, no swerving."

"It makes absolutely no sense, whatsoever."

"It makes less sense than you think," Nick said.

"What do you mean?"

"Well, Jean, those weren't the judge's words. What he did was quote from a previous case. Judges come to decisions by using the law as it is written—known as statutory law—as well as decisions handed down in previous cases which is called *stare decises*."

"I remember that the cases quoted were cited in parentheses after the statements."

"The quote that you referred to before was taken from a decision originally made by Justice Botein in a case similar to ours. I've got the papers here somewhere. Let me see. Ah, here it is. I'll read it to you, but this time I' ll start one paragraph ahead of Ascione's quote and I'll continue a little beyond.

"For what is this moral claim of a mother to her child? On what does it rest? What is it which makes motherhood so precious a boon that society chooses to leave a child even with the most poverty-ridden and ignorant of mothers rather than give him over to even the wealthiest and most cultivated foster parents? What is expected of a mother which is of such incalculable worth as to outweigh all else in the world? What except a fullness of love for the child; totality of dedication to it, an all-embracing consecration that knows no wavering, no swerving. This is a mother's gift, for which, society holds a child may well count all the world well lost. And it is in just this that the petitioner is found wanting. She is a person of intelligence and socially acceptable character. She is in my opinion a person no more unstable than a multitude of other persons. But she gave up her child of her own free will, to implement a reconstruction of her personal life; not after her last dollar had been spent and her last resource drained, but with a sizable sum at her disposal."

"Nick, are you telling me that Ascione cited a case to support his position in which the exact opposite decision was made?"

"That's exactly what I'm telling you! Of course, the opinion might very well have been researched and written by his secretary/clerk. That is very often the case."

"Nick, it doesn't make him any the less incompetent in my eyes."

"Nor in mine, but I think it is only fair to point out that New York State has always given great weight in their decisions to the primary right of mothers."

"And what about the children involved?"

"I'm afraid for the most part the courts have

paid only lip service to the best interests of the child. Mr. Spencer and his Adoptive Parents' Committee attest to that. True, the cases for the most part involve private placements rather than agency, but I don't see how that would change the best interests of the child. What is needed are stronger and better laws governing not only the mother's change of mind, but the rights of the child in question."

"I couldn't agree with you more, hon, and even though it can't help us personally, I think we both should lend our support to Pisani and the Adoptive Parents' Committee."

In the meantime, there were others who without our knowledge lent support to us. The *Home Reporter and Sunset News*, a local Bay Ridge paper printed a petition on the front page. The headline read "You Can Help the DeMartinos Keep Their Baby." There was room for 10 signatures and the petition was directed to the Appellate Court. Of course, that decision had already been rendered, but they cared and that's really what mattered most.

In order to have a little time for ourselves, we took the phone off the hook on Sunday. But on Monday it started all over again. Nick finally managed to get through to me at home. "Jean, that picture of you and Lenore with the St. Jude medal which appeared in Saturday's paper is causing a fervor all over town. Every one of my phones is ringing off the hook. What about you?"

"Same thing here, hon."

"Jean, things have been happening so fast that it's hard keeping up with it all. Let me bring you up to date. First of all, John Farro picked up on the petition idea from the *Home Reporter* and he's printing a batch of petitions. He decided to convert his store into the head quarters for the committee to help save baby

Lenore. A lithographer also got in touch with him and has made a plate of the St. Jude picture and added to it, "Help Save our Baby." He told John that he will get several packages of pictures and posters to him today. I am now referring all calls to John at his place of business. I think you ought to do the same. I'm also going to order another phone for our home. I'd like to keep this one for our personal use, okay, hon?"

"I'm bewildered and what about John? How will he conduct his own business?"

"He's turning off the presses and won't open for business until he sees this thing through to its just end. People have already shown up at his store to offer whatever help they can give. Oh, and you might like to know that he just dropped off a copy of the petition. I'll read it to you: 'TO WHOM IT MAY CONCERN: We the undersigned having been informed of the facts involved in the case of Olga Scarpetta against the Spence-Chapin Adoption Service feel that the DeMartino family should have their day in court as a simple matter of justice. No family should be torn apart and especially in this case where the best interests of a child are at stake. The oral un-investigated statements of a party should not have been enough in so important a case. We, therefore, urge that the DeMartinos be allowed to come into this case which so vitally affects them and their Baby Lenore.'

"There's room for 75 signatures below the statement." "Nick, I don't know what to say."

"I told you we have just begun to fight." So he had. But I must admit that at the time he said it, I had doubts. John did indeed close his place of business and hung a new sign in his window which read COMMITTEE TO HELP SAVE BABY LENORE.

As the days progressed, the signatures came in by the hundreds. People organized groups and took turns waiting outside of movies and bowling alleys. The picture of Lenore clinging to me with one hand and St. Jude with the other appeared everywhere. Even our family doctor took a batch of petitions and waited outside an E. J. Korvettes department store in the cold evening collecting signatures. The TV stations heard about the activities of the Committee and interviewed and gave out telephone numbers which led to more people calling and more people offering their help. An extra phone had to be installed in John's office to handle the inquires. People mimeographed the original petition and brought them back signed. My brother called from upstate New York to say petitions were signed there before he even had a chance to receive the ones that the committee was to mail to him. Mr. Reardon was shocked to answer his doorbell and find a young lady requesting his signature on a petition. They came by car, they came by bus, they came by train, and they all said the same thing: "They cared." One elderly crippled lady traveled an hour and a half from the Bronx to Brooklyn to sign her name to a petition in the Committee Headquarters. To say that Nick and I were overwhelmed would be an understatement.

Of course, Lenny, Barry, and John and their wives were busily engaged in running the Committee, but there were also a lot of faces I didn't recognize. There were many people that I met for the first time. One was Violet Johnson who manned the phone the first time I entered the Committee office. It seems that when Violet heard about the Committee being formed, she merely informed her husband Charlie that she was leaving their Staten Island home for a week stay with her mother in Brooklyn so that she could help the DeMartinos. Knowing Charlie, she knew that he would take good care of the kids while she was gone. Charlie did better than that. He even found time to give to the Committee.

"Are your children adopted?" I asked.

"No, we're simply here because we hate injustice and we love children, and it's not enough to talk about it. You've got to do something."

Along with the petitions came letters that gathered at the Committee headquarters as well as at home. All were sympathetic. All wanted to help but weren't sure how they could be of assistance. Many of the letters, which we had sent out the week before were now being answered. One senator called and informed us that he had been away and had just walked into his home to be greeted by his wife and daughter who presented him at once with our letter and the newspaper account that we had sent him. They wouldn't even let him take his hat and coat off. "How can I help you?" he asked. That was the rub. There was really nothing he or any of them could do. But just knowing people cared enough meant a great deal. Letters and phone calls from all walks of life poured in. I not only set out to read every one but attempted to answer as many as I could. Every time I had a few spare moments, I jotted a note to some well-wisher. It was the very least I could do to show appreciation for all the wonderful support. Besides, answering kept my mind occupied and left less time for grief and worry. I asked them all to pray for us!

Nick and I finally got to read the Appellate Court's decision certain parts of which stand out in my mind.

> *. . . the welfare and interests of the child are the paramount consideration. The policy urged that if surrender maybe undone, authorized agencies*

> *will be inconvenienced or even frustrated in their placement of children is not a sufficient counterweight. This disposition must be confined in its effects to the case immediately before us. . . .*

"Nick, what did the court mean by that last statement?"

"It means, honey that they do not want to set precedent with our case. Their decision is not to be cited and used as case law for others to follow. In short, the decision applies only to us and to no one else!"

"Terrific! It sure makes you feel like that secretary knew what he was talking about when he said they had it in for the agency. They'd be happy to just sweep us under the carpet and have the whole issue forgotten. If we hadn't gone to the newspapers, I'm sure that's exactly what would have happened. Thank God we did!"

Nick and I were believers, and although we were going through a great deal of heartache, we felt ourselves being drawn more and more to God. When we went to church that week, I felt overwhelmed by His presence. I hung to every word of the Gospel which seemed directed to me exclusively. I left church with a great sense of comfort, a feeling that in the end all would be put right, not only for Lenore, but for others as well.

Chapter IX

Repeatedly, Nick and I were asked by the reporters, "Have you met the natural mother?" The words stuck in our throats, but we were people of our word and we had to answer *no*. It wasn't that we wanted to discuss our meeting because, in fact, we did not want to become a mere tug of war between Miss Scarpetta and ourselves with Lenore suffering the battle scars. On the other hand, we experienced the inner turmoil between honor and honesty.

The agency attorneys, in the interim, drafted a *Writ of Certiori* which means, we believe you should hear this case, and directed it to the Court of Appeals which met in Albany. Although seven justices preside, only two signatures were required for Certiori to be granted. We lived on borrowed time.

Nick had difficulty keeping a cap on his frustration and anger at a court system which had him legally tied and gagged. Since the reporters constantly called and questioned, I wasn't surprised to read the following in the newspaper:

"Yesterday, DeMartino, 36, was upset that neither he nor his wife has been allowed to make a personal appeal in the courts that have ruled against the adoptive parents. 'If this were a refrigerator or a washing machine or a car that the courts repossessed, I would be offered every legal recourse to speak on our behalf,' he said.

'As the adoptive family we have had no legal right to enter into any of the proceedings to date. It is unbelievable in this day and age that my daughter can be ripped from my home and those who love her without any of us given a legal right to prevent this.'

"DeMartino vowed to mortgage his home and

pursue the matter to the United States Supreme Court, if necessary."

Nick meant it. Yet we waited on tender hooks. If the agency attorneys could not convince the Court of Appeals to hear our case, all would be over. The waiting got more difficult all the time. We returned to our normal routine and gave the children more time. There had been some really hectic days for them. We managed somehow to appear cool and collected on the outside, but on the inside uncertainty gnawed away.

The letters and petitions still came by the sack full. Mr. Spencer, Nick, and I hoped that the proceedings would allow us to intervene. Through the advice of a friend, we sought the legal assistance of another attorney who had experience in addressing higher courts. Jacob D. Fuchsberg, Esq. being familiar with our case through the media and hearing our plea, agreed to assist free of charge. Our only costs were expenses incurred. It was ironic like owning the best cookware available and having no stove to cook on.

On February 3, the New York papers announced the addition of Jacob D. Fuchsberg to the legal fighting team to assist the DeMartinos. They pointed out that Mr. Fuchsberg petitioned the Court of Appeals to allow the DeMartino family to take part in the legal proceedings in conjunction with the motions from the attorneys for Spence-Chapin Adoption Service who petitioned the state's top court for permission to appeal the decision.

A press conference at the offices of Mr. Fuchsberg made public steps he planned on our behalf. Mr. Fuchsberg proved fast talking, sensitive, and intelligent. We were confident in his abilities and comfortable with his approach. Nick and I were asked the same questions previously asked a hundred times. I felt shaky answering rapid fire questions thrown from all directions and was nervous and upset not because of the interviews—they were no longer trying. All you had to do was tell the truth and repeat it—but because of waiting for decisions, roller coaster ups and downs, sleepless nights. Being on stage caught up with us.

Nick and I met a sea of reporters. Reporters come in all sizes, shapes, sexes, and different temperaments. Some were solicitous, some indifferent, and some suspicious, but most attempted to keep an objective air. Nick and I were aware that the coverage stirred the conscience of the public. Therefore, we cooperated as much as possible. During a lull in the questioning, I said quietly to a lady on my right, "I wish to be far away from here, sitting in a sandpile with Linda and Lenore making castles."

"Then why aren't you doing that, Mrs. DeMartino?" she asked.

"It's one thing to sit in a sand pile with your children; it's quite another to bury your head in it," I replied.

"Sounds as though you feel a 100 percent right about what you are doing."

"Anyone convinced he or she is a 100 percent right is either a fool or deluding herself. We are convinced, however, that we are doing what is best."

She smiled. She was a reporter who had previously been dubious about our sincerity.

"What do you think of Miss Scarpetta, Mrs. DeMartino?" asked another reporter.

My thoughts raced back to our meeting. What did Nick and I think? We felt pretty self righteous that day as we left Mr. Zalk's office. I was proud of Nick and told him so. He'd shown his colors with "Jean, I'll protect Lenore with my life, and yet for all my anger somehow underneath I feel sorry for Olga."

"I understand because I too felt both pity and anger for her during that meeting. I don't believe Olga really wants Lenore back."

"She certainly said, 'I want my baby,' enough times."

"Nick, I don't think Olga knows herself why she wants the baby and why she clung to that one phrase. She didn't even discuss Lenore. It was 'I want my baby.' I read that as saying I'm guilty about what I've done and want to turn the clock back to do the right thing. After all, the image of a mother giving away her own flesh and blood is not a pretty one to live with." In answer to the question, I said, "I honestly believe that if Judge Ascione ruled against Olga Scarpetta, he would have solved her problem. She could say, `I made a mistake and I tried to correct it, but the judge wouldn't let me.' It would free her to face Lenore as a young woman.

"When you and I think of losing our children, we panic. But there are women who give away their children. If we put ourselves in their shoes, we might understand the emotional turmoil wrapped in a horrendous decision. It must be similar to what one feels when a close relative who suffered a terminal disease finally passes on. You wonder, am I relieved for my loved one or for myself. And guilt sets in.

"The kindest and the fairest thing the law can do is make perfectly clear that once a surrender is agreed upon, it sticks," I said confidently. "The finality frees the birth mother from further indecision and anguish and permits her to reconstruct her life. It frees the adoptive parents to love and cherish their new baby the day she enters their home. And finality humanizes the baby by turning her from a possession into a person."

"What happened, Jean, is that there were cracks

in the law and all of us unfortunately fell through," Nick added.

"Mrs. DeMartino, I asked you what you thought of Miss Scarpetta."

"I bear her no ill will. She did what she believed she had to do."

The reporter looked at me incredulously.

"Please," I replied, "let's not turn this into a personality contest. The issue is what's best for Lenore. If your daughter were drowning, would you concern yourself with how it happened or would you set about rescuing her? That's exactly what we are attempting to do—rescue Lenore."

In four days, the Committee gathered 87,000 petition signatures, and a C.P.A. firm offered its services to authenticate the count. John Farro and the Committee decided how the petitions could best be used. The original premise was to present them to the judiciary, but our attorneys agreed with Nick's original appraisal and advised against it on the grounds that it would appear we attempted to strong-arm the court. Not that we wouldn't love to strong-arm the court. Their second delivery choice was Governor Rockefeller, but the final decision was to present them where they were sure to do the most good—the state legislature. That many signatures would certainly serve as a mandate to review adoption laws. Meanwhile, the signatures continued to come in. Newspapers and TV programs editorialized on the case and demanded that new legislation protecting all parties in adoption cases get underway.

Assemblyman Pisani took to the air as well. When asked what he thought about our chances with Lenore, he replied that we had launched a long uphill battle and could really use a miracle.

Dr. Haim Ginott, child psychologist and author of the book *Between Parent and Child*, appeared on TV and commented on children taken away from adoptive parents.

"What does an infant experience when he is suddenly separated from the only parents he has known? The answer is loss, profound loss. The kind of loss a child, any child would feel if suddenly separated from his parents by death. Now some people may say, 'He's only an infant. What does he know? It doesn't make much difference. He'll forget." Not so! The tragedy is that an infant experiences loss but has no way of coping with it. He cannot ask questions. He cannot demand answers. The situation doesn't make sense to him. And here is the danger. He may not be able to reconcile himself to the loss."

Needless to say, our spirits were low. I was about to sink even further into despair. On February 4, the daily newspaper ran an article which made reference to the many petitions signed for the DeMartinos. My attention went to the article alongside which read:

ADOPTION CASE ENDS IN TEARS

Above the caption was a picture of a young long-haired girl holding a bewildered boy in her arms. That old sinking feeling returned, but I read on:

> *Three-year-old Richard John Ferro struggled with the blond-haired woman who led him into the elevator yesterday, crying over and over, "I want my mommy. I want my mommy."*

The story revealed that the adoptive mother had to hand the child over to its natural mother. Judge

Albert A. Oppido reluctantly carried out a January 7 directive from the State Court of Appeals that the boy be turned over to his natural mother, Mrs. Elizabeth Ferro, twenty-two, of Brooklyn. Mrs. Ferro wanted to leave through a side door to avoid reporters and photographers. But Judge Oppido refused her request stating, "The public is better served to see the terrible tragedy that comes from situations such as this."

Mrs. Ferro had the boy out of wedlock and signed an adoption consent form two weeks later. The case was handled by private attorneys and not county or private adoption agencies. Frank and Helen Bacile of Bayport, Long Island, New York, became the child's adoptive parents. They were assured as much as a year later that the mother would allow them to adopt Richard legally. But the natural mother became engaged to a nineteen-year-old named John Ferro whom she married. She decided to hire a lawyer and get her son back. Her attorney maintained that she decided she wanted to keep her child the same night of signing the adoption consent form but followed through because of parental pressures.

The trial was heard before Justice Joseph A. Suozzi and despite medical and psychiatric testimony that the child would be psychologically hurt by returning him to his natural mother, the judge ruled that the child be returned. The decision was upheld by the Appellate Division and the Court of Appeals, the same courts that we were appealing to hear our case.

Well there you had it. If a three-year-old boy could be taken from the only home he'd ever known and given to his natural mother even after psychological testimony presented at the trial said it would be detrimental to the child, then what chance did we have?

Poor Richard! Poor Mr. and Mrs. Bacile! Two

others shared their despair. Nick's and my phones became busier than ever. Did I read the account of the three-year-old? What did I think? I finally could stand it no longer, so Marie screened all calls. I couldn't find the emotional strength to answer.

The Committee persuaded me that the two cases were different. Richard Ferro had been adopted privately, and ours was an agency adoption. Even though the court was inhuman to have returned such a decision, judges might view our case differently. The Committee tried hard and yet was repulsed by the tragic decision. Some of the wind came out of their sails, too. I was pleased to hear, however, that they had immediately gotten in touch with Mr. and Mrs. Bacile and offered help. But unlike Lenore DeMartino, Richard Farro was already gone.

John, the proverbial optimist, made arrangements for him and his wife, Glenda, to fly to Albany and present the petitions. A local travel agent provided free transportation. So, on Tuesday, February 9, John and Glenda, as representatives of the Committee to Keep Baby Lenore, arrived in the State Capital with a bulging suitcase containing more than 87,000 signed petitions requesting legislative action to make our case the last of its kind. Their presentation was made to Assembly Speaker Perry B. Duryea at a press conference in the lobby, called by Assemblyman Joseph R. Pisani. An unprecedented number of legislators met them.

Pisani announced that he filed two bills to make a natural mother's surrender agreement permanent and irrevocable thirty days after signing, one directed toward agency placements, the other toward private placements.

I was, of course, pleased about the proposed legislation, but my morale was low. The letters which

had been such a great help were beginning to upset me. Some people meant well, but they wrote across their letters: "Don't let what happened to the Baciles and Little Richard happen to you!"
OF COURSE, WE DIDN'T WANT IT TO HAPPEN. BUT WHAT MORE COULD WE DO? We felt so frustrated, so helpless.

Our precious Lenore was so big now she held onto the playpen and walked around; she danced up and down and clapped her hands and became more lovable with every day that passed. And still, the waiting.

On February 12, a local newspaper, *The Bensonhurst News*, ran a new petition on their front page directed to the judges of the Court of Appeals. An inside story by Charles F. Otey was particularly awakening. It began:

> *If I were Nick DeMartino, the courts would have to get past a twelve-gauge shotgun before they could take my daughter away. . . . Laws need not be made in hidden rooms by men with hidden hearts. And if made there, they can be changed by anyone with the guts to stand up for human rights whether the challenge came in the form of intimidation of a fellow man or himself. The DeMartinos and thousands of other parents have been thus intimidated. . . . Heaven help them, The Baciles, The Ferros, the Olga Scarpettas and those who aid their causes.*

Feelings became quite intense. A Bronx

Assemblyman, Alan Hochberg, asked us to appear at a rally to promote new adoption legislation. My mind and body wanted to stay home, but my heart told me I had to go. It was hectic but not as bad as imagined. Shoppers signed petitions and offered solace and hope.

I went home determined to get some rest and to hide from the public for a while. We were asked by the *Today Show* to appear. I said *no*. But Nick and the Committee said *yes*. "The people of this state know about little Lenore and Richard Ferro. This is an opportunity to let the country know."

So at 4:00 a.m., Nick and I walked the empty streets of Manhattan to appear with Barbara Walters and Assemblyman Pisani on the *Today Show*. I actually felt detached in a side room next to Barbara Walters who got last minute makeup touch ups. The makeup artist wanted to apply some to me and comb my hair. I wasn't there to look pretty but to tell my story and get the interview over and done with. Miss Walters gave a warm smile when I refused.

We took our seats in the TV Studio. Everything seemed unreal. The show opened with a film of Richard Ferro taken from the courtroom and crying, "I want my mommy."

I answered all the questions, but as soon as the show ended, I couldn't even remember what I'd been asked, much less what my answers were. When I told that to Nick, he said, "You did fine, honey. You spoke from your heart." Evidently he was right because more letters poured into our lives, this time from all parts of the country. People were fantastic!

David Susskind was the next personality to request an appearance on his program. Even Nick had it by now. His endless energy waned. He had circles under his eyes and had lost a considerable amount of weight. We finally agreed, however, to go for an interview.

We met Mr. and Mrs. Bacile for the first time in Mr. Susskind's office. I knew the hurt that Mrs. Bacile felt and yet didn't because I still believed that some hope remained for our family. The Baciles reached the end of the line. Helen Bacile was a courageous and rather unique woman. The Lord gave her a heavy cross, but He most certainly knew that she could withstand it. As for Frank, he was a quiet man whose soft eyes could not hide the hurt.

On his show, Mr. Susskind wanted to interview the four of us at the same time. But since his was a controversial show, which is to say, that it usually consisted of people with opposing views, he wanted another party to contrast our opinions. He wondered whether the Baciles or we could suggest someone. I saw the shocked expression on Mrs. Bacile's face. Nick quickly rose and gave Mr. Susskind contrasting opinions. He took me by the hand, and we left the office with the Baciles trailing behind.

We went to lunch although very little was eaten. "Well, that does it," Nick said. "We deserve a rest. Besides we're not going to be much good for the kids if we don't feel right." Helen's face saddened but seemed to liven up as she talked about little Richard. I remember commenting it was courageous of the final judge in her case to insist that the natural mother exit from the front door rather than the side.

"Yes, that really upset all the natural mother's plans," she commented.

"I could tell by the startled expression on her face," I said.

"Oh, yes, that's true," she continued, "but it goes deeper than that. According to Mrs. Ferro, no friends or family knew about Richard. So she prepared by telling them that she was in the process of adopting a child."

"What?" I heard my voice go up an octave. "A as far as Richard was concerned, he went from one adoptive family to another, and what's even worse, he went from an honest situation to a dishonest one."

Helen said bitterly, "We must remember the natural mother's primary right." I listened to Helen tell her story from beginning to end, and all I could do was shake my head. This is not the Dark Ages, I thought. This is America, 1971. We live in a country founded on liberty and freedom, a land where the just get justice. Aren't children entitled to equality under the law? Or is the Scale of Justice really a tape measure to assure only those over a certain height get the right to be heard and protected under our laws.

Lenore and Richard and Lord knows how many children are treated like chattel and passed on to their owners under the guise of being in their best interests. Perhaps Lady Justice needed to take off her blindfold and take a long hard look around.

I never saw Helen and Frank Bacile from that day on although we kept in contact with one another for a little while, but the picture of their grief-strained faces coupled with their magnificent courage remains with me to this day.

Nick and I remained at home and out of the public eye. We didn't get much rest, though. I kept busy around the house, and he, in his office. Keeping busy took our minds off the future. We forgot, however, the promise made to the Italian-American Anti-Defamation League to appear at their meeting. They called when our story appeared and asked for a batch of petitions to pass around and have signed. John Farro received the call this time. The league reminded us about the upcoming appearance. John explained our wish to remain out of the public eye. Since they worked so hard, however, John said that he would attend on our behalf.

The phone rang again. John answered. It was the League, only this time Joe Colombo whom many believed was a Mafia boss wanted to speak to Nick personally. I heard Nick say, "Okay, we'll be there."

I protested, "Nick, you know how exhausted we are."

"Colombo merely said, 'Nick, my people worked hard gathering signatures and expect you to be there personally. I think you'd do well to remember that dying men grasp for straws sometimes only to find that there are no straws to grasp for.' That's when I said, 'Okay, we'll be there.'"

"Nick, what did he?"

"I don't know, but I don't want to find out. We're going." So, tired as we were, we went. We didn't need anymore uncertainties than we had at the moment!

February 18, Lenore was nine months old. The Court of Appeals reached its decision to hear the Agency's case.

The DeMartinos, The Adoptive Parents Committee, The Child Welfare League of America, and the Community Council of Greater New York, would each be permitted to enter an *Amicus Curie Brief* (Friend of the Court) but not be allowed to intervene (enter into the case itself.) In other words, we could ride our car alongside the train, but we couldn't come aboard as a passenger.

It was a breakthrough, and we were ecstatic. Mr. Fuchsberg held a press conference at his office issuing the following statement: "This is good news for Baby Lenore and the DeMartinos. They still have a long way to go. But this is their first legal ray of hope. Our highest State Court, the Court of Appeals, recognizes that legal and public importance regarding the questions involved as well as enough doubt as to the correctness of the Trial Court's decision to return the baby to its biological mother warrants a public hearing of the appeal." When questioned by the press how he felt about this decision, Nick replied, "Even a journey lasting a thousand miles must begin with a first step."

We still had a really high hill to climb but had reliable Mr. Spencer and dynamic Mr. Fuchsberg guiding us along. We felt good. We waited this time until early March when our case would probably be presented to the Court of Appeals. Our neighbors were super. One by one, they shared the day's good news.

Feisty, red-faced Barry bounced into our home. He gave Nick a hug which was unusual for Barry and said, "I've got something special." With that, he took off the gold medal from around his neck. "Jean's got hers and now you've got one." Nick, who grew up in a Jewish neighborhood, recognized at once the Hebrew letters for eighteen which also signified *life*.

"Barry, I can't let you do this," Nick said.

"Listen," Barry said, "my son gave it to me, so that tells you I wouldn't give it up easily. But I want you to have it, and what's more important, my son wants you to have it. You know, I've always teased about your talk about God. Remember, I told you that whenever a religious fervor came, you should spare me the details and just say *32B,* and I'd fill in the details for myself. Well, this is my *32B* to you. Lenore was born on the 18th of the month, you brought her home one month later on the 18th, and now, this decision, comes down on the 18th of the month. So maybe God does have a plan. Please wear this symbol with my compliments."

Our friend Clair Anderson, minister of the

Lutheran Church around the corner, stopped by with a batch of petitions that his congregation signed. His friendship meant a great deal to Nick and me and we were comforted by his visit. Although the petitions had been presented to the legislature, new ones were still circulated and forwarded. There were no new accounts to report in the newspapers, but people talked about the case and letters pro and con appeared in "The Voice of The People" section of the *Daily News*. One letter stands out in my mind. It went like this:

> *It's about time newspapers gave up on the weeping DeMartinos. I, for one, am tired of seeing their face staring back at me every time I open up my morning paper. If you ask me, they are nothing but publicity seekers.*

Whoever the writer was, she had a point. God only knew how much we wanted to put an end to all of this. On Sunday, February 21, a friend presented an article which appeared in the *Long Island Sunday Press*. It was the most hair-raising article yet. I can't tell you how many times I read and reread that article to put myself into the head and mind of Justice Suozzi. But the more I read the more muddled and upset I became. The article presented the facts of the Bacile case: Richard was born in October, placed with the Baciles three days later, and his natural mother sought his return in December of the following year when he was over a year old and very much a part of the Bacile family.

In defense of his decision, the judge said: "Not withstanding the expert advice offered, this court is not satisfied that a change in custody at this time would have such a detrimental effect on this two-year-old child that it must be avoided even at the sacrifice of the natural mother's primary rights." So there we had it. The natural mother's PRIMARY RIGHTS took precedence.

Judge Suozzi felt compelled to discuss our case as well. The paper stated that cases like ours caused a widespread demand for change in adoption law. The judge's response to new legislation was, "Nothing is further from the truth. On the contrary, if these changes were in effect at the time of the Ferro and DeMartino decisions, the results would be the same."

For obvious reasons that statement frightened me.

In a letter written to New York Assembly Majority Leader, Justice Suozzi suggested how the law could be changed. "A provision requiring an authorized adoption agency to serve notice upon prospective adoptive parents in every action or proceeding involving the adoptive child, and mandating that the adoptive parents be named as necessary parties either by their real or fictitious names, and further providing for the appointment of a guardian to represent the child's interest as opposed to the foster parents' interests."

On the surface, a fine proposal—at least the child had representation. But let us read on. "Had the agency done this in the DeMartino case, they would have been aware of what transpired though wouldn't effectively be able to do any more than the agency." Were not the Baciles parties in the adoption controversy over which he presided? Although Little Richard did not have an appointed guardian, experts spoke on behalf of the child's well being. As for the DeMartinos being made "aware of what transpired," it appeared that the judge's proposal sought not to remove the adoptive parents from the firing range but merely to remove their blindfolds! Justice Suozzi and Justice Ascione had a lot in common! A great deal of confusion rested in the courts and their judges.

On the heels of the Bacile case came another decision which confused the issue. The New York newspapers brought to light another case of a natural mother—Mary Roe (Fictitious name)—who became intimate with a married doctor and father of four children. She went to Puerto Rico to have the child, brought it back to New York, and placed with the New York Foundling Hospital for adoption the following May with an executed written surrender. The hospital placed the child with its adoptive parents on May 31. The natural mother subsequently sought his return which a lower court granted, but the New York Appellate Court Judges—the same court which decided our case—overturned the ruling and said, "We hold that petitioner voluntarily surrendered her child and consented to his adoption. He has a good family life with the adoptive parents. On this record, we conclude the petition should be denied and custody of the child continued with the adoptive parents."

Was mother love no longer a basis for returning children to their natural mothers? The law which governed the Baciles and us hadn't changed. More and more cases came to light. I received letters from women in other states who had lost their adoptive children. Heart-rendering stories broke in the press continuously. In upstate New York, Mr. and Mrs. Gary McAlpine lost custody of their nine-month-old baby whom they cared for since she was less than two weeks old.

It is easy to understand that with so many conflicting decisions and many more conflicting articles, that the press, the public and even lawyers were confused.

Case law (Decisions in older cases which give

merit and weight to new cases) boggled the mind and confused the issues even more. For example, cases used by the Spence-Chapin Agency on behalf of Lenore (People ex rel. Harris v Commissioner of Welfare,188 misc. 919,924 70 N.Y.S. 2d 389,395 (New York County 1949) ". . . when a mother knowingly and understandingly surrenders her child to an authorized agency to be place out for adoption, and her act is not induced by fraud or mistake, she may not thereafter come into court and, upon a mere assertion that she now wants the child and is able and fit to care for it, have the child back. To get that relief, she must show by convincing evidence that the child is in circumstances which compel the conviction that its welfare requires that the court undo what she has done." And (People ex rel. Anonymous v New York Foundling Hospital,17 AD 2d 122, 126, 232 N.Y.S. 2d 479 483-84 (12th Dept 1962) ". . . the change of mind by a natural parent is not an evil thing; instead, the change of mind is to be accorded great sympathy, and in a proper case, encouragement and favorable action. This does not mean that a mere change of mind is sufficient, prior to adoption, to justify return of the child."

    The more confused I became, the clearer the need for new adoption laws became. *Best interests* had a wide interpretation that judges given approximately the same patterns came up with opposite decisions. Both positions were upheld by the higher courts. I decided to read more about case histories. I needed time to relax and be me, so I turned to my yesterdays and thought of happier moments.

Chapter X

On March 1, 1971, the New York State Court of Appeals, the highest court of the state and comprising seven justices, heard the appeal for Scarpetta Vs Spence-Chapin Adoption Agency. Nick and I awoke early. For no apparent reason, Nick's eye pained him and finally became so intense that he drove to a nearby hospital for treatment. When he returned, he wore an eyepatch and assured me that he was all right. I could tell he was in great pain. I had to concentrate on the day ahead he told me.

We arrived at the airport in time to have breakfast with Mr. Spencer. We were all hopeful and joined Mr. Fuchsberg waiting on the plane. An hour later, we landed in Albany. A member of Assemblyman Pisani's staff drove us to his offices.

The overall attitude was optimistic. People in the halls shook our hands and wished us well. Attorney Frank Della Posta introduced himself and asked if we heard about the unhappy fate of his clients, the McAlpines, and their nine-month-old baby. Della Posta blamed himself for what had happened. He shared with my husband and our attorneys the legal actions taken on behalf of his clients. He felt that the right decision in our case would help his clients get their daughter back. We prayed for the right decision.

Soon after lunch, we arrived at the outer chambers of the courtroom and met Mr. Arthur Friedman of the Adoptive Parents Committee and Mr. Reardon, Attorney for Spence-Chapin, who was to give the legal presentation on behalf of the agency. It appeared as though our case finally penetrated Mr. Reardon's cool. For the first time he appeared nervous. I knew that he did his homework this time and really put into his brief. We greeted one another warmly and walked into the huge courtroom. I felt insignificant. The room, two stories high, was authoritative. Pictures of justices hung around the room, and from the spectators' seats behind a railing in the rear of the room, the judges seemed a great distance. They sat on a platform so high that you looked up to observe. When you place seven judges together on one long platform, the result is overpowering. I was terribly frightened and couldn't believe that this was really happening. I was brought back to earth by the appearance of a clerk who approached and asked on behalf of the judges, not to have any pictures taken in the court room. We didn't expect any would be taken but had someone wait at the door to pass on the judges' sentiments just in case.

  I wondered whether Miss Scarpetta would appear. My wondering ceased when she walked in accompanied by a stately woman with carefully groomed, short, gray hair who wore a fur coat. We later discovered that the strange woman was her mother. Miss Scarpetta looked as fragile as ever maybe even more so. She had little make-up; her hair was pulled back, and she wore a dark coat which hung down to her ankles. On either side, someone held her elbows and arms as though she needed assistance walking. She looked like an old lady being helped to a seat.

  The judges entered from a side door, and after sitting, peered down from their lofty perch. The courtroom was called to order. Mr. Reardon did his best but his best wasn't good enough. His sounded as though he spoke about crude oil or another inanimate object. He presented the details of the case, then went on to question the primary right of the natural mother. He was interrupted by Chief Judge Stanley Fuld who pointed out that the lower court had the discretion to rescind the surrender if it deems the natural mother fit and if it is in the best interest of the child. Reardon argued that the lower court had abused its discretion in this case and that the adoption agency operated within the framework of the law.

Then Mr. Zalk's took the podium. He stated that the lower courts decided that the best interests of the child would be served by returning her to her natural mother. He said, he was aware of the emotional content of the case which resulted in a number of bills being introduced in the state legislature affecting the time in which a natural mother can reclaim her child and pointed out that the natural mother in this case indicated she wanted her baby returned three weeks after placement by the agency. Mr. Zalk added that if the agency immediately said to the adoptive parents, "The mother wants her child back," the emotional problem might have been avoided.

My thoughts flashed to Nick's answer to a reporter about that same possibility, "It's easier," Nick said, "to lose a fingertip than a finger, a finger than an arm, but do you think any mother, adoptive or otherwise, should be put in the position of losing a child at any age?"

Zalk cited a case which held that adoptive parents have no legal rights until the adoption is final. I had been holding Nick's hands and he felt me flinch when Zalk called us nonpersons. He whispered in my ear, "Easy, baby. Take it easy." I looked at his patch over one eye and his face so drawn and felt a great surge of love for him. I smiled and nodded to let him know that I was all right then turned my attention to Zalk's presentation.

Each attorney spoke for an allotted time in a hearing which lasted ninety minutes. Mr. Fuchsberg addressed the court for the last five minutes. As he approached the bench, a number of justices leaned forward in their seats. Unlike the other two attorneys, Mr. Fuchsberg breathed life into the proceedings. He talked about real people with real needs not corporations or nonpersons or chattels. "How can the welfare of the child be determined," he asked the court, "if the DeMartinos are not permitted to testify? Too many questions are unanswered in this totally inadequate court record." He argued that the lower court should have inquired into the mental and physical condition of the infant, the effect of removing her from the only home ever known, and the fitness of the natural mother as opposed to the adoptive parents. In short, he concluded, "This case must be sent back for a new trial so all questions are answered."

Although Mr. Fuchsberg gave the hearing its first spark of life, he didn't have time to develop a watertight case. I studied the judges as he spoke and knew, just knew, that we lost. Back in the chambers, everyone felt elated because Mr. Fuchsberg turned the tide, everyone, that is, but me! Well, the trip home just confirmed my uneasy feelings. An airplane strike caused Mr. Spencer to drive back with Arthur Friedman of the Adoptive Parents Committee which left Mr. Fuchsberg, John and Glenda Farro who had accompanied for moral support, and Nick and I to find a way home. What else could go wrong? We rode a taxicab to an auto rental agency which had no cars. We thought to try another rental agency a short distance from the first. We found out, much to our dismay, that what should have been a short distance turned out to be a long distance. When finally reaching the rent-a-car, we were regretfully informed that they were not renting cars for long distances.

Our taxi driver then took another short cut to

the train depot, but the train to N.Y. pulled out as we arrived and another wasn't due for hours. Finally, in desperation, Mr. Fuchsberg, who had a pilot's license, suggested we locate a private plane rental service but we were unable to locate one. After endless hours of driving in and around the outskirts of Albany, we returned to the bus terminal. This time we were in luck. A bus readied to leave in ten minutes.

The only seats were scattered. Mr. Fuchsberg and I sat near the aisle. Nick appeared so tired and old and, of course, a patch over his eye didn't help his appearance. "How's your eye?" I called. He gave a thumbs up and blew me a kiss. As the bus moved onto the highway, Mr. Fuchsberg told me about the decoding work he'd done in the service and about his archaeological interests, but finally I asked, "Mr. Fuchsberg, what will be the outcome of today's trial?"

He hesitated then said, "Jean, I'm not a betting man, but if I were, I'd bet against this one." Our eyes locked for just a moment and then I said almost inaudibly, "I see." I could no longer pretend to be sociable and indicated that I wanted to sleep. Mr. Fuchsberg gave an understanding nod, and I kept my eyes closed the rest of the trip. It would have been wonderful, but sleep never came.

Nick's brother Vinnie met us at the depot in New York and brought us home. Everyone talked about success. The last time we waited for a decision, I knew we were to lose. This time I felt so strongly that we were going to lose, that once again I waited without hope.

There was talk about our case in the papers for the next few days anticipating the Court of Appeal's decision. On the whole, our home was as near normal as possible. Even Marie stayed home. Nick, whose eye no longer gave him any problem, went to work. I brought Linda to nursery school three mornings a week and took care of the children and our home. The girls seemed a lot happier with less confusion around the house. The phones rarely rang except for reporters from time to time to find out when the decision from the Court of Appeals would be handed down. During this lull, Spence-Chapin contacted us and asked us to meet with them. It felt strange entering the agency doors again like meeting with a childhood friend whom you shared youth and innocence with after years of tragedy and maturity. You're anxious to meet but wonder if you'll be able to recapture the past or whether the years will make a difference.

The receptionist directed us to the inner waiting room where we were shortly greeted by Mrs. Jane Edwards who gave us a strong, friendly greeting. As we walked through the corridors, people stopped to wish us good luck. Mrs. Edwards said, "We've all been praying to St. Jude for you."

I knew that few Catholics were connected with the agency and found their prayers a generous expression of support. Mrs. Edwards introduced a member of the Board who assured us that under the circumstances and that given the same set of facts, they took appropriate action. Mrs. Edwards explained their records showed that when Miss Scarpetta spoke of the return of her child, her conversation was clouded with troubled feelings and doubt. In subsequent meetings, she spoke continuously about her uncertain decision. Since it was common for natural mothers to have these feelings, the agency offered help to resolve her doubt. They thought she came to grips with her ambivalence because there was no further contact with her until August 3 when she corresponded through her attorney. That was the first time she clearly stated without any reservations about wanting the child back.

"She presented us with a *Writ of Habeas Corpus* on September 21, 1970," Mrs. Edwards explained, "more than three months after the surrender. In view of the time given to her prior to the surrender, the fact that we were abiding by her request to place the baby as early as possible, and, more importantly, that her request for return was shrouded in uncertainty, we had no recourse but to respond as we did.

"I know that point wasn't as clear as it should have been in the original trial, but after everything I've read in the newspapers, Mrs. DeMartino, I'm not sure that it would have mattered anyway."

I was inclined to accept what Mrs. Edwards told me because it interlocked perfectly with my appraisal of Miss Scarpetta, but I wished to know for certain! I had only one more question to ask Mrs. Edwards. "Did the agency refuse to let Miss Scarpetta see the baby when she was in foster care that first month?"

"The mother made no such request," Mrs. Edwards said emphatically.

"Now that you've cleared up those points for us," Nick said, "perhaps you will tell us what measures you intend to take should there be another unfavorable decision?"

The answer was *none*. They checked with their lawyers who advised that no further recourse seemed plausible beyond the state courts. They would, therefore, be bound by the state's decision. Their response was exactly what Nick anticipated, so we amicably took our leave.

As the weeks moved on, the weather was still cold and windy. We spent a great deal of our time indoors. I looked so drawn and tired that Nick took me literally by the hand to the office of our family doctor. After an examination, he told Nick the best medicine would be peace of mind and total relaxation. The next best thing would be to get away. When we got into the car, Nick said, "Well, a trip to Miami is in order."

"Oh, Nick, don't be silly. I can't go to Florida."
"We've talked about moving to Florida."
"Right."
"Well, this is a perfect opportunity to combine business with pleasure. You can go with the kids, relax, and forget what's happening here and at the same time find out about living there."

"Talking about living someplace and actually moving are different things. My heart is just not in Florida right now. Maybe after the appeal decision."

"You ought to go now! But if you won't, then at least start thinking about Florida and making plans."

I really didn't do much about making plans. Oh, we talked about moving. First, we thought to just move to a more countrified area. So we investigated Staten Island. As a matter of fact, we had placed a down payment on a "Village Green" home and put our home up for sale. But before ours was sold, we decided to leave the city. Nick became disenchanted with his law partner, Hal. He liked him as a person, in business, however, his attitude was never do today what you can put off until tomorrow. Nick talked with Hal about the problem, but it did no good. Nick wanted a new start. So, we canceled our Staten Island purchase and headed to upstate New York to investigate areas. Then the subject of moving to Florida came up. When Nick and I were honeymooning there, we were captured by the weather and the environment, and each and every time we returned for a vacation, we talked about relocating. I didn't think of Florida seriously. We were both close to our families in New York, a major consideration for us and the girls. Now, however, Nick seemed serious about the move. There was determination in his voice which was unsettling. I wasn't ready for any abrupt change in my life right now.

I guarded my solitude lately. So when we received a request from a Mrs. Hughs representing the *Ladies' Home Journal*, I refused to be interviewed. As the newswoman intended to do an in depth report interviewing not only us but also the Spence-Chapin Agency and Miss Scarpetta, both Nick and I agreed. Maybe time had come to report a whole rather than chopped up and confusing versions appearing piecemeal in the press. Mrs. Hughs scheduled three visits. She intended to report her findings truthfully and asked to borrow the legal information on hand. She immediately gained my admiration. I thought that any woman who cared enough to do that kind of homework would do a responsible job of reporting.

On April 7, 1971, I wished Nick a Happy Birthday. He turned thirty-seven. "Maybe you'll get the best birthday present of your life today," I said hopefully.

"I sure hope the court's decision comes soon, Jean. I'm getting edgy." He was at a trial that day and left me a telephone number. It was another cold morning. I dressed Linda and Lenore and ran around the corner to drop Linda off at nursery school. With Lenore in my arms, I opened the front door, heard the phone, placed Lenore, coat and all, into the playpen, and rushed to answer.

"Mrs. DeMartino," a voice said. "You are on the air," he said, "and our listeners want your response to this morning's decision."

"I don't understand," I replied.

"I'm referring to the Court of Appeal. I'm sorry, Mrs. DeMartino, I thought you knew."

My heart dropped, "No. No one told me."

"The court ruled unanimously that Lenore be returned to her natural mother."

"Oh, I see," I managed to say.

"Would you like me to read the bulletin?" he asked.

"Yes, please."

"The Court of Appeals, the state's highest tribunal, concluded unanimously that the record before us supports the findings of the lower courts that the surrender was improvident and that the child's interests—moral and temporal—will best be served by a return to its natural mother. Mrs. DeMartino, are you there?"

"I must go now. You'll have to excuse me." Once again the media and not the courts reported findings to us. I honestly don't recall how long I sat trying to understand. When I called Nick, I was told there was no way to get a message into his courtroom. I explained who I was and the message and the woman assured me it would get to Nick.

Our family flooded the front door. Then the committee came just ahead of a line of reporters. I didn't cry! I was angry! I remember walking up and down and spewing. "Gentlemen," I said to the reporters, "today's ruling was unjust to Lenore and an insult to the DeMartinos. The lower court reached its decision based upon mother love which they believed me incapable of, and now the Court of Appeals says Lenore must be returned because her best interests will be better served by so doing. The court made a moral judgment about the DeMartinos without ever meeting or hearing one word of testimony from us.

"This whole thing is a farce, and I don't intend to dignify the ruling by quiet acceptance or by tears." I got the last word out when Nick walked in the door. Despite all my fancy heroics, I threw myself into his arms and cried uncontrollably. Dear Lenny, who hid behind the scenes, called Nick to offer solace. Mr. Spencer offered legal hope and all our friends, irate, saddened, and bewildered, offered their continued support.

The next day, April 8, Mr. Jacob Fuchsberg issued the following release:

> *So far as Jean and Nick DeMartino are concerned, the case just started. The issues of adoptive parents and what is best for Baby Lenore are clearly neglected, in effect, in the restatement by the New York Courts in its determination to stick to what the DeMartinos regard as outworn ideas. The court's decision marks the beginning not the end of the legal proceedings.*
>
> *Basically, if the New York decision is allowed to stand, adoptive parents who have given a child love and care almost from the time of birth have no standing to even present proof as to what is in the best interests of the baby or fair to those who have made her their very own child.*
>
> *Jean and Nick DeMartino have not been allowed to present an iota of truth. They have not been permitted to testify. They have not been given the right to call witnesses or have the court hear experts or to prove a single fact.*
>
> *Not a word has been heard as to how the child fared. No one, other*

than the DeMartinos, has been concerned, has asked a single question about how the child has been during a single day of her life since the unwed mother voluntarily gave her away.

The case has been solely between the unwed mother and the adoption agency. The child's welfare has been treated so impersonal that she might as well be a piece of stone instead of a very young and sensitive human being. No court even saw the baby or asked about what effect tearing her out of her home will have.

It appears to the DeMartinos that the decision treats New York parents who adopt children as second class citizens. That is not true in many other states. The court endorsed the old idea that an unwed mother is preferable to a family unit. Jean and Nick DeMartino believe that in this age of the proliferation of illegitimate children needing homes, it is essential to recognize the idea that mother love does not come from the womb but from round-the-clock loving care. Mother love must be more than a vague idea of pretty sentiments. In this case, love comes from hard, real-life family ties between Lenore and Jean and Nick DeMartino and their four-year-old daughter Linda. The bonds have now almost a whole year of development. They appear as important as the legal title sought by a woman who gave a

> baby up almost before the child came from her body.
>
> In refusing the DeMartinos a trial, the court talked of secrecy in keeping the names of unwed mothers and of adoptive parents from one another. The DeMartinos believe that to be unrealistic. A legal proceeding brought by an unwed mother is bound to flush out the names as it, in fact, appears here. Theory or fiction yields to fact.
>
> Jean and Nick DeMartino wanted an open trial on the merits—for the baby and for themselves. This has been expressly denied. They believe adoptive children and adoptive parents have rights. They believe the constitution protects these rights from being taken without a trial.
>
> Therefore, they begin a suit in federal court to secure the protection of fundamental rights for Baby Lenore, for themselves, and for all other adoptive children and parents similarly threatened. They are determined to keep their family from being torn apart.

This statement preceded one from the Committee to Help Keep Baby Lenore:

> We, the Committee to Help Keep Baby Lenore, on behalf of more than 100,000 people who signed petitions asking, "The DeMartino

family be given their day in court," demand that opportunity as a simple matter of constitutional justice.

We refuse to tell millions more that their voices fall on deaf ears, that the highest court in New York has, like Pontius Pilate, washed its hands of the matter.

By so doing, the court permitted the well being of a little child to be determined only by unsubstantiated statements of one party, the unwed mother, and continuously refused to hear the voices of the only parents this child has known.

By refusing to heed the petitions of more than 100,000 voices, the courts placed themselves in CONTEMPT OF THE PEOPLE!

The papers printed the committee's statement, but across town the headlines read, *The DeMartinos Lose Their Adopted Daughter.* Seeing the words in print was more than I could handle. Meanwhile, Fuchsberg filed suit in U.S. District Court. He sought a *stay* and an injunction barring enforcement of the State Court of Appeals ruling. He contended that we had been denied our constitutional rights under the Fourteenth Amendment which guarantees due process. If granted, the *stay* stopped the surrender of Lenore.

Nick and I were frightened, really frightened. We thought that any minute a knock on the door meant Lenore's removal. "Is this Nazi Germany?" I screamed. "Are they coming into my home and ripping Lenore from my arms?"

"Don't worry, Jean," our neighbor who lived in the corner house said. He was a big burly truck driver and told us that if they tried to remove Lenore that the members of his union prepared to pave the entire street with human bodies over which the Marshal needed to walk in order to reach our door. Feelings got more and more intense. We needed time by ourselves to think things over.

Everyone but our immediate family left. We settled down when the mailman delivered a formal notice to pick up a registered letter at the post office. I panicked! At the post office, two people in front of me waited to be served. I felt blood rushing to my head. TIME! —how heavily it hung on us and moved slowly as though everything took place in slow motion. I felt the urge to move up front and demand that I be taken care of first yet was afraid to find out what awaited. I felt my hands get clammy, my body tingling. Was he ever going to finish with the man in front of me? I shifted from one foot to another not to show any annoyance. That would only work against me in getting the clerk to speed up. I looked at my watch. I'd only been in line for ten minutes, but it seemed an eternity.

"What can I do for you?" I heard the postal clerk saying. I handed the request to him and held my breath. As he placed the envelope on the counter, I managed to read the return address. *Department of Motor Vehicles*. "I love you," I shouted. He looked at me in a very strange way. I signed for the letter quickly and ripped it open. It was a parking ticket which, in all the confusion, Nick neglected to pay. Praise the Lord! I bounced into the house to an agonized family which shared my relief.

Nick insisted, "You've been through enough. Take Lenore and Linda and go down to Florida."

I looked at Nick in disbelief. "Can I just take Lenore to Florida? And what about the money? We've spent so much already."

He grabbed me gently by the arms, looked directly into my eyes, and said, "You must take the children and go."

I was about to object when Doris interrupted. "Bud, Lisa, and I are going with you. Bud will drive and fly back and Lisa and I will stay with you. Marie agreed to take care of Laura."

I looked from one face to another, heaved a sigh of surrender, and said, "Okay."

The following day, I got some things together for myself and the kids. Both girls had grown so that there was very little to take. I managed to pack whatever clothes were available and we were ready. Mom reminded us that Miss Hughes of the *Ladies Home Journal* was scheduled to arrive that morning for her third and final meeting. Now that I made up my mind to leave, I wanted to get started, but Nick and the others convinced me not to leave any loose ends, so I went ahead with the interview. Needless to say, I was tense through it.

At the end of the interview, the kids and I headed for the back door to meet Doris, Bud, and Lisa with a packed car and the motor running. It was a tear-filled goodbye with mom and dad by the back door waving goodbye. They had worried expressions. Mom registered special concern because Linda tripped in the living room and hit her head against an end table. I tried to give her some quick assurances, but she was distraught. My final words to Nick were, "Are you sure you'll be all right? What will our attorneys say?"

"Trust me. I'll tell Fuchsberg and Spencer when I think it advisable. In the meantime, we still have legal custody of Lenore and there is no reason in the world why you can't leave the State. Take care of yourself, darling, and write to me as soon as you get settled."

As soon as we left the State, peace settled over me that I had not experienced in a long time. It was Good Friday of Easter weekend and one of those rare times when the Jewish Services coincided with ours. I thought of Barry giving Nick his medal and telling him, "Now, you've got all bases covered, Nick." It brought a smile to my face. A bright yellow sun hung in the sky late into the evening, and guided our way southward.

Bud did all the driving. Doris and I rested and the children played in the rear. My thoughts wandered back to happier times with the children. Who possibly imagined all that had taken place? Could it be a dream? It was late Saturday evening when we arrived in Miami. We stayed in a motel and called our friends Ira and Dotty Greenfield who offered to find an apartment. Easter Sunday, we set upon our search. Finding an apartment in Miami in mid-April was next too impossible. We searched the entire day. "Come back in May" or "I'm sorry, we don't accept children." To add to our problems, the air conditioner in our car quit and we became tired and irritable.

After riding around in the heat with cranky children who needed attention, Ira finally located a one room efficiency in a complex on Treasure Isle. It was cheery, air conditioned, and had a pool which the children would enjoy. We unpacked our belongings, got the children comfortable, and then immediately shopped for food. It was a great sense of relief to settle in. We finished putting the last package away when there was a knock at our door. It was the manager's wife.

"I'm terribly sorry," she said "but my husband tells me you have children and we do not rent to people with children." I tried to answer but the words wouldn't come out. Doris was the one who asked, "Why didn't your husband tell us that before we went out and bought food?"

"He didn't realize the children were staying. You can stay the night at no charge but must leave in the morning."

The next morning, we packed our goods and once more roamed the streets of Miami Beach. The addition of food packages in the car—some of it perishable—added to our already complex problems. We turned to our friend Ira who suggested we stay at a motel for two weeks until the season ended. He located the Moulon Rouge on Arthur Godfrey Drive, a nice inexpensive place. The room was small with two double beds and a tiny efficiency, but the motel had a lot to offer. Since we merely slept in the room, living there worked out fairly well.

I determined, however, to find an apartment, so as soon as we settled in the motel, we set about finding one. Our luck changed. We found a nice two bedroom furnished apartment on Harding Avenue available on May 1, and the landlord welcomed children. I told him we planned on relocating to Florida and expected to buy a house and hoped to stay however long that took. He was a dear soul and most agreeable. We now had our ducks in a row. Bud flew back to New York, and Doris and I and the children took full advantage of our vacation.

The days were beautiful. We sat by the pool relaxing. The children had a ball. It was especially great for Linda. No longer upset by the upheaval, she really enjoyed herself. As for Lenore, she immediately captured the hearts of all who saw her and had the time of her life. We had a few anxious moments when picking up New York papers left pool side and saw

Lenore's face continually. But, fortunately, no one at the motel made a connection. Doris and I took no chances, however; we scooped up the papers and discard them or took the telltale pages. For the most part things were nearly normal. But every night reality set in when I checked with Nick into the day's happenings. "How do things look, Nick?"

"Everything is fine. The federal stay is still in effect, and a hearing is pending. Please get in touch with William Colson. He's a well-respected attorney. Everything is going along as planned here, but just in case we need an attorney in Miami, I'd like him lined up."

"How much should I tell him?"

"Fill him in on what took place with the court of appeals and ask if he'll represent us if we need him. In the meantime, I'm going to remain in Brooklyn and arrange for our house to be sold and our belongings sent when we need them. Then I'll join you. So long for now, and stop worrying about legalities. Leave the sweating to me."

I wasn't worried anymore. For some strange reason, the events of New York didn't make an emotional border crossing. I followed Nick's request and made an appointment to see William Colson. The elevator door opened, and I found myself face-to-face with the receptionist for the law firm of Colson and Hicks. Their offices took up the entire floor of a building located downtown on Flagler Street directly opposite the courthouse. I was directed into a large office decorated in dark wood and sat on a couch, a rather informal living room type. The length of one wall had glass windows which overlooked Flagler Street and the courthouse.

Mr. Colson, a tall attractive gentleman in his mid-forties, gave a broad, friendly smile and shook my hand.

He had a definite southern drawl. "My husband asked me to see you about our adoption case."

"That's not exactly my field."

"Please, can I assume that anything I tell you will remain between the two of us on an attorney/client basis?"

"You have my word." Mr. Colson listened attentively as I filled him in on events. He interrupted me only once to ask if another attorney might join us to hear the details. I then met Robert Orseck whom Mr. Colson introduced as the legal brain. Mr. Orseck appeared quite ordinary. He was younger and shorter than Mr. Colson, slightly built, had an overall average appearance, and when speaking, he stuttered slightly. In any event, I brought Mr. Orseck up-to-date and continued my story. Mr. Colson heard about our case from his wife and daughter who, it seems, viewed us on the *Today Show*. The legal aspects of the case shocked him. He found it difficult to believe that Lenore's adoptive parents never received representation in courts. He asked the question so many had asked, "How could Lenore's best interests be determined by the court that never permitted her adoptive parents to appear and testify?" I could sense that he developed some interest.

"The case is now going into federal court," he observed. "Where do I fit in?"

"Nick, my husband, and I will remain in Florida regardless of future decisions. This nightmare made our plans to move to Miami a reality. We hope that you will represent us should the need arise."

"You tread on dangerous and uncharted grounds. Your husband as an attorney knows that, Mrs. DeMartino."

"Mr. Colson, how many more surprises can be

left for us? We've made up our minds and made our moves accordingly. Now, we choose to follow through to the end. Will you help us?"

"I'll talk with Bob and let you know. If you don't hear from us by the time your husband gets into town, be sure to have him call me."

I was grateful for the time given and told him so. Mr. Orseck joined me at the elevator. During a short trip to the parking garage, I appreciated Mr. Orseck's pleasing smile and his gentle conversation. The next evening, I called Nick person-to-person at his brother's house anxious not only to hear what he might report but also to tell him about my visit with Colson. To my surprise, he wasn't there. No one answered the following evening either.

The next day, I told Nick in person. On May 1, midday, Nick and Charlie Johnson arrived at the Moulon Rouge Motel. I saw a tall, tired man leaning against the glass doors looking at me. I ran to Nick's side. He looked terrible and beautiful. How wonderful to have him back again.

My questions tumbled out one after another.

"Our case is in the federal courts. There is no reason that we can't move our family anywhere within the continental United States. So far, we haven't even been served. There is some question in my mind how people who are nonpersons in the eyes of a court can suddenly be asked to materialize and follow the dictates of that court."

What Nick said reminded me of the time I saw two little boys fighting over who was to play with a red, toy truck that a third boy owned. They socked each other and rolled in the dirt. In the meantime, the third little boy's mother took him and the truck home. The other two youngsters still fought. The analogy seemed appropriate to Nick's point. After lunch, Nick filled me in. "On April 20, Judge Constance Baker Motley of the federal court issued a *stay* for ten more days pending a decision on whether her court had jurisdiction. A week later, on April 27, Judge Motley ruled that the injunction sought by us through our attorneys did not come under the jurisdiction of her court but that our case could be taken to the U.S. Supreme Court and that is what Fuchsberg and Spencer are working on now. Judge Motley's decision, however, ended the *stay* in effect and meant that Judge Ascione could set a date for Lenore to be returned. He lost no time. I heard that he immediately issued an order that Lenore be returned Monday, May 3. But nobody told me officially, and I was never served. Anyway, Judge Motley came to our rescue again when on April 29, he issued the agency another temporary *stay*.

Since we applied to the U. S. Supreme Court, I thought it advisable to have a constitutional lawyer on our team. I hired Leo Pfeiffer, a well known civil rights lawyer, to work along with Fuchsberg and Spencer."

"Nick, how can we afford this? I heard that going to the Supreme Court costs a fortune."

"It'll all work out. Come on. Let's move to that apartment you found. All I want to do is soak up sun and sit around with you and the kids."

Doris, Lisa, and Charlie flew back to New York, and Nick and I and the children set up home on Harding Avenue.

I told Nick about my meeting with Mr. Colson who asked to let him know when Nick arrived. The place we rented was large and airy and only a block from the beach. We spent the entire weekend relaxing and pretending that all was right with the world.

On Monday, Nick called Colson and Orseck

and got an appointment. The fact that they were able to speak to Nick, not only as the father but also as a brother attorney, gave credibility to our story and weighed heavily in our favor. Nick related that he heard a New York Court ordered the return of Lenore to her natural mother on May 3, but a federal stay had gone into effect on April 29 negating the need to comply. Besides, he wouldn't oblige them anyway since we were all in Florida.

    Mr. Colson advised us to let our New York attorneys know of our whereabouts. He also suggested that since we intended to move permanently, we might make our location publicly known. Nick agreed to write Fuchsberg but opted to wait before letting our whereabouts be known. He felt our family needed time for rest and rehabilitation.

    Colson and Orseck gave us our first official welcome as residents in the Sunshine State and assured us that they would help on whatever legal matters presented themselves. Colson offered Nick per diem work through his office. Nick thanked and told him he would probably take him up on it.

We spent the next days familiarizing ourselves with Miami Beach, namely; Surfside. Nick and I got Florida Driver's licenses; we joined the Surfside Beach and Pool Club ($25.00 for the first year for the entire family.) I got a library card for books to read to the children. When we went clothes shopping, I became cautious about money and went to the least expensive stores to buy the girls and me much needed summer wear. I was disappointed in the quality but felt it was the best we could do at present. I always took pride in my appearance and that of the girls, but these proved different circumstances to make the best of.

    Nick wrote a letter to Fuchsberg and gave him a P.O. box. We awaited anxiously news of our legal position. Our only source of information was New York daily papers.

I held Lenore in one hand and a newspaper in the other and read that our request for a *stay* from the U.S. Supreme Court Circuit Judge, John M. Harlan, had been denied and that Mr. Zalk, Miss Scarpetta's attorney, contacted Mr. Fuchsberg to set up the return of our child as soon as possible.

I sobbed as Nick whispered, "Well, hon, we'll continue our plea to the Supreme Court but expect to do it without Lenore." Nick's brows furrowed, and his eyes got a far away look. There was no way to possibly hide the pain and worry he experienced.

The following day, the New York Times reported that Judge Ascione re-entered the case and ordered our appearance in court to show cause why we should not be held in criminal contempt for failure to surrender Lenore the previous Monday. "The previous Monday?" Nick shouted. "That was the original turnover date but a federal *stay* was in effect. What the hell is he talking about? Besides, that bastard never had any official contact with me. Aren't I entitled to be served like anyone else, or am I supposed to respond to court rulings based upon newspapers articles or reports over the air waves?" On the heels of discovery, we received a letter from Mr. Fuchsberg requesting that he be permitted to tell the courts that we were no longer in New York but residing elsewhere.

Nick gave him the go-ahead and, at the same time, wrote to Marty McLaughlin of the *New York Daily News*, the reporter who printed the original story and who continued to faithfully report it.

We planned a little party for Lenore's birthday. It was a far cry from the party for Linda when she was a year old. By this time, we also learned that a new judge entered the scenario. He certainly was a lot more compassionate than our friend Ascione. The new judge ordered the Spence-Chapin Agency to prepare a gradual transition by which Lenore could be turned over to her natural mother. Evidently, Mr. Fuchsberg told the court that the DeMartinos left the State of New York.

On May 25, the *Daily News* carried a front page headline: DEMARTINOS FLEE WITH BABY. Underneath in Nick's scrawl was a handwritten letter to Marty McLaughlin:

> *Dear Marty,*
>
> *I don't think that I forgot you or believe that you are yesterday's hero. I will never forget you and you are always in my prayers.*
>
> *I am, as you know, literally fighting for my life. I must use every available means to protect my family and at the same time protect those hundreds and maybe thousands of other threatened families to follow.*
>
> *I have not lost my faith in God and maybe we were chosen as His tool to fight the archaic thinking of our court system. I read where the laws have already changed, but I do not intend to have my daughter become a sacrificial lamb.*
>
> *Marty, you know that I would give my life for my family. You would do the same. In the final analysis, nothing is more valuable than those a man holds dear.*
>
> *Be patient with me until the end. You are a credit to your*

profession and great things lie in the future for you. Someday perhaps I will brag to my friends, 'I know Marty McLaughlin.'

Jack Fuchsberg will keep you posted. He is a good man and recognizes how much you have done. Fear is often the father of courage, and I know that Lenore belongs with us.

God bless you and your family and love from Jean.

Sincerely,
Nick

Nick never meant for the letter to be published, but Marty was a newspaperman, after all, and under the circumstances, Nick's letter was news. I am particularly proud of that letter, and, to this day, keep it handy. I reread it whenever Nick forgets to put the cap back on the toothpaste.

Indeed, a new adoption law awaited Governor Rockefeller's signature. The Dunne Pisani Bill allowed a mother thirty days to change her mind after giving up her child for adoption. Some question arose, though, whether Rockefeller would sign it or not.

Once Mr. Fuchsberg announced our move from New York, and Nick's letter hit the newsstands, there was much conjecture as to where we moved and what happened to us. A *New York Times* article reported, "One of the things he (Miss Scarpetta's attorney) considered was criminal action against the DeMartinos and seeking abduction or kidnaping charges against them."

I shook all over. Nick pointed out the illogic of

attempting such charges. But, I knew he worried too. After all, nothing about our case ever appeared logical. We felt that it was time to make our whereabouts known and met with Mr. Colson to make the disclosure to Marty McLaughin. On May 27, Marty flew to Miami and met us in Colson's office.

"I'd like to make one thing clear from the start," said Nick. "We are not hiding from the law or the courts. If we were, we wouldn't be talking to you. We made Florida our home and this is where we plan to stay."

New York found out the following day that we were in Miami to stay! Since we failed to comply with the New York court order to return Lenore, pressure from Mr. Zalk formed the following decree: "ORDERED, JUDGED, AND DECREED that the motion to punish Nick F. DeMartino and Jean DeMartino for contempt of court be granted. As punishment for such contempt, the said Nick F. DeMartino and Jean DeMartino be imprisoned in the county jail for a period of thirty days."

Since we were no longer in town, the court served the order to our attorney, Jack Fuchsberg. We were officially criminals in New York!

"Nick, I'll bet criminal charges and imprisonment of adoptive parents is a first," I said rather haughtily. "Mr. Zalk now has the dubious distinction of attempting to send a nonperson to jail." I spoke rather flippantly, but underneath, was panicky.

Miss Scarpetta became hysterical upon receiving word that we had left the jurisdiction. She shouted and screamed in the courtroom that we were ruining Lenore. A hard moment for her, I'm sure, and I understood her lashing out. The day after we announced our whereabouts, I saw the first picture of Olga in the newspapers. She looked much like I remembered at our meeting. I read that Mr. Zalk intended to ask the Florida courts to give full faith and credit to the decision of the New York court and, by so doing, felt Lenore would be returned quickly and without a fanfare. The *Daily News* quoted him, "The DeMartinos will be disappointed if they think to get personally before any New York court. I think the Florida court will be bound by New York court rulings." With that in mind, he saw no need for Olga to fly to Florida and would advise against it.

Colson suggested that we hold a press conference in his office. How thankful I was to have a few weeks of near tranquility with family. But we were again thrust into the public eye and meeting reporters old and new and experiencing the same anxieties and frustrations and some new ones to boot. We had an added handicap of speaking to Florida reporters who came in the middle and, therefore, unwittingly treated the case as a personality contest. The big question became, *Who is Lenore's mother?* — the natural one or the one who reared her?

We tried desperately to explain what was best for Lenore—Lenore's rights —little as she was—and our rights as adoptive parents was what we fought for. "Mr. DeMartino," one of the reporters asked, "will you return to New York if asked to do so by the authorities?"

"I will respectfully decline," Nick said. A dozen reporters stood in that office and almost as many microphones.

But Nick was in control of the situation. We stood between Bob Orseck and Bill Colson. One reporter asked Mr. Colson what was to happen next. Colson smiled broadly and in that slow southern drawl said, "I see no need for legal action on behalf of the DeMartinos. They will be initiated by Miss Scarpetta and her attorney. When that happens, my staff and I will give the DeMartinos full legal support." Mr. Colson related that Mr. Fuchsberg, in Washington the previous week, filed an appeal to the U.S. Supreme Court charging that our constitutional rights were violated by the New York courts.

We finally ended the interview and slipped out the back entrance to an adjacent parking lot. Bob Orseck waited. We got into his car and headed for home. We hadn't gone very far when we realized there was a car of reporters following. Bob zigzagged in and out of side streets, but the car was right behind us at every turn. He picked up speed but they still tailed and finally got caught in a cat and mouse chase.

"Slow down, Bob. You'll get us all killed," Nick shouted. It brought Bob to his senses. He slowed down then stopped and permitted the other car to come alongside. The reporters quickly wanted to interview further. We recognized them as the two from Life Magazine. We had met them before in New York. If they would stop following us, we'd make arrangements through Colson for another interview. The chase ended.

News from New York continued—talk of extraditing us—but Florida's Deputy Attorney General recommended against it. Then Zalk brought kidnaping charges again, but a U.S. Attorney in Brooklyn declined to authorize an investigation. He was quoted as saying "Federal authorities believe that the DeMartinos had legal custody of the child when they left the State."

Doors closed again only this time behind us. The U.S. Director of the Department of Health, Education, and Welfare, Child Development Division, at a press conference at the White House, condemned state adoption laws that arbitrarily favored the biological parent in custody disputes. Such laws paid only lip service to the child's welfare.

Not only were doors closing, but the climate changed as well. Florida boasts government in the sunshine. Laws and decisions cannot be behind closed doors. Nick and I readied to bring everything out into the open. We prayed for our day in court.

Mr. Colson received many requests from the media to talk with us. Instead of calling another press conference, he opened his home and invited them to individual sessions. As promised, Life Magazine was first to interview us. For two days, we spoke to a steady stream of newspaper, TV, and radio people. We braced to answer the same question answered so many times before, but this time few caught me off guard.

"Mrs. DeMartino, why did you refuse to accept the jewelry that Miss Scarpetta offered for Lenore?" asked a lady reporter. "Miss Scarpetta offered some gold jewelry which she wanted Lenore to have and said you refused to accept it. She also said you have consistently refused to let her see the child."

I gripped the arms of the chair tightly. I tried desperately to control the surging anger. "What else did she say?" I said curtly. "I'll answer all her allegations at one time."

"Mrs. DeMartino, you and your husband claim not to have met Miss Scarpetta personally, but she met with you and your husband in her lawyer's office. She thought you were an intelligent lady who seemed sincere but didn't understand that a baby belongs with its mother. When she asked about Lenore, you were evasive. She was pleased, however, that you had followed through with her request to name the baby."

"What?" I shouted. "Let me tell you the facts. We met with Miss Scarpetta in her lawyer's office but the condition set by Miss Scarpetta was our promise not to ever disclose to anyone, otherwise she'd not meet us. We lived up to our word. Evidently, Miss Scarpetta saw no need to do the same. And what's more, she not once during our meeting asked to see Lenore or say one word about my daughter. I brought medical information and photos and never discussed or showed anything because Miss Scarpetta didn't care. As for jewelry allegedly refused, I won't even dignify Miss Scarpetta's fantasy with a response. But I will comment on my daughter's name. If you check the records, you will find that the only name Miss Scarpetta gave Lenore was *Female* as her birth certificate shows. And it just so happens that the agency gave her a baptismal name of Lisa. If Miss Scarpetta wanted the name Lenore, she had every opportunity to name her. If Leonor is her mother's name, pure coincidence and nothing else." My voice became really tight.

Nick squeezed my shoulder then said, "This conversation is unproductive. With everything my wife said I concur, but stick to important and germane issues. What is best for Lenore is best for us as well as Miss Scarpetta. We need a courtroom to present our testimony and a judge to evaluate and decide on our daughter's welfare.

"Permit me to remind you in a courtroom under oath, the questions asked of my wife would be answered exactly as today. Please continue."

I took a deep breath and started again. It was a tiring two days, not only for us, but also for the Colsons. Mrs. Colson's routine was completely disrupted, but she stood in heroic silence after graciously welcoming hordes of people. Their teenaged daughter, Cathy, befriended our girls and entertained them while during interviews. One son, Dean, filled in when Cathy wasn't available.

Although Mr. Colson maintained calmness, he became emotionally involved. He saw a family, a closely-knit one. Over the mantle piece hung a picture of the entire Colson family in tennis attire. They were not only beautiful outside but, as we discovered, inside as well.

The pace really picked up for us. Miss Scarpetta anxiously awaited the media to tell her story. A number of New York papers carried pictures of her on the front page. Some people wrote letters of support printed right alongside letters from people who supported our move to Florida. In a two-state tug-of-war, we knew things in their proper perspective became difficult. Lenore developed a severe cough which she couldn't shake. A pediatrician feared she might have pneumonia and suggested x-rays. On the way to the laboratory, I prayed for God to let her be well. Fortunately, the x-rays proved negative. The pediatrician provided necessary medicine, and shortly Lenore sounded and looked healthy.

Since we felt we had said all there was to be said to the press and media, we once again kept the children and ourselves out of the public eye. We left the apartment only when absolutely necessary. So far no one discovered our whereabouts. We cooperated with the press but considered how it affected the children. Since having more time to think about our needs, I focused on getting Lenore a pair of walking shoes. As she walked, her right foot turned inward. I arranged to see a foot specialist to prescribe proper shoes.

For obvious reasons, we avoided a phone but now felt that our attorneys needed to contact us, so we had one installed. We did not un-list the number. As we were about to leave our apartment for the doctor's office, our phone rang. Delighted to hear from a childhood friend, Nick asked how the man got our phone number. He'd merely called information and received not only our number but our address as well.

Nick complained to the telephone company, but the damage was done, and we knew it probably created problems for us.

Because he couldn't find a parking space, Nick dropped me and the girls off. After examining Lenore, the doctor explained that Lenore's problem originated from the hip and both legs needed casts. My mind had trouble registering. Suddenly, tears flowed. My mind raced from Lenore running barefoot across Mr. Colson's lawn into her Daddy's arms to pictures of her in the newspapers with legs in casts.

"Hasn't she been through enough?" I asked.

"What do you mean, Mrs. DeMartino?"

"Forgive me, Doctor. We recently thought Lenore had pneumonia. Today, I expected a prescription for corrective shoes not casts. I've taken her to a pediatrician for monthly visits, and he never mentioned any problem. It wasn't until she started to walk that we noticed her foot turned."

"Mrs. DeMartino, in three to six months, she'll be as good as new," he assured.

"If we delay treatment, will the condition worsen?"

"You can have it taken care of anytime within the next year. But I wouldn't go beyond that if I were you."

As I left the office, Nick knew I was upset. He asked if the doctor showed me x-rays. The doctor hadn't taken any x-rays.

"What?" Nick shouted, "no child of mine is having her legs in casts on the say-so of one doctor who, as it happens, diagnosed without an x-ray!" I stared as he went on, "As an attorney, Jean, I know many cases where improper placement of casts caused permanent damage. So, before we run that risk, I need convincing that casts are the only correction available."

His reaction brought me to my senses. A second opinion was essential but could wait a while. I hadn't asked the doctor, though, about shoes for Lenore.

"Perhaps Colson can recommend another doctor, and we'll find out about shoes then. Speaking of Colson, the reason I took so long getting back to you is that I called to tell him about our phone. We should move. He also had news, Jean." Nick stopped and faced me. I braced myself. "Olga is flying to Miami. She retained a Florida attorney, a Mr. Stanley Rosenblatt. His offices are in the same building as Colson's. Colson expects a *Writ of Habeas Corpus* filed in circuit court here. We will be even busier than of late."

"I thought Zalk said that she wouldn't be coming to Miami."

"That's what he claimed, but we all knew she would eventually show up here. Don't look so glum," he said giving me a little shake. "This is what we've been waiting for. We may just get our day in court." I was pensive as we headed back to the apartment, but when we arrived, the sight of wall-to-wall people in front gave me a jolt. Nick didn't even stop the car. He pretended to be passing traffic. We drove aimlessly for a while. We put a respectable distance between ourselves and our apartment. We wound up in a motel on Dixie Highway near the Serpentarium, a good half-hour to forty-five minutes from the apartment.

We were exhausted and had nothing but the clothes on our backs and a bottle for Lenore. We drove to a drugstore where I bought Pampers, toothbrushes, toothpaste, and books for Linda. Poor little thing had been an angel throughout most of this, and I felt guilty because she really needed more attention from me.

Back at the motel, Nick called our attorney to give him our new location and then our landlord to inform him that unfortunately, we would have to move elsewhere. We would pick up our belongings and settle our bill later. He told us not to concern ourselves and to get in touch when the moment was right. He was a terrific person. When he and his charming wife first read about us in the papers, they offered help and support. If there is such a thing as love at first sight, I loved these people from the moment I met them. Just the fact that they welcomed my children when all others turned them away was enough to endear them to me. They were hardworking people who struggled in the Old World then came to America in search of a new life. They understood our pain without ever having to tell us.

Our landlord thanked Nick for the call. He told us about a steady stream of people at our door all day. Many sought to question him, but he told them politely that he knew nothing.

The following day Olga arrived and held a news conference in the offices of her attorney. Nick spent the day at Colson's office, but I remained with the children. I went with them to the park across the way from the motel. I hoped to relax them after a hectic pace. Since Nick was not a member of the Florida Bar, he couldn't practice law in Florida. But, Colson knew someone in Commercial Real Estate looking for a manager to oversee several of his buildings and recommended Nick. Again we were indebted to Mr. Colson.

We returned to our apartment for our clothes and things the following day. Once more reporters and people backed up outside. So we headed back to our motel. Nick stopped for gas along the way called Colson, who asked us to come to his home immediately. He didn't go into details. When we got there, Mr. Colson reported that Olga had been interviewed on TV and made certain rash statements that he wanted to clear with us. Miss Scarpetta said among other things, that the adoption agency charged fantastic fees for children which led the interviewer to discuss unscrupulous practices between lawyers and agencies whereby babies are bought and sold.

She also stated that prospective adoptive parents sat in a room and picked children like shoppers. "She sounded," Colson said, "like you went to a supermarket." Colson turned to us for answers. I blurted, "Spence-Chapin Adoption Service has placed children since the turn of the century. They enjoy a fine reputation. As to the allegation that they charge fantastic fees, we paid $650.00 which no where compares to the amount spent by the agency for care to Miss Scarpetta and the cost of social workers involved in our case. They are a nonprofit organization. Let me further clarify that we did not pick Lenore. We endured months of interviews and investigations before the agency called to inform us that they had an appropriate child. It was done by selection all right, the careful selection of the agency. But, you know all this Mr. Colson. I don't understand—"

"You're right Jean," he interrupted. "I don't like misinformation bantered about. You've been asked to appear, live, on the same TV show this afternoon, and I recommend that you tell the interviewer just what you've told me now."

I stood in the Colson living room in a dress that hadn't been changed in two days, the belt had somehow been misplaced, and the sandals slipped off my feet as I walked only now they had the added distinction of dirt from the park. I thought of my hair which hadn't been properly combed. I sighed and asked, "Where do I go from here?" I freshened up as best I could at the Colson home and went on my way. Colson and Nick, who were at home watching the program, were pleased with its outcome.

Later that night, we slipped into our old apartment on the beach and rescued clothes. Colson suggested, now that Miss Scarpetta was in town, that we permit some reporters to see us. So the following day, we met at the Colson home and talked. I felt particularly up that day, had on a clean outfit, the girls were sparkling clean, and things broke well. This new optimism reached the surface, and relaxed, I greeted the reporters warmly and without stress.

One local reporter, whom I never met, watched carefully as I spoke. Finally, he said rather curtly, "Do you know, Mrs. DeMartino, how much hurt and sorrow you brought Miss Scarpetta?"

I studied his face and caught the disdain. We had been asked direct and disturbing questions, but his seemed aimed for the gut. I lowered my eyes, and said softly, "Miss Scarpetta experienced a great deal of sorrow and pain, and I have no desire to minimize it, but please be aware, we have had our share of heartache."

He contorted as to say, "I'm having trouble believing you." I knew there was nothing to convince him otherwise. In the days and months following, he championed Miss Scarpetta with added zeal. Years later when the DeMartinos and Scarpettas were forgotten, I read an article about his retiring and spending his childhood in an orphanage. Then I got some inkling of his fervor in our case. Perhaps, like

Annie, he hoped that his mother would materialize.

When the interviews ended, Colson told me that he received a request from Miss Scarpetta's attorney for her to see Lenore. The blood drained from my face. "I don't recommend it, Jean," he said "but felt I had to let you make the decision. Nick checked with your pediatrician who doesn't think it's a good idea right now, but we're leaving it up to you."

"I wonder if the idea was hers or her attorney," I snapped. Mr. Colson shrugged his shoulders. Olga finally asked to see Lenore. My mind wrestled with the thought. Could I deny Olga's request and still respect myself? On the other hand, was Lenore ready for such a meeting? My mind flooded with unanswered questions. When and where would the meeting take place? And could we be sure Olga wouldn't take Lenore and run to South America? I abruptly stood and said, "She saw no need to see Lenore for over a year, so she'll wait until this whole thing is resolved. There isn't much sense to placing all of us through emotional upheaval right now."

Nick agreed and we headed for the tiny motel room called home. We wanted a permanent place but unfamiliar with the area and didn't get a chance to look. We had been told, however, that the Southwest section of Miami was a good place to bring up children, so we got in touch with a real estate broker whom Colson recommended. She might have a furnished house available to rent. On the day we were to see it, Mr. Colson called us to his office.

"Jean, something needs discussing. As Nick already knows, a petition for a *Writ of Habeas Corpus* was filed in Dade County Circuit Court. A hearing is scheduled for tomorrow before Circuit Judge Ralph O. Cullen. Jean, I want you to understand that the attorneys for Olga are going to present their case on unlawful possession of Lenore and the Florida courts should give *full faith and credit* to the New York decision. We will argue the point, of course, with good legal precedent as back up. On its merits, we hope to get our case heard.

"If, however, the judge does not assign a trial date and proceeds to hear the case that afternoon then prepare for the worst. What I'm saying is Lenore might be lost to you this weekend."

Colson's words either didn't register or didn't convince me because instead of fear, I felt elation. We were going to court for the truth to win. About to leave Colson's office, a call came from the real estate broker that another house became available. Although the owners weren't prepared to rent just yet, she convinced them to move as soon as possible, and they agreed to let us in the following morning. THANK YOU, GOD!

Chapter XI

On Friday, June 10th, we finally went to court. We awakened early and packed our belongings. We had breakfast at a nearby Pancake House then headed for our new home. We met the owners, a pleasant couple in the process of removing a brother's personal items still in the house. The landlord explained that his brother had lived there as a bachelor who died of cancer. The house held memories, and he had been unable to return until today. He intended to have the house cleaned prior to renting but since we needed to move in quickly, he apologized for not tending to it.

We tried to assure him that we understood. Nick and I and the girls sat as quietly as possible on the couch while the owner and his wife sorted his brother's items. The children became restless, so Nick and I explained our situation. We were due in Court that afternoon. The couple took leave. I took a look around the two bedroom, one bath house with a small Florida room. We had a home! The tub and the walls around it were black. I later realized that it was mildew which is common to Florida. I did my best to clean it before bathing. We began to feel like members of the human race again.

At 3:00 p.m., we headed for the Dupont Plaza in Downtown Miami. Mr. Colson felt that the children had to be nearby in case the judge asked to see them, so he arranged for his son Dean to stay with them at the hotel. Having safely secured the children, we headed for the courthouse. We entered a small room with a long table. Mr. Colson, Steve Rossman, from the law firm of Colson and Hicks, Robert Orseck, Nick, and I sat on the right. Opposite, sat Olga Scarpetta with her attorneys, Stanley Rosenblatt,

Richard A. Schwartz, Mallory H. Horton, and Joseph Zalk.

My knees shook as Judge Ralph O. Cullen entered. It's funny how images stay with you. Judge Cullen looked exactly as I pictured right out of the Andy Hardy movies of my youth. Holding Lenore's future in his hand, he sat at the head of the table, and we were all introduced. I looked at Olga, but she avoided my eyes. She stared ahead. Mr. Colson asked that the hearing be rescheduled and that the Judge set a future date to hear the merits as to what was best for Lenore. Mr. Rosenblatt pressed the judge to abide by the ruling of the New York courts.

Mr. Colson showed legal precedence for hearing the merits. I heard him—Southern drawl in tact—quoting a previous Florida decision, "The court, when asked to restore an infant, is not bound by any mere legal right of parent or guardian but is to give it due weight as a claim founded on human nature, and generally equitable and just. The court is in no case bound to deliver a child into the custody of any claimant but should in the exercise of sound judicial discretion, after a careful consideration of the facts, leave it in such custody as the welfare of the child at the time appears to require."

Mr. Colson made his appeal, "We respectfully request a week from Monday prepare our plea or before that, Your Honor, if you desire. We wish to present a day and a half of testimony." Mr. Rosenblatt interjected, "Judge Cullen, here is Miss Scarpetta's petition for *Habeas Corpus*. The merits of the case and the welfare of the child were litigated in six courts in New York. The respondents have no legal standing and no claim for custody. As a matter of fact, Colson's reply to the *Writ of Habeas Corpus* reached our hands fifteen minutes before this hearing. They admitted no blood relationship to the child and have not as yet adopted her. It is our position, therefore, that they have illegal possession.

"Of course, the argument in Mr. Colson's return and one made throughout the case is that the welfare of the child is best served by remaining in the possession of the DeMartinos because they had the child for so long. Now, they ask for additional time and will say, 'We had the child an additional month.' We feel it is appropriate to determine whether or not the respondents have any legal basis to keep this child from the natural mother who has been awarded legal custody by the highest court of the State of New York, and we object strenuously to any motion for a continuance.

Mr. Colson, laid back and easy going, stepped on the heels of Olga's attorney with, "We wish our petition for *Habeas Corpus* heard and would like an early determination so that custody can be determined. If Your Honor wishes to hear case law on why a full hearing would be appropriate either now or in twenty-one days, we can go into that. Whatever your pleasure, Judge Cullen."

The Judge shouted, "We will hear the petition now." Mr. Rosenblatt sighed with relief and sat back. I slumped over in my chair. My head burned as though on fire. "Is this it?" I asked myself. Colson said we should expect the worst if this turn of events took place. So was this the end? Had all these many months of praying for and shouting for a day in court amounted to this? I heard Miss Scarpetta sworn in as a witness on her own behalf. As she answered the questions, I raised my head. A light, which caught my eye, distracted me. I turned slowly and gleaming brightly across the face of Robert E. Lee whose picture hung on the wall was a bright cross of lights. It was obviously caused by the overhead fluorescent fixtures, but for me it was a reminder that God was still with us and no matter how bleak, He was by my side.

So with renewed hope that this was not the end but a beginning, I relaxed and listened. Mr. Rosenblatt finished asking Miss Scarpetta her New York address. He continued:

Q. At birth, what was the name of your child?
A. Female Scarpetta.
Q. What do you know her as now?
A. Lenore.

Q. At some point in time did you give possession and custody of your child to an adoption agency?
A. I did.
Q. When would that have been in relation to the day your daughter was born?
A. June 1, two weeks after.
Q. Have you seen your baby since that time?
A. No, I haven't.
Q. Who has your baby now?
A. Mr. and Mrs. DeMartino.

Mr. Colson cross-examined her.
Q. Miss Scarpetta, where are you a citizen?
A. Colombia, South America, Bogota.
Q. Your mother and father live there?
A. They have their permanent residence there. Right now they are in New York.
Q. Are you presently married?
A. No, I am not.
Q. Have you ever had children other than Lenore?
A. No, I have not.

Mr. Colson was interrupted by Mr. Rosenblatt who objected to the line of questioning. He said Colson went well beyond the scope of direct examination. The judge reminded Rosenblatt that in the interest of time he would not limit Mr. Colson nor stand on technicalities. However, he asked Colson how much longer a presentation. Colson said it would take several hours.

"I want to give everybody an opportunity to put what they want on but certainly can't have a hearing that starts at four o'clock and runs past daylight hours," the judge said. Colson seized the opportunity. "Exactly my point. We need to fly people in from New York. This is a tremendously vital thing." As Mr. Colson pressed on, Mr. Horton interrupted. "Your Honor, could I make a suggestion? We have Mr. Zalk with us today who was counsel in all of the proceedings in New York and he has certified copies of all the New York proceedings. This case went through the Court of Appeals in the State of New York. They found Olga Scarpetta was the lawful mother, entitled to possession, and the court issued a contempt citation against these people.

"Now, as they admit in their petition, Your Honor, they are not the lawful parents of this child and are not related in blood. We do not have a *writ of habeas corpus* based on the illegal detention. This testimony is immaterial at this point, Your Honor."

Mr. Horton paused, and Bob Orseck followed up with, "Mr. Colson's office is involved in a special hearing which they will gladly give up for this hearing." Everything happened rapidly. Mr. Rosenblatt insisted that the court proceed on the hearing for the *writ,* and Mr. Colson insisted that the court's duty must to go into what was best for the child. As Colson raised his hand for emphasis, it shook. Behind that calm Southern exterior, a tense, caring human being pleaded our case. "All we ask and beg for," he said, "is a chance to present witnesses."

Mr. Rosenblatt sarcastically responded, "All we

beg for, judge, is lawful custody—all we beg for is that six orders from New York courts and an order from the highest court of the state be complied with by the DeMartinos who are in contempt where they adopted this child, the state they resided in, and the state they were happy and content to remain in until the court awarded custody to Miss Scarpetta."

Mr. Colson countered. "The case is currently in the United States Supreme Court."

After bringing the Judge up-to-date on details in New York, Mr. Horton summed up, "Your Honor, these people have no claim to the child whatsoever, and you don't go into whether the child is better off in their custody when they have no legal standing. They are strangers to the blood.

"We have the final orders here. When the DeMartinos admit that the child is not theirs lawfully, the decree of the State of New York, if not Res Judicata; namely, unappealable, the blood mother, Olga Scarpetta, is entitled to custody at least by comity between Florida and New York if not outright recognition of New York's adoption laws. We simply say here that the question my friend wants to raise is a waste of the court's time."

Robert Orseck, in a shaky voice, said: "Fortunately for our clients and for Lenore, we are in a Florida court. What Mr. Horton contends does not reflect the law of our state." Mr. Orseck had at least four decisions from the Florida Supreme Court and the Appellate Court involving people in the 'Posture of the DeMartinos.'" He discussed Fielding against Highsmith, a 1943 Supreme Court Case. In a *habeas corpus* proceeding involving an infant, the primary consideration above all else was the welfare of the child. "At no time," Orseck continued, "in the New York proceeding was the child's well being or medical history presented." Orseck raised another case, McKinney against Weeks. The adoptive parents had the child for three weeks prior to the *writ of habeas corpus*. The Court said in its decision, "A court is not bound to deliver the child to any claimant, but should leave it in such custody as the welfare of the child at the time appears to require.

"All we ask, Your Honor," Orsek said, "in this very serious and far reaching case, is an opportunity to present the welfare of this child. As far as full faith and credit to New York law, Your Honor, it just ain't so, if you will pardon the colloquialism. Full faith and credit to laws of another state when relating to a child does not exist in our state. The DeMartinos never had their day in court.

"The fact is, the DeMartinos received lawful custody at the time they obtained the child. Their rights terminated under some peculiar aspect of New York law without any opportunity to be heard. This fact is in those records Mr. Horton holds of the proceedings in New York. Fortunately, we are in Florida where a pre-adoptive parent does have the right to be heard, and under Florida Law, the welfare of the child governs.

"Now, I could speak for another half hour and cite case seven where, Your Honor, the pre-adoptive parents are in violation of a custody order of another state, parties in violation, but the DeMartinos have never been a party.

"Your Honor, this is a case where welfare of this child is vitally important. As attorneys, we accepted service on one day's notice. The *writ* required twenty-four hours return without any opportunity to present our case. We plead that this one day in court not become a futile gesture for the DeMartinos."

A hush came, but Mr. Rosenblatt quickly broke

it. "Your Honor, counsel said, 'Fortunately, we are in Florida.' So he takes the position that Mr. DeMartino, who is an attorney licensed in New York, by being in contempt of the highest court of his state should be rewarded. Carrying that logic out, if he gets a decision in a Florida court that he doesn't like, he will go to Michigan to have a next hearing.

"I call Mr. Zalk as a witness to describe the New York decisions."

Mr. Zalk addressed the court. "If I may be heard at this time, I would argue that the DeMartinos never had their day in court because of New York law, and the court of appeals ruled on this point in a decision handed down on March 7—the consent agreement by which Miss Scarpetta surrendered her child to the Spence-Chapin Adoption Agency was an agreement between Miss Scarpetta and the agency. Under New York Domestic Relations Law, the whereabouts of the child is confidential. Therefore, when the *habeas corpus* proceeding was brought after the consent had been revoked, the only ones against whom we could proceed was the adoption agency.

"The DeMartinos raised a motion to intervene in the New York State Court of Appeals. The motion was denied, and the court said specifically that they had no legal standing under applicable statute. When they claim not having a right to intervene, it is because they don't have legal rights as prospective adoptive parents.

"They supposedly had legal custody according to my esteemed colleague. Legal custody never lay with the DeMartinos, only provisional custody, and it was revoked. As a matter of fact, we have a letter from the Spence-Chapin Adoption Agency's attorneys to the DeMartinos requesting that they cooperate in returning this child in compliance with the court order of the State of New York."

I thought of our visit with the agency, "We have called you here," they said, "because we have no further recourse beyond the state courts and will therefore be bound by the state's decision." I realized that Zalk was not finished with his testimony, so I turned my attention back.

"I argue," Zalk continued, "that full faith and credit may not apply in this decision by New York courts. However, the issue of Miss Scarpetta's fitness was part of the first decision in the New York State Supreme Court. It deemed her fit, competent, and able. And *best interest* indicated that the child be returned to her natural mother. That was November 20, 1970. The DeMartinos now say, in effect, that 'because we had the child for a period of time, the best interest indicates she stay with us.' They take advantage of their own wrongdoing. Had they complied with the order of the court on November 20, the child would be with Miss Scarpetta.

"Now, the DeMartinos say, 'We were never parties to the proceedings.' That is incorrect. The order of the Supreme Court directed specifically Nick F. DeMartino and Jean DeMartino to turn over the baby to Miss Scarpetta. When the order of contempt was issued, it directed Nick F. DeMartino and Jean DeMartino to surrender the child. While they may not be technically parties in the caption of the proceedings, no question whatever exists that the DeMartinos were named specifically.

"I understand that this is a court of equity, and, Your Honor, I don't know anything about Florida law. I do know axiomatically that when you come in, you come in with clean hands. The DeMartinos do not have clean hands. They ran from the New York court and came here on the pretext of enjoying fresh air and sunshine. Next, they will enjoy the fresh air and sunshine of California and then the fresh air and sunshine of another state. How far must Miss Scarpetta be forced to pursue them?

"I think the buck should stop in this particular court. If they want their day in court, the DeMartinos have an opportunity this afternoon. While the court has jurisdiction because the child was snatched away from New York, the DeMartinos do not have the right to challenge the findings of the New York court that Miss Scarpetta is fit, competent, and able, unless, perhaps, they maintain that between March 7, the last date the Court of Appeals affirmed the decision of the lower courts, and today, some change occurred with regard to Miss Scarpetta.

"I submit that no such change occurred. Anything brought before this court will predate all the court orders in New York. I believe it unconscionable for these people to say, 'We never had our day in court.' They had days upon days.

"The issue in the U.S. Supreme Court—to dismiss the appeal which cannot be heard until October—is only the DeMartinos being entitled to notice pursuant to the Fourteenth Amendment which guarantees civil rights. I don't want to argue the Supreme Court Case." Mr. Zalk, did, however, cite one case allegedly used by our lawyers before the Supreme Court. He did not feel the case applied because it involved natural parents entitled to notice while we were strangers to the blood with baby Lenore.

Everyone listened quite intently to Mr. Zalk. I wondered why he had referred to March 7 as the day that the New York Court of Appeals reached its decision. The only decision I knew about was put forth on April 7. But then, did it really matter?

The judge remained poker faced. He rocked back and forth in his straight back chair and stared at a pencil held between both his hands.

Mr. Colson quoted a ruling, ". . . since a child custody award is subject to modification, it is not within the coverage of the full faith and credit clause. I ask you, judge," he said, "to let us present testimony we want to proffer, but not on Friday afternoon at five o'clock.

"We ask you to hear of the child's daily life. It isn't any different from the day New York made its decision. Our testimony would take about a day."

Bob Orseck spoke again. "Your Honor, what our adversaries contend is the very same thing that the Florida Supreme Court reversed in the case Mr. Colson cited. They reversed and said that no testimony was taken on the interest and welfare of the child. That is exactly this case.

"Secondly, Your Honor, it is an anomaly that the DeMartinos were ordered to turn over the child when they were not parties proper to that case."

Orseck quoted another case, Fox against Webster, where a mother took two children against the orders of Ohio and California and brought them to Florida. Though she violated court orders, the Florida court considered only the welfare of the children." Orseck turned his attention to the pending Supreme Court Case. "I am not as old or experienced as Mr. Zalk, but I know a little about constitutional law, and I think due process was violated. When someone is deprived of something substantial to his life as the DeMartinos are—love for the child—then they are entitled to be heard on the merits and the welfare of that child."

The judge showed clear signs of tension. He heaved a sigh of annoyance, then Mr. Horton addressed him. He spoke about *full faith and credit* and that a natural parent doesn't stand on the same basis as a stranger. He then followed with a quote from Roy vs. Holmes. "Parents are by no means required to face strangers to their blood on equal terms in contention for the parental right to their children.

"Nevertheless, and this is italicized," he said, *"except in cases of clear, convincing, and compelling reasons to the contrary, the child's welfare is presumed to be best served by care and custody in the natural family relation by its natural parents, and that transitory failures and derelictions of the parents might justify temporary deprivation of custody by appropriate proceedings but seldom the permanent deprivation of parental rights with the finality of an adoption decree."* Mr. Horton presented another case where a grandmother and natural mother sought custody and the burden of proof rested with the child's grandparents to show entitlement rather than the burden of proof resting on the mother.

Referring to Miss Scarpetta, he said, "I know, Your Honor, an explanation of whether or not she is a fit and proper mother or whether these people can give the child a better home is immaterial. Roy vs. Holmes clearly establishes that parents should not have to contend with a stranger on the same level."

Mr. Colson reminded the judge that Judge Futch of the Florida Supreme Court reversed a lower court ruling because that court did not go into the welfare of the child.

Mr. Rosenblatt spoke, "Your Honor, that case and all the others talk about blood relationships to the child."

The judge, obviously disturbed, moved forward in his chair and said, "We will have a full hearing."

Mr. Colson: "Thank you, judge."

Steve Rossman and the judge spoke about a date for the hearing. Mr. Rosenblatt, in a state of shock, asked, "Your Honor, in effect, the DeMartinos may continue possession of the child. Not so?"

The judge: "I am not upsetting it."

Mr. Horton: "Judge, shouldn't they be under some admonition not to take the child from the State of Florida?"

The judge: "Mr. Colson, do you give assurance?"

Mr. Colson: "Judge, the DeMartinos submitted to your jurisdiction. Order them to stay here, and I will—"

"Your assurance is all we want,"

I grabbed onto my St. Jude medal and silently offered a prayer of thanks.

Chapter XII

We settled in at home, and my mom and dad wasted no time getting to us. Waiting in New York and not knowing what happened was hard on them. At the airport, we read relief on their faces as they embraced the children. We brought them up-to-date. At home, mom and I stacked the remainder of the previous owner's belongings in the garage. Then we scrubbed! We felt good in a home again. The girls were excited that Granny and Grandpa stayed with us. For a short time, we forgot what lay ahead. But then the pace changed.

Colson asked us to bring the children to a pediatrician for complete physical checkups. Then, we had them tested scholastically and psychologically at the Mailman Clinic, a hospital specializing in children. Linda tested above average in intelligence, and Lenore's results were average. In addition, Nick and I took intelligence and psychological tests. I don't know how either of us concentrated.

At Colson's request, a well-known child psychologist spent an afternoon to view us as a family unit, and a photographer from his office took motion pictures as we tended the children. Colson had young law students working for him, and they threw themselves into the case. Mr. Colson's partner, Bill Hicks, and a young law student, who acted as his interpreter, flew to Colombia to investigate. And, of course, Robert Orseck became very special to us. He appeared average looking and slight, but now was ten feet tall. He was, indeed, a legal brain yet *human* in every sense of that word. Bob was Jewish, and a Yiddish word describes him best, *mensch* (a good human being.) From the very beginning he cut through red tape and emotional aspects of our case and put the emphasis where it belonged, on Lenore. He, too, had young children, and you felt his warmth and affection for them.

It was obvious that everyone worked hard, but not until the trial, did we understand how much Mr. Colson and his staff put forth on our behalf. On Tuesday, June 22, 1971, we arrived bright and early at the offices of Colson & Hicks. Mr. Colson took me aside. "Jean, child psychologists and psychiatrists will be at the trial today. Each gives opinions on what is best for Lenore and what separation from her family means. I know separation is more difficult should the proceedings not turn out as we expect—" His voice trailed off.

I patted his hand and said, "God brought us this far, Mr. Colson. You and I have done all we can. Now it's up to Him."

He smiled, and we all left for the courthouse. As we crossed the street, we saw the steps of the courthouse packed with reporters. With Colson on one side and Nick on the other, we approached.

"Are you ready, Jean?" Colson whispered.

"Yes," I said softly. "I've been ready for months."

Light bulbs flashed, and reporters pushed and called out questions. We finally made our way into the corridor to face more crowds of reporters, who, in turn, packed into the elevator. The flash bulbs bothered my eyes. Thank God the children were safely tucked away at home in the care of grandma and grandpa. Soon it will be all over, I thought, and we can relax and do things other families do. We made our way into the judge's chambers. Wall-to-wall people stood there as well.

We sat with our attorneys, Bill Colson, Bill

Hoppe, Robert Orseck, Jacob Fuchsberg, and Joseph Spencer. Across the table sat Olga Scarpetta flanked by attorneys Stanley Rosenblatt, Joseph Zalk, Malory Horton, and a young man resembling Mr. Zalk. I recalled a humorous long distance conversation with Barry Tash. "Watch out," he said. "Rumor has it that Florida is not only going to see the *Return of Zalk* but also *Son of Zalk*!"

Olga Scarpetta, who, as usual, avoided my glance, was unusually neatly attired. She wore a blue and white suit which went well with her coloring. Her hair was neatly pulled back in a ponytail and she wore white gloves. Aside from white gloves which seemed an affectation, she looked the best I'd ever seen her look. She sat erect and self-assured. I hadn't slept, and the stress and strain of the past few months settled in at that moment. I had to present the proper image, and it was crucial to be alert, so every bit of energy sat me up attentively for the trial to begin.

Judge Ralph O. Cullen entered the room at 9:00 a.m. promptly. He took his seat at the head of the table, and the hearing began. Mr. Colson introduced our two New York lawyers, Jacob Fuchsberg and Joseph Spencer. Judge Cullen reminded the attorneys that he expected a summation by the end of the day.

Mr. Rosenblatt addressed the judge. "Your Honor, before I call Miss Scarpetta, I want to make a brief statement about our position. "We contend that the respondents have no lawful right to raise the issue of fitness. The *Writ of Habeas Corpus* does not allege that the petitioner is unfit or has any change of circumstance since the rendition of the New York order. The return to the *Writ* admits that Mr. and Mrs. DeMartino are not related by blood to Miss Scarpetta's baby and admit that they have not formally adopted the child. In view of Your Honor's ruling indicating that you permit Mr. Colson rather lengthy cross examination, I intend, under that circumstance, to be more lengthy." He then called Olga Scarpetta as a witness on her own behalf.

Under direct examination by Mr. Rosenblatt, she related her educational background as follows: She came to the Untied States and started Junior High School in Cleveland, Ohio. She moved to New York and went to a boarding school in New Jersey which enabled her to visit with her parents in Flushing, New York, on weekends. But her parents decided to return home to Colombia, and since she still had two more years of high school, Olga stayed with an uncle who lived not far away from school. She returned to Colombia and studied philosophy and literature. She did not finish college, but instead went to France where she studied French Civilization at the Sorbonne for a year and a half. Afterward, she returned to Colombia, worked for two and a half years, and became interested in the social sciences. So she moved to California and majored in social science at California State Polytechnical College. Following that, she worked toward her master's degree in Latin American Affairs at the University of the Americas in Bogotá.

Having established her educational background and credentials, Rosenblatt questioned about her employment.

Q. Could you tell us generally what types of employment you held either in the United States or Colombia?

A. Right after school, I worked as a teacher of English and Spanish literature. During that time, I also worked in a home for abandoned boys doing recreational activities and helping find the parents for the boys and getting them adjusted to the family so that they could start living a normal family life.

When I returned from France, I worked at this job part time. This was voluntary work. I started a finishing school and a modeling school which I owned and ran and worked at in the afternoon.

When I came to California, I did volunteer work at a mental hospital, a mental institution for men, and our work prepared people just about to come out to behave socially. I worked at the Foreign Institute Desk counseling foreign students to adjust with life in the United States. After I finished college, I returned to Colombia and worked at the Bank of Bogotá. This is the largest private bank in the country. I headed the social services department. This included counseling employees and their families, programming, and recreational activities. During my last year in Bogotá, while working for my master's, I taught at a secretarial school and junior college and also did some counseling for the students.

I was impressed with her credentials but how many different schools and jobs had she mentioned? In light of her testimony, would Judge Ascione still believe that she was unsure of her ability to get a job and that a girl who counseled so many people would allow herself to be manipulated by an agency into giving up her child for adoption?

Rosenblatt changed the direction of his questions and asked Miss Scarpetta about the birth of Lenore and the events leading to the time she gave the baby to the Spence-Chapin Adoption Agency.

Q. Have you ever seen your baby in person since she was four days old?
A. I asked the agency on various occasions to let me see the baby, and they refused. Since then I asked them on other occasions and have always been refused.
Q. Whom have you asked on other occasions?
A. Mr. and Mrs. DeMartino. (I let out a low, audible

gasp and looked at her in disbelief. I wanted to say "once" and through her attorney, but Nick patted my hand to assure that it really didn't matter.)
Q. And who has your baby now?
A. Mr. and Mrs. DeMartino.
Q. Do they have the baby with your consent?
A. No, they do not.

The direct examination by Mr. Rosenblatt continued as Miss Scarpetta related many of the same things said in the first trial. She said her parents didn't know she was coming to New York to have a baby, but in August of 1970, after the baby was born, she returned to Colombia and told them. She spoke about her family having a high standard of living. When asked whether anyone in her family held a position of importance in Colombia, she replied that her sister's father-in-law had been a president of the Supreme Court of Colombia.

I looked at the judge to see if any reaction, but his expression was unreadable.

Rosenblatt turned his questions toward the signing of the consent form and the subsequent revocation by Miss Scarpetta. She testified that her change of mind progressed from June 1 on and that by June 18, she called the agency to say she wanted the baby back.

I wished at that particular moment I could climb into Miss Scarpetta's mind and find out what she thought. Did she really have an early change of mind? Was she as definite about getting Lenore back as repeatedly stated or was the agency's version the correct one? As I recalled, they said Miss Scarpetta indeed talked about getting Lenore back from the very first visit, but she obviously hadn't convinced herself of what she really wanted. In view of continued uncertainty, the agency couldn't consider turning

Lenore over.

For my own peace of mind, I would like to know, for sure, what actually took place.

Q. Miss Scarpetta, are you now in a position to care for Lenore?
A. Yes, I am. Miss Scarpetta explained that she had an apartment with a large living room divided to use one half as a studio and the other as a bedroom. In addition, the apartment had two bedrooms, one for Lenore and one for a family friend to take care of the baby. She confirmed $20,000 in savings in Colombia. Then said an additional $5,000 sat in a U.S. bank.

Mr. Rosenblatt posed his final question.
Q. Miss Scarpetta, once you wanted to revoke the consent in June of 1970, have you ever changed your mind?
A. No, I haven't.
Mr. Rosenblatt: I have no further questions, Your Honor, at this time.
Mr. Colson began:
Q. Miss Scarpetta, you are not a citizen of the United States, are you?
A. No, I am not.
Q. And have you made up your mind to become a citizen of the United States since the last time that you testified?
A. I have to live in the United States for five years before I can make that decision. I still have three years to think about it.
Q. At the time baby Lenore was born, she was illegitimate. Did you hear in the last twenty four hours on TV that the father of this child was to show up in Miami and marry you?
(I hadn't heard. But evidently Colson had. Before Miss Scarpetta answered, however, Mr. Rosenblatt objected

to the question.)

"I have no objection to that question," he said, "but to refer to the press reports as a predicate or basis of the question is objectionable."

The judge asked Mr. Colson to rephrase the question.

Q. You don't have any plans to get married, do you, ma'am?

A. I am thinking about somebody in New York. I am talking about marriage, but it is not the baby's father. Right at this moment, I couldn't tell you who I am going to marry.

Q. You are not engaged?

A. No, I am not.

Colson turned his attention to the town where Miss Scarpetta and her family lived. Evidently in the original trial she referred to Sedellin (really Medellin) as her hometown. She said that she misunderstood the question at the time.

Q. Now, your father's name is Luis?

A. That is right.

Q. What is your Mother's name?

A. Lenora

Q. And Lenora is spelled differently than baby Lenore's name. Is that correct?

A. Yes, it is.

Q. And do you know anyone by the name of Condellera Scarpetta?

A. No, I don't know

Q. Do you know any other Olga Scarpetta?

A. No, I don't.

I knew why he had asked her about Lenore's name, but I had no idea why he was asking about these other Scarpettas. Had his investigation in South America turned up information pertinent to the case?

Colson continued:

Q. You were raised by a lady other than your mother—not that your mother was not there, but some lady would come to the United States to help raise the baby if you got the baby?
A. Yes.
Q. What is her name?
A. Omelia.
Q. Sanchez?
A. Right.
Q. And Omelia Sanchez is how old?
A. She is about sixty-five.
Q. While working during the day, Omelia Sanchez would care for Lenore, is that your intention?
A. She lives with me and has for the past two months.
Q. Does she speak English?
A. No, she knows a few words.
Q. And is she a resident of the United States?
A. No, she is not. She is here with me as a friend.
Q. Are you aware that you cannot bring people to work in the United States as domestics?
A. She is not working for me.
Mr. Rosenblatt interrupted, "Excuse me, Miss Scarpetta, don't be so fast to answer. The question calls for a legal answer. I object. It is not a proper question."
    Mr. Colson nodded his head and continued.
Q. Do you intend for her to work?
A. She will not be working.
Q. But she will take care of Lenore during the day?
A. She will take care of Lenore during the day.
Q. When you came to the United States pregnant, you did not tell your parents?
A. I didn't tell them that I was pregnant.
Q. And you changed your mind and told them?
A. I went back home, yes, and told them, yes.
Q. The decision was not to keep the baby as your own?
A. No, that was not my decision at that time when I

first left Colombia.

Q. When did adoption become your decision?

A. After a referral to the Spence-Chapin Agency. The social service department at the New York hospital suggested the agency. I had no plans to give my child up for adoption. The Spence-Chapin Adoption Agency talked about all the advantages and counseled me. Through counseling at Spence-Chapin, I decided to give my baby up. But in no way was that my intention when I came to the United States or in my first visit to the Spence-Chapin Adoption Agency.

Q. What I am trying to establish is that at first you wanted to keep the pregnancy a secret, is that right?

A. When I went to the Spence-Chapin Adoption Agency, I had not talked to my parents. I had not decided whether I would or would not tell my parents that the baby was born.

Q. When did you decide to tell your parents.

A. I decided to tell my parents when I started doing everything to get my baby back.

Q. As a matter of fact, when the baby was born, it is customary to tell your parents, to notify the parents and you said, "Don't do it." Is that right?

Mr. Rosenblatt took the floor, "I object to what is customary, Your Honor."

Q. Did anybody ask you, "May we." or "Should we tell the father of the child?"

Mr. Rosenblatt addressed the court again, "Your Honor—"

A. No, nobody asked me.

Mr. Rosenblatt said, "Excuse me, Miss Scarpetta." Then he addressed the court. "This is hearsay, what unidentified people from the adoption agency told Miss Scarpetta."

Mr. Colson replied, "I am not talking about the adoption agency. I am talking about the hospital. But we will go on."

Mr. Rosenblatt issued the same objection.

At the judge's direction, Mr. Colson went back to his cross-examination.

Q. Now, the father of this child lives in Bogotá, is that right?

A. As far as I know. I have no idea.

Mr. Rosenblatt broke in. "She doesn't know where he is."

Q. At the time you went with him, where did he live?

A. He lived in Bogotá.

Q. And did you know that he was married?

A. No, I did not.

Q. And how long did you go with him?

A. I knew him two years. We started going seriously for about the past eight or nine months.

Q. And you talked about marriage?

A. Yes.

Q. Now, isn't your family custom that when somebody goes with a person and discusses marriage that they meet your mother and father?

A. They meet—he met my parents. My parents never approved of him, and therefore I never told my parents that I planned to marry him. We planned to elope.

Once again Mr. Rosenblatt interrupted, "I object to the relevancy. The relationship between Miss Scarpetta and this unidentified man, has no—"

Mr. Colson interrupted. "Miss Scarpetta had alternatives and, in effect, if the adoption agency persuaded—" The judge interjected. "I will permit her to answer."

Q. We established that you did not know that he was married and, secondly, you planned to marry. Is that correct?

A. Yes.

Q. Thirdly, your parents did not approve, and,

therefore, you avoided his seeing them.
A. He went to pick me up at the house and took me back. He visited with my family a few times, but I never discussed plans with them, plans of marriage until the very end.
Q. Did you ever meet his family?
A. No, I did not.
Q. Even though you were planning to marry, you never went to his home and met his family and talked about the marriage?
A. No.
Q. You already picked out the name for the child, the two of you, before you married?
A. We had not talked about children.
Q. What was the name of the child going to be?
A. Margarita.
(I was vindicated in Mr. Colson's eyes. I had to admit it strange that we named our daughter Lenore and her maternal grandmother had the Spanish equivalent of the same name.)
Colson pushed ahead.
Q. At first, did the father offer you an abortion?
A. Yes.
(The thought of Lenore being aborted sent shivers up my spine. Once a child exists, the thought of it never being is hard to handle. Little chance abortion being considered by Miss Scarpetta because she practiced Catholicism and abortions were illegal in New York.)
Q. Secondly, did he offer to take the child and urged that you give him the child and not place it for adoption?
A. He wanted to take it to his wife, yes.
Q. You knew that there was no such thing as a divorce for Catholics in Colombia, is that right?
A. There is no such thing as divorce for Catholics anywhere in the world.

Q. That applied to him, and to you, right?
A. Yes, he was married through the Catholic Church.
Q. And how many children did he have?
A. Two.
Q. When did you find out?

Mr. Rosenblatt objected to the line of questioning on the history of the natural father.

Mr. Colson explained that he intended to show that the natural father fought against adoption.

The judge admonished Mr. Colson: "Stick to this thing somewhere."

Mr. Colson requested permission for two more questions along the same lines. The judge agreed.
Q. Haven't you testified that you didn't like the way he raised his children and therefore didn't want him to have your child?
A. That is right.
Q. How did you know how he raised his children?
A. Because he told me.
Q. Told you after Lenore was born or after he told you that he was married?
A. We had a few discussions after I knew that he was married.

"This is your third question," said Mr. Rosenblatt, "and you told the Court that—"

Mr. Colson said, "I'm changing the subject."
Q. I don't think it would do any good to put his name in the record. May we agree on his initials?"

Mr. Rosenblatt: "No, I will object."

Mr. Colson responded that he wanted to talk about the natural Father's trips to the United States as relevant.

Mr. Rosenblatt addressed the court. "Your Honor, this is far afield and ludicrous—the father's trips to the United States, his discussions with Ms. Scarpetta. Mr. Colson broadened the hearing far beyond the scope of *habeas corpus* and to a man that they are not calling as a witness and we are not either. He has no relevancy to any conceivable issue before Your Honor."

Colson responded, "Miss Scarpetta already described conferences with him, and I wish to test her credibility about these visits to the United States. She saw him before and after the birth and leads into her decisions about the formal surrender document. She had all the counseling in the world from this man."

"You're Honor," interjected Mr. Rosenblatt, "the New York courts held that the consent was revoked. We admit and will stipulate that many options open to any pregnant, unmarried woman. She chose one. Eighteen days after signing the consent, Miss Scarpetta changed her mind, the very same day that the DeMartinos picked up the child, I might add."

Colson countered. "What this lady told the New York judge is false testimony. I think that material information has to do with the trips of the father to the Unites States."

Mr. Rosenblatt: "I stipulate the entire transcript before the Supreme Court of New York go into evidence."

"We will so stipulate," said Mr. Colson.
The judge: "Ask the question."

Mr. Colson said, "I ask if the real father with the initials *ARC* made trips to the United States to counsel about this adoption while you were pregnant."
Mr. Rosenblatt objected to the form of the question. "Mr. Colson talked about perjury. Let him read what Miss Scarpetta said in New York and ask if that is accurate or not accurate."

"I don't see how he can impeach unless he asks her first," replied the judge.

"I object. Let him use—"
Colson picked up the record in front of him and

directed his attention as much toward Rosenblatt as Miss Scarpetta. "Okay, we'll do it your way."

Before he continued, the judge, displaying the same air of patience throughout the hearing, turned to Rosenblatt. "He can ask his question now, and then refer to the record. I think that he has to lay predicate." Rosenblatt slumped back in his chair, and Colson went on with his questioning.

Q. I ask if a Mr. *ARC* came to the United States and counseled with you about this adoption problem?

A. The first time he came to the United States was December. At that time, we discussed a possible marriage. In April of 1970, we talked about adoption. He opposed it and asked me to give him the baby. I said, *no* because I did not want—I did not want my baby brought up by his wife. I did not think that right.

Q. Did you know his wife?

A. No.

Q. Did he come in July?

A. He came, I think, the end of June or the beginning of July.

Q. That was, of course, after the baby was born?

A. Yes, and then I told him that I tried to recover the baby.

Q. Ma'am, in your testimony you stated that the Spence-Chapin Agency talked you into this adoption.

A. I went with no intention of giving my baby up for adoption. They counseled me, and I signed the surrender papers, and that is all.

Q. Wasn't your voluntary decision to go to the Spence-Chapin Agency?

A. Nobody pushed me.

Q. Did they give you this book which I hold in my hand?

A. Something like it, yes.

Q. Take a look at it, please, ma'am.

A. Yes, apparently the same book.

Q. Does anything herein say that the agency in any way makes money for an adoption?

A. No.

Q. They certainly charged you nothing.

A. They told me, as a matter of fact, that—

Mr. Rosenblatt interrupted, "This is improper cross examination—not within the scope—not within the farthest reaches—not within the farthest reaches of the scope of direct examination. How much latitude is given? If we want to finish in one day—they have several doctors to call upon."

The judge said, "I heard nothing to indicate that the finances of the adoption are in question."

Colson continued.

Q. Didn't the agency propose that you put this child with a foster home while you worked?

A. They mentioned it. They mentioned a few possibilities, yes, and the first thing that I discussed with—

Mr. Rosenblatt broke in again, "Excuse me, I just understood you ruled that he was not to persist in this line of questioning about the booklet."

Mr. Colson established that she had made up her mind prior to the birth, to place the child for adoption. He then asked during the four days in the hospital, if the child was brought to her to feed or touch. She said it was.

Q. After touching and seeing the child, you then took her to the adoption agency. Did you take the girl physically?

A. Yes.

Q. Did anyone talk you into that?

A. Into taking the child?

Q. To the Spence-Chapin Adoption Agency?

A. That day?

Q. Yes. Was it a voluntary act?
A. That day when Miss Daniels came, I agreed to take the child. It was—I went there, yes, voluntarily with Miss Daniels.
Q. Your sister stayed with you throughout the birth, did she not?
A. She came a week before the baby was born. She is here.
Q. And you turned the baby over voluntarily at that time?
A. Yes.
Q. Now, on May 29, you returned to the adoption agency to sign a formal surrender, did you not?
A. Yes.
Q. After fifteen visits, namely, the sixteenth visit, you signed this surrender document?
A. Yes.
Q. On the fifteenth visit, without going into it, you did not sign the document, did you?
A. I could not sign because I could not stop crying.
Q. And so, on May 29, you went home to think and make sure?
A. I went home and made an appointment for June 1.
Q. And signed this surrender document?
A. Yes.

"Your Honor," interjected Colson, "I don't believe you read this document. While Miss Scarpetta is on the stand, I would like her to it."

"I will stipulate" said Rosenblatt curtly, "that she read and understood it before signing, yet eighteen days later, she revoked it."

Colson read from the document, ". . . that it was done voluntarily and unconditionally and absolutely and that she was unable to provide a suitable home. Will you stipulate to that?"

"No," Rosenblatt said sharply. "I stipulate that

Miss Scarpetta read the document and signed it."

Colson, once again read from the surrender. "Finding that I am unable to provide a suitable home for said child and feeling that the welfare of the child will be promoted by its adoption." Then, turning to Miss Scarpetta, he asked, "Did you sign that document and read it?"

A. That was my feeling at the moment, yes. I read and signed it.

Through further questioning, Colson elicited from Miss Scarpetta that she was thirty-two when signing the document and that she realized it was a final surrender.

Q. And no one told you ever that you had six months to change your mind?

A. I found out by myself when I checked that law.

Q. The reason you wanted to go with the adoption and felt you should place your child up for adoption was for the best interests of the child?

A. At that time, I felt adoption saved her from every problem in this world. She was in a little glass cage where nobody could get to her, hurt her, and I wanted a good life for my baby. I offered her complete happiness through adoption.

Q. You don't have any idea now that she wasn't in a glass cage, completely protected, and happy, do you?

A. I think she was hurt an awful lot.

(I felt my whole body stiffen and peered over at Olga waiting anxiously for what came next.)

Q. Hurt by whom?

A. All the propaganda in the press.

Q. Is she aware of the propaganda?

A. She will grow up and be very much aware of the propaganda.

Q. There is no question that will happen. Ma'am, do you believe anything changed since, in its best interests, you put the child up for adoption?

A. Yes, adoption is hard for a child to face. As long as the natural mother is fit and capable and loves and wants the child, the best place is with its mother because babies have a right to their own heritage. My baby has a right to know who she is, to be among her people, and if the mother loves the child and is able to take care of her and if the whole family wants and loves and desires to have the child, that child should not be with strangers.

Q. At the time you signed this formal surrender, didn't you feel the best interests of the child were served by having a home, a mother, a father, other children around, in short, having a family? For those reasons, you gave up your child, didn't you?

A. At the time I signed, I felt tremendous strain and guilt—gilt for not providing a home and family. The tremendous strain caused me to sign the papers.

Q. Respectfully, ma'am, I still wish an answer to my question. We understand your guilt. Yet, weren't a stable home with two parents, an environment with siblings and friends, a family unit—weren't those the reasons you signed the surrender?

A. I think all the things we discussed at the agency, yes.

Q. Yet, you changed your mind after the agency met your wishes?

When Mr. Rosenblatt interrupted the long cross examination, the judge granted him a brief recess.

Chapter XIII

I was grateful for time to rest. Concentration on Miss Scarpetta's testimony included tedious repetition, but, of course, the judge heard her story for the first time. I hoped to see some reactions on his face, however, he maintained a blank but pensive look. When Miss Scarpetta, flanked by her attorneys, left the room, Nick spoke in hushed tones to ours. I wished for reality to come out of an unreal situation. Since my mouth was terribly dry, I looked for a water cooler when my eye caught Life Savers on the table. Irony is everywhere if we just look for it. Zalk's son sat opposite me. "I wondered if you might pass a Life Saver?" I asked.

"Certainly," he replied and raised the package in an exaggerated manner and let them fall on the table just short of my hand. The snide expression on his face showed him greatly pleased with himself. I returned his smile and nodded acknowledgment of his *act of defiance and disdain* and took a Life Saver. His childishness made me confidently grateful for our attorneys and friends. As I said a silent prayer of thanks, Miss Scarpetta and her attorneys re-entered.

Mr. Colson resumed and established through his questioning that other than higher pay, Miss Scarpetta's circumstances remained the same, ". . . as far as the agency, the baby's welfare, or your desire for a home with both a mother and father?"

A. All I knew about the prospective adoptive parents was that she was a nurse and he was a lawyer. Aside from that, I didn't know what type of family life, what type of psychological makeup, what type of moral standards, what type of beliefs they had. The agency also told me they were Catholics, but I had nothing to assure me about the baby's moral upbringing.

(By this time I wasn't particularly upset by what she said. I realized her responses were emotional and of the moment. But what made her think that I was a nurse? Colson didn't think it important and dropped it.)

Q. I believe you told the court that you had a poor job before the birth and that is what led to the adoption.

A. I could not live on $20,000 all of my life. I needed a good job. What brought me to adoption was a state of mind which changed afterwards, sir.

Q. I would suggest that you filed a lawsuit that says you notified the agency on June the 30th of 1970, and you stated here that you notified them eighteen days after June 1 which would be June 18.

A. I called the agency on June 18. They told me there was nothing to be done. I checked the law and went to the social worker at the New York Hospital. She called on the 23rd—and I believe the 23rd is there—and they told me to contact my social worker for an appointment. On the 29th of June, I returned to the agency to formally request the return of my baby.

Q. On page thirteen of the Petition for the Writ of Habeas Corpus that was filed in New York, you swore in front of a notary public.

A. That was the date that I formally requested the return of my baby. There were previous calls.

(Mr. Colson made reference to other places in her testimony where the 29th of June was her request date. Miss Scarpetta held firm that she made earlier calls. I wondered why he pushed so hard on this point. With some additional prodding, she said that after the original discussions with the agency in June, she agreed to go to there four more times. Each time she reached the same conclusion. She wanted her baby back.)

"All right!" Colson said raising his voice, "You had four visits in July. Did you not also agree to have a visit with the psychiatrist on August the 28th about the subject?"

(A Psychiatrist? What psychiatrist? Nobody told me that she went to see a psychiatrist. I felt my pulse quicken and waited anxiously for an answer.)

A. I did not agree to anything concerning a psychiatrist. The agency said if they could not dissuade me, they'd recommend a psychiatrist. I did not agree, however, though the social worker did make an appointment for the psychiatric clinic.

Q. To discuss your change of mind?

A. Yes.

Q. And instead, you went to Colombia?

A. No, I went to the appointment.

Q. You did go to the psychiatrist?

A. I went to the appointment.

Q. What happened?

A. I talked to—to the psychiatrist, and we discussed the problem. She felt I was right and once the situation was fixed with my family—I told her that I was going home to talk with my parents. She felt I needed no psychiatric care. I was well on my way to solving the problem.

Q. Did she advise you to take the baby from the adoption home?

A. We only talked about my state of mind.

Q. And what was her name?

A. I don't remember. I could find out.

(So there it was, laid out before me. I wished to read Miss Scarpetta's mind to find the truth about the psychiatrist's evaluation. It was obviously just as the agency said. Miss Scarpetta talked about the return of the baby, but her requests, they said, were "shrouded in uncertainty." I didn't know whether to respect them or resent them for not telling me about her visit to the psychiatrist, but then again, maybe they didn't know because she initially refused to take their offer and instead went on her own through the hospital.

The visit took place on August 28, so obviously, as late as August, she was still confused and unresolved about her state of mind. I looked at Nick. Our eyes met briefly and confirmed the importance of the moment. We each knew that we did the right thing for Lenore, and I once again felt a certain inner peace.) Meanwhile Colson pressed on with his questions.

Q. Have you been examined by a psychiatrist before or since?

A. No, I have not.

Q. We offered an examination, just as the DeMartinos and the children had—not to find anybody unstable—just for psychometric testing, and you refused.

(Mr. Rosenblatt objected. He said that Mr. Colson never made a formal motion for psychological testing.)

Mr. Colson went on with Olga:

Q. You had a meeting with Mr. Zalk, your attorney, a secret meeting agreed by the parties never to be discussed, did you not?

A. The contents of the meeting were never discussed.

Q. And you disclosed that meeting, didn't you?

A. The contents of the meeting?

Q. Yes.

A. I did not. The meeting was not secret, but the contents were confidential. It was never agreed to remain in confidence. That day we met with Mr. and Mrs. DeMartino—

Mr. Rosenblatt interrupted, "Your Honor, if the contents, as Mr. Colson says, were confidential, let's respect that."

Mr. Colson cut in, "We waive any confidentiality. Miss Scarpetta already discussed the meeting with the press."

Mr. Rosenblatt raised his voice, "It is not

material, Your Honor."

Miss Scarpetta spoke up, "I have not discussed anything with the press."

Mr. Colson said, "Didn't you refuse at that time back in New York several months ago at a secret meeting to see a psychiatrist or even read about the subject?"

Mr. Rosenblatt objected, "Immaterial, Your Honor."

The judge sustained the objection.

Colson looked over some notes written on a paper in front of him and then continued.

Q. Now, ma'am, did you offer the adoption agency any jewelry for this child?
A. Yes, I did.
Q. Where is the jewelry?
A. I have it. The agency told me the adoptive—the prospective adoptive parents—refused the jewelry. They said the family had not accepted the jewelry or the other things for the baby.
Q. Can you tell us the date you left the jewelry for the baby?
A. June 1.

(Had I been offered the jewelry which she spoke about, I certainly would have followed Miss Scarpetta's wishes and seen to it that Lenore received it.)

Mr. Rosenblatt became impatient. He said, "Your Honor, I object to this line of questioning as immaterial. This jewelry—we stray far from any issue."

Judge Cullen nodded his head.

Mr. Colson asked, "What was the name that the father wanted for the child?"

Rosenblatt objected.

The judge sustained it.

Then Mr. Colson asked Miss Scarpetta if she continued to see the father after the birth of the baby.

Mr. Rosenblatt objected.

Mr. Colson explained, "I want to know why she continued to see the man who deceived her."

Miss Scarpetta volunteered, "I saw him once."

"Afterwards?" Mr. Colson asked.

A. I think it is in the testimony. I saw him once and told him that I was planning to get the baby back.

Mr. Colson said, "That is all we have at this time, Your Honor."

Rosenblatt started by asking Miss Scarpetta her religion.

A. Catholic.

Q. Are you a practicing Catholic?

A. Yes, I am.

Q. Why didn't you tell your parents when you found out that you were pregnant and came to New York? Why didn't you tell them?

A. I was awfully ashamed. I had failed all my moral principles. I had done something wrong. I had never thought of having a relationship with a married man.

Q. Mr. Colson referred to a Miss Daniels who testified in a previous hearing in New York and talked about thirteen or fourteen visits with this Miss Daniels. How old is this Miss Daniels?

A. I believe at that time she was twenty-two years old.

Q. Twenty-two years old and this is the lady who you had all those conferences with, is that correct?

A. That is correct.

Q. She is employed by and paid by the adoption agency?

A. That is right.

Q. Miss Scarpetta, you testified about going to the adoption agency to sign a consent on May 29, 1970. Why didn't you sign the consent at that time?

A. I couldn't stop crying and read the papers.

Q. And this crying was taking place in the presence of

whom?
A. Miss Daniels.
Q. When you signed the consent, did you have a lawyer with you?
A. No, I did not.
Q. Did you have any legal or professional advice with respect to the import of the words that were on that form?
A. No, I did not.
Q. Who provided that form?
A. Spence-Chapin.
Q. Before coming to New York in 1969 and before your experience with Spence-Chapin, had you ever had previous experience with any adoption agency anywhere in the world?
A. No.
Q. Had you ever been pregnant before?
A. No.
Q. You said that before you went into the hospital, the job in New York was, take home, $48.00 a week?
A. That is right.

  (Mr. Rosenblatt announced that he had no further questions. Mr. Colson, however, wanted to recross-examine.) He asked Miss Scarpetta:
Q. You failed your moral principles. This affair with a married man was not your first, was it, ma'am?
A. Yes, it was.
Q. You never had any other love affairs including California when you were there?
A. No.
Q. You never had any love affairs in Paris when you were there?
A. No.
Q. This love affair resulting in a pregnancy at the age of thirty-one was the first in your life?
A. That is right

Mr. Colson thanked Miss Scarpetta and the judge excused her. Miss Scarpetta weathered the questioning rather well. She returned to her seat as composed as before. Mr. Zalk was called to the stand as a witness by Mr. Rosenblatt. Although our attorneys objected to his being called as a witness on the grounds that he was Miss Scarpetta's attorney, he was nonetheless permitted to testify provided he kept to the legal events which took place in New York. I don't know whether it was because I was tired or because we seemed to cover this ground so many times before, but Zalk's testimony went on forever. Our attorneys continued to object, not only to his testimony, but to the legal documents presented to the court. They maintained as before that we were never parties to any of the legal proceedings which took place in New York.

Finally, Mr. Fuchsberg's cross-examined. First, he addressed the court very quietly and slowly then raised his voice to Mr. Zalk, and in a series of rapid fire questions, began to interrogate. He spoke so quickly that it appeared he wasn't going to wait for an answer.
Q. It is a fact is it not, that in the proceedings tried on November 2, it is your understanding that the baby was about five and a half month's old. Is that correct, sir?
A. The baby was born on May 18 and November would make it about that.
Q. She is now, of course, past her thirteenth month. Is that correct, sir?
A. Yes.
Q. Is it also a fact that the DeMartinos—just say *yes* or *no* and we will get along much quicker—were not named as defendants in that suit when you started your petition? Is that correct, sir?
A. Yes, that is correct.
Q. Is it a fact, since they were not named, they were not served? Is that right, sir?

A. Yes, that is right.

Q. Is it also a fact that they were never called as witnesses? Is that right, sir?

A. That is correct.

Q. And exact, sir. Is it also a fact that other than a summary question put to the social worker, no inquiry as to the status of the child in the home of the DeMartinos was made at that New York hearing in November of 1970? Is that right, sir?

A. Yes, that is correct.

Q. Is it correct that neither the family physician nor any other member of the DeMartino household nor anyone else who had any direct contact with the child on a continuing basis was called by either the adoption agency or your client as a witness in that trial? Is that right, sir?

A. The only witnesses at the trial were Miss Scarpetta and some employees of the agency.

(I looked around the room at attorneys, newspaper reporters, some old and some new, and wondered how many who just heard that testimony realized the importance. "This is what I've been telling you," I wanted to shout out. "Can't you see how the court system pays lip service to the best interest of the child? Don't any of you recall being overwhelmed by the big world? Haven't any of you experienced a little lost tot whose anguished face and cries of fright say it all?" How is it that adults show so much compassion and understanding for a child caught in that momentary fear but think nothing of being the instrument which condemns a child to that same experience permanently? PLEASE, GOD, DON'T LET THE UNCARING WORLD SWALLOW LENORE.)

In the background, Fuchsberg hammered away at Zalk by asking him to confirm the various stays which were in effect during the court hearings.

Q. When the court of appeals made its decision and an order signed pursuant to that, a stay was in effect. Correct?
A. Not against the DeMartinos, against the Spence-Chapin Agency.
Q. There was a stay at all times into April of 1971 against that order. Is that right, sir?
A. Against the Spence-Chapin Adoption Agency, yes.
Q. At that time there were never any direct orders to the DeMartinos, were there?
A. Not until April 28.

Fuchsberg was quick to pick up on Zalk's answer. He got Zalk to admit that he had our name added to the order on that date thereby enlarging upon the original decree and that it was done without any prior notice to us. With prodding from the judge, Fuchsberg continued his questioning.

Q. And then, sir, that order directed the DeMartinos by name to deliver the child on May the 3rd. Is that correct, sir?
A. Yes.
Q. Between April 28 and May 3, an order had been obtained for a stay in the federal court in existence on May 3 at ten o'clock?
A. There was some kind of a stay in existence at on May 3. I don't believe the stay precluded the return of the child to Miss Scarpetta.

Mr. Fuchsberg looked at Mr. Zalk incredulously and asked, "I was the one who, on behalf of the DeMartinos, applied for that stay. Is that right, sir?"
A. Yes. I was the one who opposed you.
Q. Federal Judge Constance Baker Motley granted my application, didn't she?
A. If Your Honor pleases, this becomes technical, and I

don't know if I can answer by saying *yes* or *no*. If I can explain, perhaps it would be easier.

With the judge's approval, Zalk explained that when he and Fuchsberg appeared before Judge Motley, she wrote across the application, "My judgment above is stayed," and in Zalk's opinion her action did not become a stay of the lower court's proceedings. "I think," he said, "Mr. Fuchsberg is correct in assuming it a stay for turning over the child on May 3, but the point is arguable."

Fuchsberg reminded Zalk that the judge signed a copy to make the stay effective immediately and that Zalk got a copy at the time. Zalk continued to sidestep the questioning, however, as best he could.

I realized it was important to show that we were not fugitives from justice but was worn from hearing the issue discussed at such length. Fuchsberg finally left the subject and began discussing the proceedings in the federal court.

Rosenblatt objected by stating that the issue was far beyond the scope of direct questioning and continued to object as the questions moved ahead.

Finally, Orseck spoke up, "The DeMartinos never had their day in court, in the federal court, or any place else. The purpose of the cross examination is extremely relevant since Mr. Zalk testified that a complaint was dismissed that the DeMartinos filed in the federal court. That is a damaging and misleading implication."

So, with the judge's *go ahead,* Fuchsberg continued. After a re-questioning of the witness by Rosenblatt and then again by Fuchsberg, Zalk was excused. Rosenblatt rested his case after telling the court that he would object to our side calling medical witnesses. If, however, we were permitted, in rebuttal, he would produce his own medical testimony.

Finally, it was Colson's turn to present our case! "Your Honor," he said, "the respondents will call as our first witness, Reverend Anderson."

I was startled to hear his name and could tell by Nick's the expression that he was just as surprised. Then, Bob Orseck, who consistently kept his eye on target, addressed the judge in that familiar shaky voice. "We would move to dismiss or quash the written petition on the grounds that under the law of Florida on a habeas corpus proceeding involving custody of a child, the paramount issue is the best interest of the child, and we have not heard one iota of testimony on that key issue."

The judge reserved ruling on the motion and the trial continued. It felt good to see an old friend sitting in the witness chair. Obviously, Reverend Anderson was a character witness.

As Colson directed his questions toward our first meeting and the build up of our friendship, I thought with fondness of the little happenings in our nursery school: how Linda and I made a game of racing around the corner to see who got to school first; the frustration on winter days of bundling up two kids in heavy coats and boots only to peel them all off seconds later; Reverend Anderson strutting around the little house like a proud peacock and pleased that he got this little nursery off the ground; and me sitting on the floor of the nursery school doing exercises with the kids.

"We asked Mrs. DeMartino if she would become a member of the board and she agreed," Reverend Anderson said.

Q. How did she participate?

A. She became chairman of the administration and policy committee and, last fall, served as chairman of the board.

Mr. Rosenblatt interjected, "Your Honor,

Reverend Anderson's testimony relates to the issue of fitness, and rather than constantly interrupt, I want to make our position clear. In our opinion, the DeMartinos don't have any lawful right to raise the issue of fitness. Miss Scarpetta was adjudicated as a fit mother by New York, and a contest in a proceeding of this nature that attempts a comparison as to who might be more fit is inappropriate."

The judge overruled, and Rev. Anderson continued with his testimony revolving around his observance of us as a family unit. Needless to say, he spoke in glowing terms. Shortly after, Rosenblatt cross-examined. "I take it that you do not then know Miss Scarpetta."
A. No, I do not.
Q. You don't know her parents?
A. I have just met them outside.
Q. You don't know anything about her apartment in New York?
A. No, I do not.
Q. Or her ability or the facilities that she could provide for the baby?
A. No, I don't.
Q. Do I understand, sir, that you have come from Brooklyn specifically to testify in this case?
A. I was invited to do so.
Q. Who paid for your trip down here?
A. Mr. Fuchsberg.
Q. In other words, they just got you a ticket and paid?
A. Yes.
Q. Where are you staying?
A. The Dupont Plaza Hotel.
Q. And by the same token, is legal counsel, Mr. Fuchsberg, paying for that as well?
A. Yes.
Q. Did you ever discuss with Mr. and/or Mrs.

DeMartino the expense of your trip here?
A. No, I did not.
Q. Do you know when Mr. and Mrs. DeMartino left Brooklyn to come to Florida?

Mr. Colson interrupted, "That assumes they left at the same time, Your Honor. If he wants to make it two questions, I think it would be fair."

Q. Do you know when Mr. DeMartino came to Florida?
A. About the beginning of May.
Q. And do you know when Mrs. DeMartino came to Florida?
A. I believe a couple of weeks prior.
Q. Did they discuss with you their reasons for coming to Florida?
A. No, they did not.
Q. Weren't you, as a person who is in relatively close contact, curious as to why they planned to leave their home in Brooklyn where they had close family ties and a close association with your church? Why, out of the blue, had they picked up and traveled from New York to Florida?
A. I thought *why Florida* but understood they were leaving, perhaps, for Lenore's best interest.
Q. During the entire period of time that you knew the DeMartinos prior to the publicity in New York papers concerning this adoption battle, had they ever indicated a desire to leave the State of New York?
A. No.
Q. Is it a fair statement, Reverend Anderson, that they left New York for Florida was due to this adoption case?

Mr. Colson objected, "Your Honor. The question calls for a conclusion and mental condition of somebody else.

The Court: Sustained.

Q. As I understand, you never counseled the DeMartinos on the basis of religion or spiritual advice about this adoption case.
A. That is correct.
Q. Was Lenore ever in your school or was she too young?
A. No, she was not in our school.
Q. When did you first discuss with the DeMartinos your coming to testify?

    Mr. Colson: "If he did."
    Mr. Rosenblatt: "If you did."

A. I haven't discussed it with them, period.
Q. Could you tell us, Reverend Anderson, how you were contacted and when you were contacted and by whom to testify in this case?
A. Last Thursday evening a committee which worked on the DeMartino's behalf asked if I would come to Florida as a character witness. I agreed.
Q. Could you give us the name, sir, of the individual who called you on behalf of that committee?
A. John Farro.
Q. Do you if he came to testify in this case?
A. I do not know.
Q. What is the name of that committee?
A. The Committee to Save Lenore.
Q. Is this the committee that gets a great deal of press and propagandizing in New York on behalf of the DeMartinos?
A. I read the papers.
Q. Moving ahead, let me ask if the property of the DeMartinos abuts your church?
A. Correct.
Q. Who is living in the house now?
A. It is not occupied at present.
Q. Has it been sold?
A. I do not know.

Q. I put quotation marks around the word you used in describing the DeMartinos, and you used the word, *stable*. Do you recall using that word?
A. Yes.
Q. I am going to show you some posed photographs, some of them with Mr. and Mrs. DeMartino and some only with Mrs. DeMartino and their children. Many of them are from the *New York Daily News* with the largest circulation of any newspaper in America. Reverend Anderson, do you think posing for the newspapers in photographs such as these and on television—I'm sure you watch TV also—with a baby is evidence of stability?
A. I don't see the relevancy.
Q. Is that a legal opinion or—
A. My personal opinion, Mr. Rosenblatt.
Q. Did you ever question the DeMartino's motivation for seeking an avalanche of publicity?
A. I think my responsibility is not to divulge any information about counseling.

    Mr. Colson intervened, "We would be glad to waive confidentiality on their behalf if it is all right with the DeMartinos. Nick answered *yes*. So Mr. Rosenblatt continued:
Q. My question, Reverend, calls for a *yes* or *no*. Did either or both of them ever discuss their motivation or reasoning behind being photographed for the newspapers, television, or any other media?
A. No.
Q. I am sure that living in Brooklyn you had occasion many times to see some of these photographs or to see some of the news accounts on television?
A. Yes.
Q. After observing either newspaper pictures, newspaper articles or material on television or radio, did you ever initiate a discussion with either of the

DeMartinos as to why they were doing all of that?
A. No.
Q. Were you aware, Reverend Anderson, prior to the departure of Mr. and Mrs. DeMartino from New York to Florida they were ordered by the highest court of the State of New York to surrender Lenore to Miss Scarpetta?

Mr. Colson objected. "The Order speaks for itself.
Whether it was served upon the DeMartinos, the Reverend would have no possible knowledge."

"It is very material, Your Honor," Rosenblatt insisted, "to know whether they discussed the order or—"

"I think you asked him already," the judge reminded Rosenblatt.

Rosenblatt stressed each word as he spoke. "I ask you, Reverend, if any source informed you about a duly executed court order in the State of New York for the DeMartinos to surrender the child to Miss Scarpetta?"
A. Yes.
Q. Did you discuss that fact with the DeMartinos?
A. Yes.
Q. Did you advise them to go to Florida?
A. I advised them of nothing.
Q. You didn't advise them either to obey the order or to disobey the order?
A. No, I did not.
Q. Did you suggest that they see their priest?
A. No, I did not.
Q. You knew of the order before they left. Is that correct, sir?
A. Yes.
Mr. Rosenblatt: "That is all I have, Your Honor."

Colson asked to redirect:

Q. Reverend, the three years that you described knowing the DeMartinos, had a Catholic priest come to this particular parish since that time?
A. Yes.
Q. Is he relatively new to the parish?
A. Yes, within the last year.
Q. The DeMartinos don't go to your church. They go to that parish. Is that right?
A. That is right.
(That is right, and our pastor, Father Racigliano, not only gave us spiritual guidance, but came forward on our behalf and took a picture with us in front of committee headquarters. The photo appeared in a special article in the *Daily News*. I wished that I had told Colson so he could put this questioning about our priest to rest, but I never anticipated the importance of it.)

Colson changed his line of questioning:
Q. Did you agree to come here voluntarily and completely on your own?
A. Yes.
Q. And the Committee to Save Baby Lenore is the one that gathered 87,000 signatures in New York?
A. I believe so.
Q. Did they present those to the legislature to change the law?
A. I don't know.

"Is this a petition contest now?" Rosenblatt blurted.

Colson reminded Rosenblatt that he brought up the committee issue.

"I did not bring up the committee," he said emphatically. Before any other banter, the judge asked them to move on.

After Colson asked Reverend Anderson more questions about the pictures in the N.Y. Newspapers,

Rosenblatt took over:

Q. Have you ever traveled from your parish in Brooklyn to another state to testify on behalf of anyone?

A. No, I have not.

Q. I believe counsel used the word *volunteered* as a witness. Of course, that is not accurate. You were called by the committee and asked if you would be willing to testify.

Q. When Lenore becomes eleven, twelve, or eighteen, do you have an opinion, sir, of how she would react to these photographs and articles, how she might feel about her real mother fighting desperately to have her returned?

Mr. Colson interrupted. "I object to the lawyer's speech. This reverend is not a psychiatrist."

Judge Cullen: I sustain the objection

Q. Do you consider the DeMartinos to be law-abiding citizens?

A. Yes.

Q. In spite of a violation of a lawful order of the court of New York?

Mr. Colson said, "I object to the fact that some order never served on the DeMartinos is referred to."

Mr. Rosenblatt countered, "I object to the characterization of my lengthy question as a speech. I am asking questions, not making speeches.

Mr. Colson: "I object, Your Honor."

Judge Cullen: I sustain the objection.

Mr. Rosenblatt: That is all I have.

(No sooner was Reverend Anderson excused when Colson said, "We call Dr. Libo." We were in for a lot of surprises, so I had better get used to it. I never expected our pediatrician to come to Florida to speak on our behalf.

This time it was Mr. Fuchsberg who handled

the questioning. Dr. Libo gave his qualifications which included chief resident of pediatrics at the Jewish Hospital in Brooklyn. He then related his experiences with our family. He was a pediatrician to both Linda and Lenore from the time they entered our home, and he tended them on a regular basis. When he first saw Lenore at one month, her height and weight were below normal—below 97 percent of children—but after a few months, she came up to the norm.

Needless to say, he spoke in glowing terms and said he recalled us as excellent parents. We were always calm, and our requests for help or advice were always logical and reasonable.

I was particularly pleased to hear him talk of a natural empathy between Lenore and myself. "There was no way that you could possibly know there was an adoption here or anything like that," he said. "There wasn't this overprotection that you frequently get with an adopted child." In addition, he said that the relationship between Linda and Lenore was perfectly natural.

"You are not a psychiatrist, are you?" asked Fuchsberg.

A. No, sir.

Q. In your work, have known of the effect of forced separation of children?

A. I would say so and not only that, sir, but a good part of pediatrics is being sort of a psychiatrist. You deal with mothers and their emotions and the child's emotions and the interplay. Certainly a good part of my work deals with behavior.

Q. Sir, you know, do you not, that on the 18th of June the baby came to the DeMartinos? (Mr. Fuchsberg turned to me for confirmation and I nodded *yes*.) The baby was one month of age and the only relationship she had with her biological mother was in the nursery four days. After the hospital, she was brought directly to the adoption agency and never seen again by the mother, and that the parents, the DeMartinos as you know them, have been the sole ones to care for the child from June 18 of last year until the present, more than a year.

In your opinion, Doctor, would it be a good thing to have the baby given to the biological mother who had a limited relationship?

Before Dr. Libo responded, Mr. Horton objected on the grounds that it hadn't been established that Dr. Libo knew anything about the mother. "Therefore," he said, "the question would simply be irrelevant. I further want to object to this complete line of questioning and move to strike all of the witness's testimony. It is immaterial on the grounds stated before. Whether the DeMartinos are fit or proper is not an issue."

The judge said to Dr. Libo, "You may answer."
A. Your Honor, I think it would be one of the worst things for Lenore to be taken away from her parents at this critical time in her development. Every weight of medical testimony or—

Mr. Rosenblatt interrupted. "I object. Just give your own opinion, Doctor, not any 'weight of medical testimony.'"

"As a pediatrician, I firmly believe that remaining with those who cared for the baby through this critical and formative period of adjustment, behavior, and development of the child's personality can be severely damaged if the child is removed from the home environment and mother figure."

Q. Did I ask if you would willingly come to testify?
A. Yes.
Q. Did I examine your records in any way before you came?

A. No.
Q. Is there any arrangement for you to receive a single cent for your testimony?
A. Not one penny.
Q. For time?
A. It was neither offered nor did I request it.

Cross-examination continued with Mr. Rosenblatt. "In the course of your medical practice," he asked, "how many Colombian children have you treated?"
A. I never counted but am sure, many.
Q. Can I have a name?
A. Just let me finish. I never asked the origin of any child who I've taken cared for, so I really wouldn't know if Smith was a Colombian or if Smith was an American.
Q. To our knowledge, Dr. Libo, have you ever treated a child whose natural mother and natural father were from the country of Colombia?
A. Yes, I have.
Q. How many?
A. I can think of two.
Q. Two of thousands of patients?
A. Probably.
Q. You are aware of the fact that Lenore is Colombian?

"She is what?" shouted Colson.
Ignoring Mr. Colson, Rosenblatt continued:
Q. Her natural father is from Colombia, are you aware?
A. I understand that he was a citizen of Colombia. Is that what you mean sir?

Rosenblatt's annoyance showed. He continued questioning and emphasizing again each word as he spoke.
Q. When is the last time you traveled from New York to another state to give medical testimony in a case free of charge?

A. This is the first time I have ever been called to give medical testimony in a case in another state.

Libo turned to the judge and in a conversational manner said, "For Your Honor's information, I happen—" but was quickly interrupted by Rosenblatt, "Well, Your Honor, I am going to object to this expert witness volunteering information. I am on cross-examination and would appreciate—

The judge nodded affirmation and said, "proceed."

Q. Let me see the records on Lenore. Rosenblatt looked them over and asked, "When Lenore was brought to you on June 19 of 1970, were you aware that the DeMartinos had obtained the child the previous day?"

A. Yes.

Q. How many times while the DeMartinos had Lenore had you been in their home?

A. Two or three.

Q. I would imagine for a short time since you were a busy doctor. Were you there for a specific purpose?

A. Let's see, fifteen or twenty minutes depending upon the situation.

Finally, directing his attention to the doctor's records, Rosenblatt asked, "Do you have one single solitary word where you use the words *emotional development* or where you use any word except *seems withdrawn?* Do you use any words in Lenore's record that are psychological?"

A. Yes, here. "Seems to be adjusting okay."

Mr. Fuchsberg interjected. "When was that?" he asked. "On October 8, 1970," he replied. "If you can read my hieroglyphics, the phrase is there."

Appearing to ignore Dr. Libo, Rosenblatt continued: "What is this word about an accident on this same date?"

A. Oh, I am glad you brought that up.

Rosenblatt rolled his eyes, and in a facetious tone said, "I may be sorry. If I make you glad, I get nervous, Doctor." The people around giggled. Libo answered. "This also refers to the emotional development and physical development of the child. My records say, *accident taught*. It is about this age that I always speak to parents about accident prevention. For instance, when another child is playing, parents have to be careful about little pieces of toys so that the child doesn't swallow them.

(I smiled thinking back on that occasion. Dr. Libo started his little speech, and I interrupted by saying, "Doctor, you went through all this with Linda.)

Q. All you have are the words *accident taught*. "Seems to be adjusting okay."

Dr. Libo pointed to his records, "See, these are—"

Rosenblatt turned in an exasperated manner to the judge and said, "I want the doctor to be responsive" Then back to the doctor: "I did not ask you to interpret your records, Doctor. I asked you a simple question. Did you write the words *emotional development*?

A. "Seems to be adjusting," to me means the child is emotionally up to par for her age.

Q. That is five months?

A. Correct.

Q. At five months of age in November of 1970, a court in the State of New York decided that the child should be returned to its natural mother. Did you know, sir?

Libo testified that he knew nothing about the court order.

Q. Had you ever met or talked to Miss Scarpetta?

A. No.

Q. You have absolutely no idea whether she would be a magnificent or a terrible mother?

A. No, sir.

Q Your information about the DeMartinos is based upon their visits with the baby to your office and two visits to their home.

A It might have been more but no less than two.

Rosenblatt focused on the emotional problems adopted children face as teenagers. Should they be told of the adoption? Would the doctor recommend telling a child that her natural mother changed her mind about the adoption less than one month afterward and fought in every possible court to regain her baby? "Should the DeMartinos tell Lenore that?" he asked.

A. Well, my opinion would be, yes—that they should, yes. Depending what age you talk about—perhaps four of five—the child should be informed that he or she is adopted.

Q. Well, at what age would you recommend that the DeMartinos tell Lenore the full truth because obviously she'd eventually see newspaper accounts. Is that right?

A. I think when a child becomes a responsible individual, perhaps a young adult—

Q. What age are we talking about?

A. Sixteen or seventeen if the child were mature. The child could learn the complete story from the adoptive parents.

Q. For the first sixteen years, the parents should only tell the child about the adoption, period, but should lie about the rest.

A. I never said to lie.

The judge asked if what is told to a sixteen-year-old would help the court determine the matter before it. Rosenblatt, nonetheless, continued with his speculation.

Q. What is the effect, Doctor, of removing a child from a home in Brooklyn where she lived since one month of age and putting the child on a plane and moving to the State of Florida? Does that have any adverse effect?

A. I think as long as the child is with the parents, I can't think of any adverse effects.
Q. You don't know what effects because you have not seen the child since March 27?

Fuchsberg objected. "The doctor answered to the opposite," he shouted.

The judge responded, "He answered," he said.

Rosenblatt kept the doctor on the stand for another ten minutes and questioned about Lenore's health.
Q. Did you ever hospitalize the child?
A. No.
Q. Did you ever refer the child to a psychiatrist of any kind?
A. No.
Q. For testing?
A. No.
Q. Was there any difficulty with the child's feet?
A. Not to my knowledge.
Q. Now, obviously the DeMartinos selected a pediatrician in Florida. Do you know who the pediatrician is or has that doctor ever contacted you?
A. It is possible that the doctor contacted my office. I wouldn't see the transfer of the records, so I don't know who their doctor is.
Mr. Rosenblatt: No further questions, Your Honor.

(Fuchsberg thanked the doctor for coming. As he departed, I hoped that he read the "thank you" on my face as well.

The judge called a recess until 1:30 p.m.. It was hard to believe that only the morning had passed. It felt like I was sitting in that room for two weeks and was exhausted. What happened next proved trying. We entered a private room where Colson obviously made arrangements for sandwiches. I made a beeline for Colson.

"Did you hear what Mr. Rosenblatt said about the orthopedic specialist?" I asked. "Is he suggesting that we neglected Lenore? I took her to a specialist, but Nick felt we should wait to get another opinion." By this time my whole body shook. "Maybe you should contact our doctor and find out if he'll come to testify," I shuddered.

It was obvious that Colson, in that southern drawl of his, said, "Little lady, there is nothing to get so upset about. We have everything under control. You just take a deep breath, have yourself a little something to eat, and you'll feel better."

Well, of course, I couldn't eat. I just sat in the corner and waited for the moments to tick away until the trial began again.

Chapter XIV

The hearing reconvened at 1:30 p.m., and the first witness was Dr. Andrew Samuel Watson. I had never seen or heard of him. Mr. Fuchsberg informed the court that Dr. Watson resided at the Children's Psychiatric Hospital, University of Michigan, and was formerly Assistant Professor of Psychiatry at the University of Pennsylvania. For the past twelve years he was Professor of Psychiatry and Law at the University of Michigan Medical and Law School. He was also a consultant to several government agencies including the juvenile court and the State Department of Health in the State of Michigan. He was a dark-haired, middle-aged, portly man whose bearing spoke self-assurance. Before he testified, Mr. Rosenblatt asked and was granted the right to have the courtroom cleared of any and all medical witnesses who were to testify.

With that out of the way, Fuchsberg began. Mr. Watson said that he familiarized himself with our case and read a copy of the testimony in the New York hearing. "In your opinion," Fuchsberg asked, "what would be the effect of a separation of this child from Mr. and Mrs. DeMartino and a transfer to Miss Scarpetta, the lady who gave birth to her and who never saw her since the day the baby left the hospital? Do you have an opinion, Doctor?"

"If one contrived the most devastating thing to do to a child, it would be to remove her from those who parented her these first thirteen months of life."

"From a medical as well as a factual point of view, is the original lady that birthed the child a complete stranger in these circumstances?"

"Absolutely!" Through a series of questions and

answers, Watson elaborated upon the grief that Lenore would experience if she were separated from us.

Fuchsberg paused for a moment then said, "Dr. Watson, this morning Miss Scarpetta testified here. She stated that she voluntarily surrendered this child and after four to five months of counseling—at least fourteen sessions and several post natal sessions—she placed the child—I think she used the words *in a glass cage* to protect the child from everything. I think that is the substance of what she said." Fuchsberg, who was interrupted by an objection from Mr. Rosenblatt, said, "My first question is merely whether the return has any medical significance. Perhaps the doctor will say, *no*."

"Do you think he will say *no*?" Rosenblatt asked sarcastically.

"I don't know." Fuchsberg responded in a mocking manner. Before they could continue their personal asides, the judge overruled the objection, so Dr. Watson responded:

"As you probably know," he said, "any child reared in a glass cage out of a contact with life and its problems would be in a very bad condition psychologically. I don't need to go any further." After a number of questions related to Lenore's well being and whether Lenore should be removed from our home, Dr. Watson summed up by saying, "it would jeopardize her well being."

Fuchsberg released Dr. Watson for cross-examination by Mr. Rosenblatt. Much to the attorney's chagrin, the doctor testified that he received no fee. So Rosenblatt recouped by accusing him of testifying in the case because of the press coverage which enhanced his prestige. After more superficial questions, Rosenblatt said, "Doctor, let's get down to the nitty-gritty. Counsel asked you—and I noticed in your response, you talked generally—if it's hard for a child of thirteen months to be taken from one situation to another. Are you representing to this court, based upon reasonable psychiatric or medical certainty, that if this particular baby is returned to Olga Scarpetta, this baby will be permanently scarred?"

"We have very few things about which we say with any degree of sureness," he replied. "This is certainly one where I say categorically, a baby of this age removed from a home where she lived her whole life—this child will be permanently scarred. A lot depends on variables. I could evaluate the degree of shock by examining a displaced child."

Q. Doctor, have you ever examined Lenore?
A. Never.
Q. Have you ever examined the DeMartinos?
A. Never.
Q. Have you ever examined Olga Scarpetta?
A. No.

Having made this point, Rosenblatt questioned the doctor about experiences with handling displaced children.

Dr. Watson responded with ease, "We are talking about adaptive stresses, and the clinical knowledge about this problem is known worldwide. Many experts express similar opinions. You probably could not find any issue with more agreement among experts than the risk factors of displacement."

"Are you telling this court that one-year-olds whose parents are killed in accidents grow up manic depressive or psychotic?"

"Those children will grow up with a psychological scar which requires adjustment in many ways."

Next, Rosenblatt asked Dr. Watson what would happen if Jackie Kennedy decided to fire her son's nursemaid after thirteen months of care. Dr. Watson stated emphatically that it would have a devastating effect. Not only had he encountered cases precisely in that category, but was, in fact, working on several because the initial scars were profound. "Wealthy people have problems too," he said.

With that, Rosenblatt turned to the question of when and how to tell a child she is adopted. After some long and lengthy questions and answers, Rosenblatt, using the same expression as before said, "Doctor, getting to the nitty-gritty—aren't you in total speculation? You never saw the baby or examined the DeMartinos. Yet, to determine this little girl's reaction when she is told the whole truth is speculative, not so?"

"I am no more speculating than if I were a pediatrician who would say, `For goodness sake, give your child a small pox inoculation.'"

Rosenblatt hammered away in an attempt to get the doctor to shift direction, but Watson held steadfast and was finally excused as a witness.

Chatter filled the room. The appearance of Dr. Richard Toister, who had been waiting in the hallway as directed, interrupted the onlooker's give-and-take. He was duly sworn in and introduced as a professor of psychology at the University of Miami and practicing child psychologist at the Mailman Center for Child Development at Jackson Memorial Hospital. Before beginning, Colson pointed out to the judge that he only took twelve minutes with the last witness of the thirty-five minutes allotted for cross-examination.

Rosenblatt responded. "Your Honor, I would remind the court that I objected to all this medical testimony."

The judge said, "Let's go," and Dr. Toister began. Colson asked whether he had personally examined Lenore, Linda, Nick, and myself. Toister said that he had not only met with us but that he administered psychological and intellectual tests to each of us. He revealed his findings. Lenore tested normally for her age. I scored above average, and Nick scored in superior intellectuality. Rosenblatt protested when Linda was mentioned, so her scoring was withheld although I found out later that she tested in the superior range for her age.

Colson's questions led Dr. Toister's answers to be consistent with the previous medical witness, Dr. Watson. When Rosenblatt cross-examined, asked Dr. Toister whether the tests measured our level of maturity. Toister replied that he found us both developmentally normal.

"Let me ask you this question, Dr. Toister," Rosenblatt continued. "Mr. DeMartino is thirty-eight, a practicing lawyer for sixteen years, has a law degree from a prestigious New York university, and is of better than average intelligence. The court of his state where he is licensed to practice law says, `You must return the baby to its natural mother.' He takes his wife, my client's baby, his other adopted child, and flees to Florida where he is not a practicing attorney, where he has not taken the bar examination, where he has some kind of a job obviously making a great deal less than he was making in New York. Does this flight represent emotional stability in a thirty-eight-year-old adult?"

"Yes. He acted as a father," said Toister in a very calm and deliberate tone.

Rosenblatt unabashed, pushed on:
Q. Are you able to say, based on reasonable psychological certainty, that if the child were returned to Miss Scarpetta, that Lenore would definitely be adversely affected?
A. I think the possibility is high. There will be stress, and reaction to that stress causes permanent difficulty.
Q. The reaction to stress has to be speculation because

you have no way of knowing how this baby would react in Miss Scarpetta's home in New York, do you?
A. On the contrary, we know this is a normal baby who developed normally. We know she is with a family that is normal and provides good care. We know she is attached to her mother. I would say it's a probability there would be some detrimental effects to this child.

Rosenblatt was not ready to leave the subject; however, he once again brought up the question of Jackie Kennedy and the effect on John Jr. if his nurse were fired. He also asked the doctor whether he had ever tested a child who was born of Colombian parents. His response to both questions was consistent with those given before.

How little grasp Rosenblatt had of the situation, I thought, if he believed that wealth or lineage made a difference in the world of a thirteen-month-old. But, I must admit that when he projected into the future and asked the doctor some questions about Lenore's feelings concerning her adoption, that hit a tender area. The medical experts indicated that they did not feel the truth would be a problem if handled correctly, and they believed that Nick and I were capable of handling the truth correctly. It was Dr. Toister, however, who made me more comfortable and confident.

"Isn't it typical to wonder about who a child's real parents are?" Rosenblatt asked.

"Yes, the important question is handling those feelings, not having those feelings," Toister responded.

"Lenore is going to be an adult much longer than she is going to be a child," Rosenblatt pointed out.

"But her childhood is precursory to adulthood, and her feelings and emotions are the product of early development." With a great deal of relief and admiration, I listened to Toister. Then Dr. Toister was excused, and Dr. Ben Sheppard was called. As he entered, a hum of excitement rose. Dr. Sheppard, a senior citizen, shuffled to the stand. His appearance was disheveled. He sat slowly, placed his elbows on the arms of the chair, folded his hands and leaned forward. I must admit he made a rather unimpressive sight, yet by the response in the room, I could tell he was some one to be reckoned with.

Mr. Colson broke the hum: "Everyone in the community knows Dr. Ben Sheppard because he has been in pediatrics for forty years, he is a Diplomat of the Board of Pediatrics, he was active in polio care in this community, he placed the first child in Variety Children's Hospital, he has a fellowship in psychiatry at Menningers Clinic, he was a juvenile judge for seven years, and he is the executive director of the Catholic Welfare Bureau in charge of the medical problems for adopted children in this community."

Rosenblatt, with a tone of respect in his voice, interjected: "and also the doctor who taught me workmen's compensation in law school, and I never practiced it."

Colson began his direct examination:
Q. Dr. Sheppard, tell the judge what is best for Lenore.
A. Judge, based on forty years of working with children and supervising foster and adoptive homes, following children from their homes through the clinic, through the hospital, it's my opinion that the best interests of Lenore would be served by permitting her to remain with the present adoptive parents. My studies led me to believe the most formative time of a child's future life runs from the fifth or sixth to eighteenth months. I'm a firm follower of Dr. Spitz and feel that taking a child from her present environment into a totally alien one would be traumatic, might lead to chronic illness, and certainly might leave scars for future interpersonal relationships.

Mr. Rosenblatt: Excuse me, Dr. Sheppard. I'm going to object to the entire line of questioning. It's cumulative. The doctor is narrating a summary of testimony constantly using the word *might* which is not the test in this court. It hasn't been brought out he has examined anyone, and we have had his testimony already, and it's cumulative.

Mr. Colson: Your Honor, six more doctors will take five minutes a piece—exactly what we took last time—to testify. We ask for five minutes of testimony each.

Mr. Rosenblatt: I think, Your Honor, if they seriously intend to call that many doctors, they make a farce of this proceeding, and you can get forty doctors on the other side of the question as well.

Mr. Colson: Try, if you will, to get forty.

Mr. Rosenblatt: That is not the issue. It's an issue of common sense. One doctor made your point. Why six more?

Mr. Colson: May we proceed, Your Honor?

The judge: I'm inclined to think we are getting—

Mr. Rosenblatt: I'm calling one doctor.

The judge: It's cumulative testimony. He has a valid objection. This could go on for a week.

Mr. Colson: No, sir.

Mr. Rosenblatt: Dr. Sheppard, of course, is well known in this community and well respected, and counsel blatantly attempts, as I see it, to impress and influence this court by calling big names to say that in their opinion, maybe, the return of baby Lenore to my client might—I emphasize the highly speculative *might*—do some psychological harm.

The judge: I am not basing my ruling on any such basis. I'm basing it on—

Mr. Rosenblatt: Nonetheless, I resent the attempt.

The judge: It's cumulative evidence. He signaled Colson to continue who, to speed things up, asked the witness two more questions and then turned him over to Rosenblatt. He pointed out to the court that he took only four minutes with Dr. Sheppard.

Rosenblatt's questioning of Dr. Sheppard was rather uneventful. He covered the same ground and asked the same questions. Dr. Carolyn Rabinowitz, a young attractive woman introduced as a teaching member of the University of Miami School of Medicine in child psychiatry was sworn in. Although Mr. Colson's questioning was brief, he did manage to cover the same ground as the other medical witnesses. The answers were all on target for our side.

Mr. Rosenblatt, too, kept to his same line of questioning but seemed curt. Dr. Rabinowitz, who spoke softly, hadn't an opportunity to complete answers. Colson objected that Rosenblatt was argumentative. So Rosenblatt gave the witness time, and the trial continued with Rosenblatt hammering the witness about never examining "Baby Scarpetta," and the testimony was purely speculative. The witness was excused, and the judge announced a short recess. Mr. Rosenblatt requested that upon return to call a witness out of turn.

I don't know how long the recess lasted. It seemed over before it began. Neither Nick nor I left the room. If the legal system worked to confuse people, it did its job well. If it posed as just, New York Courts proved adverse to the system of agencies, legal adoption, and parental rights. Were we winning, or, God forbid, losing our Lenore? The battle of my and Nick's lifetime, the upheaval, the havoc played also for Lenore's sister, Linda. The judge's bench, witness stand, the contentious tables from which the DeMartino and Scarpetta teams waged battle, rosewood paneled room, fancy railings behind which separated officials from curious people in wooden seats—these made a stage for emotional devastation as a theme. I tried desperately to get my thoughts in order. In the midst of confusion, I heard Dr. Leonard Haber sworn in.

Dr. Haber appeared rather nondescript. He was of medium height, slightly overweight, and could easily get lost in a crowd. At Rosenblatt's direction, Dr. Haber informed the court of his educational background. He received his college and master's degree from the City College of New York and his M.D. from Adelphi University in clinical psychology. His professional experience included work at various Veterans' Administration Hospitals. He instructed at Adelphi University in the psychology department, was a supervising clinical psychologist with the V.A., and director of Psychological Associates of New York. In private practice, he was a clinical psychologist and dealt with problems that arise between partners in business, a husband and wife, or a parent and a child. When Haber finished, Rosenblatt zeroed in on the case:

Q. Lenore was born on May18th, 1970, in the City of New York. Four days later, the natural mother, Olga Scarpetta, transferred her to an adoption agency. During the thirteen months that Mr. and Mrs. DeMartino had the child, they provided normal care. The court ruled that this thirteen month old baby be surrendered to Miss Scarpetta. Do you have an opinion that this transfer would do any permanent, long range damage to the baby?

A. With comparable mothering, the child would have no permanent damage.

Q. Could you explain your conclusion?

A. The trying time, the danger, the pain, and the

suffering belong to the adults in a situation like this. They know what is happening, and to all involved in a custody dispute, it makes a substantial difference who raises the child. My feeling is that at thirteen months, since the child has limited awareness and recognition, it's doubtful the transfer would matter if the rearing in a new environment is properly done. It's also my belief that damage is more likely related to the nature or quality of mothering than to the question of who does the mothering.

Q. Do you feel, assuming Miss Scarpetta could give the child equal care both in a material and love sense, the transference would cause any substantial temporary problems?

A. I assume that a child would be aware of a change in surroundings. I find it difficult to predict what the individual reaction would be or how long a child might react with some discomfort or stress. My belief would be that given reasonably good handling, no serious or lasting difficulty would arise and go on indefinitely.

Q. Before I contacted you, were you aware of this case from the press and from other sources?

A. Yes.

Q. Did you, before I contacted you, take a public position on the question asked today?

A. Yes. The issue of Baby Lenore came up on a radio program I host and have for five and a half years every Saturday. A listener questioned me about—

Mr. Colson: I object to hearsay.

Mr. Rosenblatt: This is the doctor's response.

Mr. Colson: About someone who called.

Mr. Rosenblatt: I'm making the point that Dr. Haber took a public position over the airwaves.

Mr. Colson: We heard that.

Mr. Rosenblatt: I want him to explain what he said publically, judge.

Mr. Colson: We object. What he said outside of this courtroom is not important.

Mr. Rosenblatt: It's important that a witness gave an opinion before he had any interest in the case or knew he was going to testify. I think that is particularly pertinent, judge.

Mr. Colson: I wasn't there to hear it and cross examine him, judge.

Mr. Rosenblatt: You are here now to cross-examine.

Mr. Colson: Not if I didn't hear what he said.

The Judge: I sustain the objection.

Q. Let me ask you, Doctor, if that radio response was essentially the same as in this courtroom today?

A. Yes.

Mr. Rosenblatt: No further questions.

I thought it ironic that Rosenblatt did not ask the one question asked of all the other doctors: Do you have any experience dealing with Colombian children? Not that I ever saw the pertinence of the question, but, I assumed, he would make us all see his point sooner or later.

Colson began questioning.

Q. Are you a medical doctor?

A. That is correct.

Q. You are not a psychiatrist and are not in any medical schools teaching or any hospitals in the community in child psychiatry. True, sir?

A. That is correct.

Q. Dr. Haber, will you be willing and are you capable of testing Miss Scarpetta as to whether she is an average, normal mother who should have this child?

Mr. Rosenblatt: I object because counsel filed papers about testing Miss Scarpetta but never set for hearing before the court. It's quite late in the day to ask this doctor such a question.

Mr. Colson: Nobody compelled us to have our side

examined, yet we did.

Mr. Rosenblatt: You apparently felt it would strengthen your case.

Mr. Colson: Absolutely. I just wanted to know if Dr. Haber is competent to do it.

The Judge: Mr. Colson can ask the question, Mr. Rosenblatt.

Dr. Haber: Yes, I could conduct an examination and professionally determine her fitness for mothering?

Q. Would you consider comparable mothering for a baby going from the DeMartinos, a home in Miami with a mother, a sister, and a father, to an apartment in New York with an unwed mother, no father, no sister, a Spanish-speaking maid, a working mother, and a different culture? Is that comparable mothering?

A. It's possible. I couldn't say for sure because I know none of the people involved.

The witness was excused, and all eyes followed Stella Chess as she entered the room from the hallway and took the witness seat. Fuchsberg said, "Brevity is the catchword. I would like to introduce Dr. Chess. I have pages of background, but I'll just name a few things."

The judge asked the witness to please state her name.

"Stella Chess, M.D." she responded

The judge signaled Fuchsberg to continue.

"Dr. Chess, you've practiced medicine since 1939; you are a full professor of child psychiatry at New York University Medical College; you did extensive research under grants from the National Institute of Mental Health, the Health Research Council of the City of New York, the Children's Bureau of the Department of Health Education and Welfare; you are the author of these books (a pile of the doctor's books sat on the table) among others that I borrowed from the University of Miami; and appended here are fifty-six articles you wrote for major medical journals. With all due modesty, is that accurate?

A. Yes, that is accurate.

Q. Dr. Chess, did you go to the home of the DeMartinos and examine Baby Lenore, her sister, and parents?

A. Yes, I did.

Q. Who decided to use the home setting?

A. That was my decision.

Q. Would you tell us—please try to condense—your conclusions about the situation of the baby and any relevant history with respect to her care?

A. Let me start with the present because that was the first thing I evaluated. I saw Lenore at home because I did not want to introduce extraneous factors and strangeness. At thirteen months, physically, she is appropriate. She is a little precocious, walks well, and uses a few words ahead of her age group. Effectively, her emotional interchange also showed age expectancy. She has clear affectionate ties with Mrs. DeMartino, with Mr. DeMartino, and with Linda, who was very much present during our examination. Lenore warmed up rather quickly to me as a stranger. She went back to home base occasionally, to Mrs. DeMartino, as one would expect a normal child of that age to do. The emotional status and health of Lenore are normal and an integral part of this home setting.

Linda, who is three months short of five—

"Excuse me," interrupted Rosenblatt, "I'll object to any testimony about Linda as not pertinent and material."

The judge stated that if the testimony had a direct relationship upon Lenore, it might be relevant. If it was just independent observation, he would sustain the objection.

With that in mind, Fuchsberg asked Dr. Chess

if what she had to say about Linda had any relevance. She said that she was about to describe Lenore's imitation of Linda.

"To which I'll object," shouted Rosenblatt.

Once again Fuchsberg asked Dr. Chess, "Is that relevant?"

Rosenblatt, obviously annoyed, turned to the witness, "Excuse me, Doctor, we have a judge. It may be relevant to you and it may not be relevant to me. This child's reaction to her sister and Linda's age are irrelevant. I object."

"She describes," interjected Judge Cullen, "the child's reaction to her sister is relevant, so I overrule your objection."

"That means you can answer," said Fuchsberg.

"My point is that Lenore's capacity for imitation is part of her development. Linda brought a book to read, and Lenore got her own and turned the pages. A youngster of Lenore's age imitates people around, and that is the way the child learns patterns of life in a family and culture. In short, I've stated essentially the observational part of my examination."

"What else can you tell us, Doctor?" Fuchsberg asked.

"Records show that Lenore was on the small side when she came to the DeMartinos and a bit slow in new situations, a bit irregular in sleep patterns, and very much in the need of nurturing. The interaction with the DeMartinos was supportive and effective. The youngster turned to her parents' side, lifted her arms to be picked up, and clearly had warm interaction with both parents.

"For a child initially a bit slow in new situations, I judge that the security in the DeMartino home played an important part in Lenore's sense of ease, security, and happiness. I observed her ability to interact with a stranger without fear, and judged that a strong development of comfort and confidence existed in the home environment."

Fuchsberg asked how she became a witness. She had first been contacted by a Mr. Chaimberlain and then Mr. Fuchsberg himself. She never met either of them and received the background information by messenger. When agreeing to testify, she insisted on permission to visit with the child first. She did not ask for nor receive money other than reimbursement for travel expenses.

"Dr. Chess, because you read the background papers, you know the length of time this child lived with the parents, and I'm talking about the DeMartinos. You know how brief and under what circumstances the child knew the original mother. I would ask this pointed question, if I may. Would it be in the best interests of the baby to take her from the only parents she ever had, the DeMartinos, and place her with Miss Scarpetta?"

"I definitely do not think it would be in the best interests of Lenore to move," she replied. At the beginning of her medical career, the first youngsters she saw were children placed and re-placed in foster homes. They developed personality disorders, had difficulty developing strong attachments and patterns of functioning. The trend in working with children has been to place babies in permanent homes as early as possible and make changes only under dire circumstances such as death or severe illness of parents.

Fuchsberg established that Dr. Chess was Chairman of the American Psychiatric Association, the most recognized association of psychiatrists in the country. He asked if permanency represented accepted standards recognized by professional psychiatric associations and medical opinion in this country and throughout the world. She answered *yes* for the country but could not tell him about world standards.

"I notice some of your works are distributed in foreign countries."

"Yes, but that doesn't tell what they think; it tells me they read."

Fuchsberg smiled sheepishly and said, "I'm glad you are so careful." He thanked Dr. Chess for coming and turned her over to Rosenblatt for cross-examination.

Rosenblatt asked if the first call she got to testify came from Mr. Fuchsberg's office.

"Mr. Chamberlain was not in his office," she said.

"Oh," Rosenblatt observed. "Is the gentleman on the Save the Baby Lenore Committee?"
A. I believe so. (I realized she had been saying Chamberlain, but meant Chaimowitz, Lenny Chaimowitz, good old "one and one" came to our rescue again.)
Q. Didn't it strike you as odd that a stranger to these proceedings would call about your availability to testify?
A. No. I am known as a child advocate, and he introduced himself as a committee member advocating children's needs, so the call didn't seem strange at all.
Q. And this Committee to Save Baby Lenore got quite a lot of press in the New York, is that correct?
A. I couldn't answer about the amount of publicity.
Q. Of course, you knew, didn't you, even without examining the DeMartinos or the child that you were philosophically in sympathy with their position?

Fuchsberg objected: The question leads the witness.

The Judge: Sustained.
Q. You pretty well decided that unless the tests really

were surprising, that you would be a witness for the DeMartinos when you came down from New York?

A. Yes. My view is that a child happily functioning and handled well in a home, a child at an age where movement is critical, should not be moved unless there is some compelling reason like abuse, illness, or death of parents.

Q. Do you think it a compelling reason that the New York courts ordered the DeMartinos to return the baby?

A. I'm talking about compelling reasons that make a child's home unfit.

Q. I'm talking about compelling legal reasons, Dr. Chess.

A. I can't answer about legality, only about medical situations.

Q. Were you aware of those orders by the highest court of the State of New York?

A. I make—

Mr. Fuchsberg interrupted. "The highest court of the State of New York never included the DeMartinos ever, didn't serve them or inform them," he said. "I must object."

Dr. Chess nonetheless responded, "I didn't try to understand the legalities," she said. "Surrendering Lenore was a medical issue."

"Are you able," Rosenblatt continued, "to predict with reasonable medical certainty what would happen to this baby if she was, in fact, transferred to Miss Scarpetta, assuming Miss Scarpetta loved the child and met all her physical and developmental needs?"

Dr. Chess explained that one can't always predict an individual case. She gave an example of a child eating plaster. He had a fairly good chance of lead poisoning though not a 100 percent chance. But she would insist on her prediction to not let him eat plaster.

Rosenblatt finally asked, "Have you treated children whose natural parents were Colombian as opposed to American?"

A. No.

Q. Of course, you never examined or talked to Miss Scarpetta?

A. No.

Q. For all you know, she might qualify more as a mother than Mrs. DeMartino?

A. I can't make any statements about Miss Scarpetta.

As with other psychiatrists, Rosenblatt questioned Dr. Chess about telling children about their adoption. At what age should they be told and should the DeMartinos tell Lenore the full truth that Miss Scarpetta, steadfast as a rock, wanted her baby back and these people not only refused but would not let the mother see her baby. When, if ever, should they tell Lenore those facts?

Fuchsberg objected. The question was argumentative and full of misstatements. "On second thought, I withdraw the objection."

Dr. Chess responded, "I would say whenever the question comes up. In general, children's questions should be answered when asked."

Asked how would Lenore react as a teenager, Dr. Chess said there was no way to know specifically but could speak in probabilities. If the parent-child relationship remained strong, whatever issue came up would be minimally traumatic. If the child-parent relationship weakened, then a high probability existed that trauma would occur.

"Of course," Rosenblatt said, "there is not any way to predict six or seven years from now based upon one visit, how their parent-child relationship will be?"

"At this point it is solid. What it will be at age

ten, again, I can't say."

Rosenblatt questioned Dr. Chess about identity and Columbian heritage. His questions fired rapidly, and Dr. Chess had difficulty completing answers. Finally Fuchsberg interrupted. "May we have one question at a time?" he asked.

"Are you having a good time, Mr. Fuchsberg?" Rosenblatt fired back.

"No. I'm trying to be a lawyer," Fuchsberg responded, "and ask you to be one as well."

"Address your remarks to the judge. Don't engage in chitchat because I'm not impressed by it," Rosenblatt retorted.

"Okay, okay," the judge said much like someone separating two misbehaving children.

"Dr. Chess, is it normal during an argument for an adopted child to say, you are not my real father, and you are not my real mother. Get off my back?"

"If the relationship is weak, 'You can't tell me what to do' or 'I'll run away from home,' is common, but the threats have nothing to do with adoptive or non adoptive status—at least, in my experience. The child's behavior is influenced by how strong the parent-child relationship is."

"Of course," Rosenblatt pointed out, "the situation I gave you would not ordinarily end up in your office because it's not major if a kid said something like that."

"Can we discuss something of substance?" she asked.

"Of course. The majority of situations when compared to this adoption are commonplace. In the majority of cases, the natural parents give the baby away and that is the end. But in this case, when Lenore learns that mommy made a mistake and changed her mind and tried and tried and tried to get her baby back, don't you think tremendous resentment will build toward the adopting parents?"

Dr. Chess pointed out that for Lenore her adoptive mother would be *mommy* and that a great deal depended on her view of the mother-child relationship.

Rosenblatt wanted to know whether Dr. Chess believed any serious setbacks would affect a baby returned at five months of age. The doctor replied that a five-month-old already shows attachments and changing environment would not be the best plan, but thirteen months would be a particularly bad time.

Rosenblatt asked, "Are you saying all children face permanent psychic scars from momentary upheaval in their lives at a very early age?"

"Not all children. I certainly hope, Mr. Rosenblatt, that traumatic changes would be avoided whenever possible."

Rosenblatt asked the doctor whether she had any continuing relationships with the adoption agencies in New York. She responded *no*. He then turned to the judge. "That is all I have." The witness was excused, and Colson quickly asked the judge if the other doctors could come in from the hall. With approval, Colson introduced Dr. Albert Solnit, psychiatrist and Director of the Child Study Center at Yale University; Dr. Peter P. Schneidau, director of the inpatient service of New York Hospital of New York; and Dr. Jay Katz, a professor at Yale Medical School. Colson explained that the judge ruled there be no more medical testimony. It would be redundant. In support of our case, Colson submitted their reports. They could not be placed into evidence but were accepted by the judge, who, in turn, explained to the doctors that he would have heard them if the court had time. Since they were "plowing the same ground," he felt compelled to make his ruling. He thanked them for coming. Colson's last request was to note that each of the doctors came without any promise of money and would maintain basically the same position as Dr. Chess and the others. I was over whelmed by the magnitude of so many prominent doctors appearing on behalf of Lenore.

Fuchsberg explained that the next witness, Mr. Spencer, would testify that in the courts of New York, he bought motions for the DeMartinos to intervene and the orders in those cases were rejected. With the approval of the opposing attorney, Mr. Zalk, it was so stipulated, and, therefore, not necessary to call Mr. Spencer.

Professor Henry Foster of the N.Y.U. Law School was then introduced. He came to clarify New York Law, "If Your Honor has questions?"

Judge Cullen indicated that it wasn't necessary and told Colson to proceed and Jean DeMartino was called as a witness.

Chapter XV

"Do you swear that the testimony you are about to give is the truth, the whole truth, and nothing but the truth, so help you God?" (So help me God? I stared blankly at Colson. Was it just last night that Nick and I and the kids knelt at an altar rail and asked God for help in a beautiful church, one to become our church? We were alone before the altar and though we whispered, our voices echoed through the high rafters. Moonlight shown through a stained glass window above a cross. The eyes of God gazed upon a loving family nearing the end of its trial. How small and insignificant I felt and yet felt a oneness with God. My eyes followed the ornate etchings which formed an arch on the rear wall of the altar, and although they were not familiar, nevertheless, gave me a sense of well being and of a journey's end. When Colson coughed nervously, my mind sprung back to the courtroom.) I blurted out, "Yes, I do."

Colson didn't want to disclose our specific address and began by asking if I lived in a home in Miami.
A. Yes, I do, sir.
Q. Describe the home and yard, will you, please?
A. It has a living room, dining area, kitchen, Florida room, two nice sized bedrooms, and a bath. There is a yard in front of the house and in back.
Q. Who lives with you?
A. My husband and two children.
Q. For the record, what are the children's names?
A. My oldest daughter Linda is four and my youngest daughter Lenore is thirteen months.
Q. What is your age please, madam?
A. I'm 35.

Q. Mrs. DeMartino, where did you grow up?
A. In New York.
Q. How far did you go in school?
A. I went to college for two years.
Q. And while you were in high school, were you elected to any offices?
A. I was vice president of the student body.
Q. When did you and Mr. DeMartino marry?
A. 1956, January 21.
Q. Is that your only marriage?
A. Yes, sir.
Q. For both?
A. Yes, sir.
Q. What religion are you?
A. Roman Catholic.

Colson asked about my parish in Brooklyn. I explained that Father Racigliano, the pastor of our neighborhood church, offered his services and support through the Save the Baby Lenore Committee. Throughout this tug of war for my Lenore, the committee, our priest, family, and friends threaded the needle that sewed our well being and emotional stability to the fabric of family.

"Now, madam," he continued, "how long have you been in Miami?"
A. Over two months. (And time away from the stress of publicity, interviews, invasions of privacy, legal setbacks, confrontational lawyers, and crank telephone calls. The only negative: I missed Nick though we talked on the phone daily until he joined us.)
Q. When you first came, what immediate family came along?
A. My children and my sister-in-law and her daughter.
Q. Tell the court about the others in your immediate family, your parents, and relatives.
A. My mother and father are visiting.

Q. Do they know Lenore?
A. Oh, yes, and love her very much.
Q. Does Lenore recognize them?
A. Very definitely. She has a special attachment to her grandfather who is retired and visits often.

Colson asked about the rest of the family and I explained that Lenore had a close relationship with them all—her aunts in particular. He then asked about our ability to have natural children. I had three unsuccessful pregnancies. With two healthy, happy daughters to raise, I'd not thought about the emotional toll of those miscarriage years, the heartbreak and depression Nick helped me through though, I'm sure, the times were hard for him as well. My voice trailed, and Colson asked me to speak up. I sat erect and listened attentively while he continued.

After establishing that both Linda and Lenore came to us from the Spence-Chapin Adoption Service, he asked, "When you adopt a child through an agency, do they investigate before either child is placed?"
A. Oh, yes, a great deal of investigation. (Not to mention long, pensive delays and difficult waiting periods for two people who wanted nothing more than to become loving parents. We have so much to give, and the investigators seemed unable to evaluate anything besides material possessions and clean home environment.)
Q. What were the highlights of the investigations for both children?
A. We were asked for medical reports. Had to show financial stability. They looked at living space and inquired about furniture purchases and immediate family support. Sometimes I felt they overlooked matters of the heart.

"Keep your voice up," Colson prodded.
We were asked for medical reports; We were asked to

get a letter from our pastor indicating we were in good standing. We were visited at home, and we were to have a special room for the youngster. We visited the agency so they could determine our knowledge of child-rearing, and we presented income tax reports as proof of our financial status and ability to support children. And we waited interminably."

Q. After you got Linda, was an additional investigation conducted for Lenore?

A. There were home studies; social workers came after the placement to see how my children adjusted. (Oh, hi, daddy. Mommy told me I could answer the phone. The lady from the adoption agency is coming today. Are you coming home to have lunch with mommy and Lenore and me? Oh goodie. When the lady gets here, we can have a party.) "Keep your voice up," Colson prodded once more.

"To see how the children adjusted," I said in a louder tone.

Q. Approximately how many visits were made?

A. The agency made three home study visits.

Q. In the adoption of Lenore, did you pick her, or was she picked out for you?

A. We spoke to the social worker and waited almost two years for Lenore because the agency sought to place the child in a home they felt most compatible. (Though we did not pick her, from the moment Nick and I saw Lenore, we knew—we held her little, warm body and knew.)

Q. So when Lenore was picked after her birth, you were advised and told you were qualified by the Spence-Chapin Agency to have this particular child, is that right?

A. Yes, sir. (The agency surely decided we were the right parents, but I think God brought Lenore. Nick felt closer than if Lenore were our own bloodline. If a man shines, he did with both our girls. I could never understand why the court branded us strangers to the blood.)

Q. Mrs. DeMartino, when you went for Lenore, who went with you?

A. My husband, Linda, and my mother.

Q. Does Linda, at four, know she is adopted?

A. Yes, sir.

Q. Did she know where she was going when you picked up Lenore?

A. Yes. It was an exciting day for her. (The image of Linda smiling and holding her sister for one brief moment at the agency will remain in my mind's eye until the day I die.)

Q. When you returned home with Baby Lenore, who was there?

A. Well, Linda told friends, and they lined up outside to meet her baby sister. We invited family and friends to have sandwiches and coffee and celebrate the occasion in our home.

Q. Does Lenore recognize Linda as her sister?

A. Oh, yes, very definitely.

Q. What do they do together?

A. Well, they play together. Lenore mimics Linda a lot. They eat together. That was a big thing in their lives. Lenore now has table food, and they sit together. They enjoy wearing the same type of clothes and playing in the yard. They bathe together and have a full sister relationship. (Mommy, I can't believe she's really here! Mommy is she really my sister? Of course, darling, she's our daughter now and that makes her your sister. I mean, will she be with us forever and ever?)

"Now as to Mr. DeMartino" Colson said in a rather loud voice to get my attention.

I tried listening carefully to a series of questions which added up to Nick being a lawyer and doing trial work in New York City. Then Colson established that Nick followed me here and had been here for the past few weeks. Our home in New York was to be sold and our furniture to be shipped to Miami.

"What will be the length of your say in Florida?"

"Florida is my home," I answered. (I never realized how much enjoyment bath time with the girls laughing and catching bubbles and splashing in the tub. The few weekends when Nick bathed them, I felt almost jealous watching the fun.)

"What about the future?" he asked.

"Florida is my home," I repeated.

"Regardless of the outcome of this litigation?"

(What did he mean, "regardless of the outcome?" Florida was my home, Lenore's home, our home!) "Florida is my home," I said once more with an air of finality. My message was loud and clear. Colson got me to say that we had changed our car license plates, took the Florida driving tests, and secured new drivers' licenses. We registered to vote and become members of our neighborhood church. I reported that the children loved it here and were quite healthy and doing fine.

Colson then established that Lenore lived with us continuously from the day we brought her home, and that I was and always had been a full-time mother and that it was my future intention to continue to be one.

Then he asked whether Miss Scarpetta personally asked about visiting with Lenore. I responded strongly, "Never! Never have I been asked by Miss Scarpetta."

Referring to the secret meeting in Zalk's office, he asked, "At that meeting, did you hear Miss Scarpetta asked to undergo psychological testing or visit a psychiatrist or read books on the subject? Were you at such a meeting?

A. Yes.

Q. Did any of that happen?

A. No, it did not. She refused.

Q. Did your lawyer ask her to do various things in that line?

A. Yes, sir. He did.

Q. Let's go on, ma'am. Are there any serious problems noticeable in the children's relationship with you or your husband?

A. No. I would say ours are happy children though Lenore was a very sensitive child and very small when we brought her home. In early feedings, I attend her needs. Also, Nick and I set up an intercom between our room and hers. We monitored, provided love and security, and modified our attention to her need to grow and be independent.

"What would happen," Colson continued, "if you walked into my living room with Lenore and I'm there, a complete stranger? What would happen if you left the room?"

"If I left the room, she would become very upset. She'd cry."

Colson asked about Lenore's baptism, and I explained that she had already been baptized by the agency, but we nevertheless spoke to Pastor Racigliano and had a special blessing ceremony so that we could give Lenore Godparents. We had to wait three weeks for her Godfather, her cousin Stephen, to get leave from the Marine Corp.

"When Linda came to your home as an adopted child, who named her?" he continued.

A. I did.

Q. And when Lenore came to your home as an adopted child, who named her?

A. I did.

Q. Spell Lenore for us.

A. L-e-n-o-r-e.

Q. And is that different from the name Leonor, Miss Scarpetta's mother, spelled for the record L-e-o-n-o-r?

A. Yes, it's different.

Q. On any occasion, did the adoption agency tell you a name to give the child?

A. No, sir, they did not. They said her birth certificate showed "Female Scarpetta."

Q. Was any jewelry offered by any adoption agency?

A. No, sir.

Q. Or discussed with you?

A. Never.

    Rosenblatt objected to the materiality of the questions. The judge nodding his head said, "Let's move ahead."

Q. Mrs. DeMartino, when was the first time you heard of litigation to remove Lenore from the DeMartino family?

A. I don't remember the exact date, but about two or three days before Thanksgiving. I remember . . . ("Come on, Linda, I'll race you around the corner to school, and when you get home, we'll go for fur-lined boots you've wanted." "Do you mean it, mommy? Really, today?" "Mommy took Lenore to the doctor yesterday, but this afternoon we'll go for boots and shop for turkey day. We'll have a fun time, I promise.")

Q. Mrs. DeMartino, please speak up. Were you or your husband a party to any litigation between Spence-Chapin Adoption Agency and Miss Scarpetta?

A. No. We didn't know about it.

Q. Were you ever served with any subpoena or summons for a lawsuit?

A. No, sir.

Q. Since Lenore's placement, were you and Mr. DeMartino ever served an order to do anything with the baby?

A. No, sir.

Q. Until this hearing today, have you ever had your story told before a judge or in court?

A. Never.

Q. Has any lawyer ever asked about the best interests of Lenore in your behalf?

A. Never.

Colson nodded and said, "That is all we have at this time."

I sighed with relief, slumped back in my chair, and welcomed a coming break. When Rosenblatt approached, I realized there was not going to be one and braced myself. Rosenblatt began immediately:

Q. Mrs. DeMartino, you know from reading testimony in the New York case that the agency knew on June 23 that Miss Scarpetta revoked her consent and wanted her baby back. Yet, you testified the agency did not tell you at that time?

A. The agency knew Miss Scarpetta vacillated which is the case with many mothers. They sought to save Nick and me from undue emotional stress.

Q. From June 23 onward, Miss Scarpetta never changed her mind. She wanted her baby. You know now, don't you?

A. I only know her testimony indicated she had many visits with the agency.

Q. Did she change her mind after any of those many visits?

A. The transcript did not say when she reached a conclusion, sir.

Q. And you are upset with the agency for not telling you in June or July or September, not only about wanting it back, but also about legal proceedings instituted in the Supreme Court of the State of New York? (I wanted to tell Rosenblatt how privileged I felt that Lenore came to Nick and me because her mother voluntarily gave her up. I wanted to ask if he ever had a child torn from his arms. I wanted to ask if he believed in Lenore's best interest. I wanted to ask if he even cared about the DeMartino family.)

      Colson objected, saying that my feelings toward the agency were immaterial. The judge sustained his objection, and Rosenblatt continued.

Q. How did the agency inform you about the legal proceedings?
A. They informed my husband. They called his office.
Q. Did the agency give background information about the natural mother?
A. Yes.
Q. You knew that the natural mother and father were Colombian?
A. Yes, sir.
Q. You or your husband never adopted Lenore, did you?
A. If we could legally adopt her, we would have.
Q. Of course, the first child had a normal adoption. Is that correct?
A. Yes, no litigation, so we adopted her legally.
Q. How long did her adoption take to formalize?
A. I think—I'm not sure, sir—nine months to a year.
Q. So you know that you could not formalize an adoption until at least six months passed?
A. I know we could not get legal papers.
Q. How much did you pay the agency for Lenore?
A. What difference does money make? Do you wish a price placed on Lenore so people see how painful any loss of a precious baby may be? My children are not on sale.
Q. Please, no lectures, Mrs. DeMartino. I don't mean to upset you. Please answer the question or I'll ask the judge to have you do so.
A. $650.00.

Q. Thank you. How much did you pay the agency for Linda?
A. I believe, $590. I'm not sure.
Q. What would explain the difference in price?
A. Whimsy.
Q. Please answer, Mrs. DeMartino.
A. At a nonprofit organization, some pay nothing and others pay a maximum fee based upon a fraction of income.
Q. What is your percentage?
A. I don't know, sir. The Spence-Chapin Agency better provides information about charges. Nick and I focused on adopting a second child. The money stayed completely out of the picture, and the agency worked with us cooperatively.
Q. Okay. Can we go on to where you were born?
A. New York City.
Q. Have you ever lived any place other than New York City until you came to Florida?
A. No sir, I haven't.
(I noticed that Rosenblatt asked questions in a more rapid way as he'd done with others.)
Q. Did you meet your husband in New York?
A. Yes, sir. We met—
Q. Throughout your marriage, you and your husband resided in the State of New York?
A. Yes, sir. In a section of Brooklyn—
Q. If the New York Courts said, "Keep the baby," would you have come to Florida?
A. We talked often about coming to Florida, and—
Q. I'm asking now, Mrs. DeMartino, if there were no litigation or problems, would you be a resident of Florida?
(More out of a sense of defiance than anything else, I stared back, head on, and said clearly and deliberately—)

A. Yes, sir. We'd come to Florida several—

Q. As I understand your testimony under oath, coming to Florida is totally unrelated to the decision of the New York Court of Appeals to return the baby to Miss Scarpetta?

A. (Realizing that I let him get the better of me, I softened my answer.) "Perhaps subconsciously the order had some bearing."

Q. You and your husband never discussed the proposition, "We love this baby and are not giving it back. We'll go to a state where things will turn out in our favor?"

A. That statement never passed my lips.

Q. Before you and Mr. DeMartino came to Florida, and you said to Mr. Colson several times, "This is my home," did your husband write the Florida Bar to find out if he could take the Florida Bar exam?

A. Not to my knowledge.

Q. Has he made any arrangements to take the Florida Bar exam?

A. No, sir, he has not.

Q. Did he have a successful practice in New York?

A. A modest one. Please slow—

Q. What is he doing now?

A. Insurance work, investigations for—

Q. Which company? Speak up, Mrs. DeMartino unless you have something to hide.

A. Colson and Hicks.

Q. Was that employment arranged through Mr. Fuchsberg when you were both in New York?

A. No, sir, it was not.

Q. Did you or your husband contact the Colson firm while in New York?

A. No, sir, I did not.

Q. Did you have any discussion with Mr. Fuchsberg about coming to Florida?

A. No, sir, I did not.
Q. Other than insurance investigator, has Mr. DeMartino had other jobs in Florida?
A. No, sir, he has not.
Q. What are they paying him?
A. You'd have to ask my husband.
("It's natural for you to be tense and uptight, Nick, but it might help if you had something to do—some work. Why don't you let me give you files to look over? We'll figure out what we owe after you give your reports," Colson offered. "You've got to be kidding, Bill. How can I charge for doing work?" "At the end, we'll tally up, and some pay we'll consider reciprocal for my services. But I insist that you take payment. You probably can use it, and besides, if asked, you can honestly answer that you are a paid employee.")

"You'll have to speak louder, Mrs. DeMartino," the judge admonished. If only my mind stopped wandering. I promised to keep my voice raised.
Q. Has your husband dissolved his legal partnership in New York?
A. Yes, sir, he has.
Q. When your husband came to Florida on May 1, the court of appeals already ruled, and you both knew if you remained in New York the baby must be surrendered to Miss Scarpetta. Is that correct?
A. No. A stay was in effect.
Q. Are you aware that you and your husband are in contempt of court?
A. Yes. I heard a ruling to that effect, but our attorney, Mr. Fuchsberg, rectified that. People are innocent until—
Q. Until a legal order is mandated that they return the baby to its natural mother. You don't work, do you?
A. No, sir.
Q. Do you have a bank account?

A. Yes, sir, I do.

Q. How much money is in it?

A. About $3,000.

(How quickly our money depleted. Though some attorneys hadn't charged for services, the expenses mounted. I hadn't checked our assets since the shock of reading that first horrid court transcripts a lifetime ago. When I approached the subject of money, Nick said not to worry. Dear Nick. If we were penniless, he'd say, don't worry and then do whatever necessary to keep me worry free. He'd sold stock. I'd wondered if my parents or his siblings gave or lent money. But I never insisted on an accounting. He believed that I had enough on my plate!)

Q. Had you and Mr. DeMartino retained Mr. Colson prior to the employment or was your husband employed first?

A. Mr. Colson works on a non fee basis. Is that what you mean?

Q. No. I want to know whether you retained Mr. Colson before your husband went to work for him or after?

A. I believe almost the same time or a few days after.

Q. In addition to living all your life in New York, do you have relatives there?

A. Yes, sir, I do.

Q. Sisters, brothers?

A. Yes.

Q. Cousins?

A. Yes.

Q. Friends?

A. Yes.

Q. Went to high school in New York?

A. Yes, sir.

Q. Your husband, the same?

A. Yes, sir.

Q. High school, college, law school?
A. Right.
Q. Did your husband, in connection with his law practice, ever handle adoptions?
A. He legalized adoptions on several occasions.
Q. When you got Lenore from the Spence-Chapin Agency, did they give you documents of any kind?
A. No, sir.
Q. Since you acquired Lenore, have you or your husband applied for a passport?
A. (Annoyingly detached, Rosenblatt used the word *acquired* as if my Lenore were a property or personal chattel.) No, sir, we have not.
Q. I believe you learned for the first time Miss Scarpetta wanted it back late in November of last year?
A. (The *it* you refer to, Mr. Rosenblatt, laughs and cries, toddles along after her sister, reaches up for hugs from mommy and daddy, and loves to play with Nick's briefcase as if she wished to become a lawyer.) That is correct.
Q. Now, the return to your petition for the *writ of habeas corpus*. Paragraph 19, which your attorney filed, gave the date as November 2, 1970. Am I incorrect, Bill?

    Colson: The paper may say that.

    Rosenblatt continued.

Q. Could you be mistaken, Mrs. DeMartino, about the date you knew Miss Scarpetta wanted it back or are you sticking to late November?
A. I learned around Thanksgiving.
Q. Do you know if your husband was informed on the 2nd of November?
A. Yes, my husband was informed sooner. The agency suggested that he save me heartache by not telling. Couples who love and protect one another—
Q. So your husband found out about the litigation on

November 2, but you didn't until three weeks later?
A. Yes, that is correct.
Q. We heard testimony about examination by certain doctors since you acquired Lenore. Did you ever see a psychiatrist or did your husband ever see a psychiatrist before that?
A. Other than the tests we took for today, no, sir.
Q. Mrs. DeMartino, I don't want to waste a lot of time showing you every photograph in the newspaper, but, I'm sure, you saw the one posed either with Lenore or with Linda and Lenore. What was your motivation for all those photographs and inviting photographers and reporters into your home?
A. Mr. Rosenblatt, I cherish my privacy. I think people normally cherish privacy, but I felt the public needed to know what was happening.

I attempted to see Miss Scarpetta at an address she gave in testimony, but she did not live there. For all I knew, Lenore might have no stable home. I was very—I panicked, was upset, and phoned the newspapers. Please understand, Lenore was surrendered to us voluntarily, and we loved and cared for her as our own flesh and blood. Miss Scarpetta was the stranger. If the court ordered my baby returned, I wanted to see the living conditions. I wished to speak with Miss Scarpetta openly and honestly about what was happening to both of us. I wanted to discuss the best interests of Lenore.
Q. You phoned the newspapers?
A. Yes, sir.
Q. You thought your husband, an attorney and investigator, would be unable to ascertain the correct address for Miss Scarpetta?
(When asked that question, I wanted to explain that both Nick and I decided to call the press. He physically made the phone call and conducted interviews.)

A. Mr. Rosenblatt, that is not what frightened me. Miss Scarpetta was not at the home she testified to in court, a home she claimed where relatives were nearby to assist a working mother. I became frightened that my daughter would be turned over to someone who gave false testimony and had, God knows what, in mind for Lenore.

Q. So you decided to seek favorable press and public opinion for your side?

A. If we merely wanted public opinion on our side, sir, then we would not have advised the committee to send their 87,000 signatures to the legislators rather than the judiciary.

(I knew what I had said didn't make too much sense, but at least I had gotten it into the record. I was getting my second wind and for the first time felt alert and in control.)

Q. The newspaper shots are not candid, pictures cuddling the baby and so forth—all posed. You did know a photographer was there and posed?

A. Yes, as Miss Scarpetta did when she posed for her pictures.

Q. Miss Scarpetta, unlike you, Mrs. DeMartino, has not posed for a picture with her baby, has she?

A. Miss Scarpetta signed away her baby one month after Baby Scarpetta was born. She didn't even bother naming Lenore.

Q. We know that. My question, Mrs. DeMartino, is, to your knowledge, has Miss Scarpetta ever posed for a picture with her baby?

A. You cannot pose with an infant you've given away, sir.

Q. So then your answer is *no*?

A. Obviously.

Q. One cannot pose with something a court ordered to be returned, can you? Unless you flee to another jurisdiction, not so?

A. That order was given to the Spence-Chapin Adoption Service, never to us, sir.

Q. But you are aware of it, aren't you?

A. That order was made with our name, but I was here at that time.

Q. Mrs. DeMartino, if you returned to New York with the baby, it would be taken away from you. You know that, don't you?

A. I know there is a contempt order which is in question, yes.

Q. What do you think as a woman with two years of college, what do you think this baby's reaction will be when she sees posed pictures and her mother's picture in the newspaper?

A. Well, she'll see an adoptive couple, her parents, who loved her greatly and fought for her well being.

Q. Won't she also see a natural mother who loved her greatly and, unlike you, had no free legal counsel but dipped into her funds to pay for representation in New York? Wouldn't the child also see that?

A. Lenore was given up voluntarily in her first month of life.

Q. Agreed.

A. A fact of life that cannot be changed. She'll see her birth mother try to undo what Miss Scarpetta voluntarily and knowingly created. My baby will also see parents who loved her greatly and were concerned about her well being, so I think the newspaper stories and pictures will speak for themselves, Mr. Rosenblatt.

Q. So there is no doubt in your mind that, even when Lenore reads those stories and sees those posed pictures, they will not bother her because she knows that you and your husband love her?

A. I think the security and love in our home that Lenore received and will continue to receive will make these stories of little consequence. As I mentioned already, Miss Scarpetta rejected Lenore, but with our love and security, she'll accept that reality with minimum, if any, emotional discomfort.

Whether Lenore is in our home or in Miss Scarpetta's home, the scar of rejection cannot be undone.
Q. Is that your medical opinion?
A. No, my maternal opinion.
Q. How do you justify keeping Miss Scarpetta from seeing her baby?
A. Miss Scarpetta never asked to see Lenore. By your own admission, the court proceedings in New York had no knowledge of us, the adoptive parents. We weren't informed about Miss Scarpetta's change of mind until November, so I don't know when or if she asked to see Lenore. She never asked me or my husband or my learned counsel.
Q. Which learned counsel?
(I heard laughter in the courtroom. Although I felt myself blush, I answered promptly.)
A. Mr. Spencer or Mr. Fuchsberg. Miss Scarpetta never asked to see Lenore, so I have no feelings of guilt about something that never happened.
Q. Didn't you read newspaper articles where my client said she wanted to see her child?
A. In May of this year in newspapers, Miss Scarpetta said—seven months after she took the agency to court—that she wanted to see Lenore. She did not ask us personally or say anything in newspapers prior to that time, and you can check, sir, and see.
Q. Would you have let her see the baby last month when I requested so of Mr. Colson?
A. I checked with my pediatricians who agreed with my attorneys that a visit would serve no purpose for Lenore and only become emotional turmoil for the

adults.

Q. You make a big point about Miss Scarpetta never requesting before May. Well, let's say—

A. I'm not making any point, Mr. Rosenblatt. You are by wrongly painting a picture that we refused.

Q. Okay. Let me ask another way. Assuming she made a request when the baby was two or three months old, would you have let her see it?

(Colson objected to the hypothesis and the judge sustained the objection.)

Rosenblatt continued.

Q. Now, Mrs. DeMartino, did you contact the Miami newspapers before coming to Florida?

A. No, sir, I did not.

Q. When did you contact them?

(This time I was very specific)

A. I didn't personally contact the Miami newspapers. Mr. Colson invited the press to his office, and asked us to come.

Q. Where is the baby now?

A. She is at home with her grandparents.

Q. Home being where?

Colson interrupted, "Do you want the address?" he asked. Rosenblatt: I want it on the record.

Colson: May we write for you and the judge instead of giving it to the press?

Rosenblatt: All right.

That accomplished, Rosenblatt turned his attention once again to me.

Q. Through whom did you arrange to get this rental?

A. Mrs. Delores Elridge, a real estate broker.

Q. What is your rent?

A. $225 a month.

Q. I show you a copy of a letter addressed to you and your husband from the attorneys for the Spence-Chapin Adoption Agency and ask if you ever received the

original?
A. No sir. I was in Miami.
Q. The letter was never forwarded?
A. Not to me, sir, no.
Q. Rosenblatt stared at me for a moment and then said, "That is all I have."

I was asked to step down. Once again exhaustion set in. I heard Colson speak but almost as though under water. "Judge, Mr. DeMartino's testimony will be cumulative, but he is available for cross by Mr. Rosenblatt.

Rosenblatt: I'd like to cross-examine him.

Chapter XVI

Nick DeMartino took the witness stand and was duly sworn. He testified as follows:
Q. Mr. DeMartino, how long had you and your wife owned your home in Brooklyn?
A. I believe four years.
Q. If not for the New York ruling, would you be living in the southwest section of Florida?
A. I would give the same answer as my wife. We always hoped to come to Florida, and I would be lying if I said subconsciously that the court order was never a factor.
Q. How about consciously?
A. I didn't actually say, "Let's run away, Jean," if that is what you mean.
Q. Consciously, did you think anything along these lines: "The New York courts said give the baby back. I don't want to give the baby back. I'm not giving that baby back. I love the baby, so I'm going to skip town." Does the thought process sound familiar?
A. I thought those things except for the last. I didn't think to skip town.
(I had trouble concentrating on Nick's testimony. I became cold and shivered. Thank God nobody noticed. Nick said he heard that Iowa was a better state for our case to be heard and Rosenblatt chided him, "a Brooklyn boy in Iowa? Living in Des Moines surely fascinates an easterner like you." I heard a glimmer in Nick's response, "Not like living in Florida.")
Q. If you stayed in New York with a court order to return the child, particularly an order adjudicating you in contempt, would you have given the baby back?
A. I have been led to believe, Mr. Rosenblatt—
Q. Could I have a *yes* or *no* before the explanation?

Would you give the baby back if you remained in New York?

A. No.
Q. Explain?
A. The order was never served on my wife and originally directed to the agency. Why the rehash. You know that later our names were on a subsequent order.

I was in Florida May1st, and that order was signed, I believe, on May 3. I was advised that order is invalid for a number of legal reasons. One was a stay by the federal court.
(Rosenblatt displayed annoyance.)
Q. You also know that if you remained in New York, you either turned the baby over or were in contempt and would be punished. You did, as an attorney, know that?
A. Mr. Rosenblatt, I know one thing. I'm a father. I'm not an attorney in this case.
Q. I'm asking you to be an attorney. We are all impressed that you are a father.
A. I'm not trying to impress you.
Q. We all are. We all are. I am. You love your children. No one is arguing. I don't doubt that for a minute you love these two children. I think that any normal American who has a baby from one month to thirteen months grows to love it. I don't have any quarrel with that.

I'm asking you as a lawyer. Would you answer my question?
A. I'm testifying as a father and a human being who never had a day in court, was never consulted, never served with any papers. You can't ask me to testify as a lawyer in this case unless you're inhuman.
Q. Testify as a father who coincidentally—
A. As a father, I'll do everything in my power to keep

my child. This is my answer to your questions.

Q. Testify as a father who coincidentally is an attorney, and I ask whether or not you were also advised or knew that had you remained in New York after May 3, 1971, you either would have turned the baby over to Miss Scarpetta or would have been punished for contempt?

A. And I say you are being speculative because no order came to me or my wife, and if the order existed, it was subject to a stay by the federal court.

Rosenblatt realized that he was nowhere with that line of questioning and abruptly asked:

Q. Have you sold your New York house?

A. It's in the process.

Q. As of this moment then, you still own it?

A. No. That house has been offered—

Q. Now you are a lawyer, not a father?

Colson objected, but Nick spoke over the objection in an angry tone. "I'm going to answer your question, Mr. Rosenblatt."

Colson said to Nick, "Be a witness. Relax and don't argue." Then to the judge, he said, "I object to Mr. Rosenblatt's argumentativeness."

Nick sat at the edge of his seat, and I could see the vein in his forehead pulsating. The judge said, "Answer the question."

A. The answer is that an offer is made, and we are accepting the price.

Q. That is not my question.

A. That is my answer to your question.

Q. My question to you, sir—

A. Is it sold? No. It is not closed.

Q. You are still the owner, and the answer is *yes*.

A. Technically, yes.

Q. Was your wife accurate with respect to the amount of money you have in Miami and in Brooklyn?

A. She was accurate about Florida. $3,000. She said under $2,000 in New York. I would say under $200 is more accurate.

(No wonder Nick was so evasive about money, but nothing mattered right now except Lenore and Linda.)

Q. Well, your wife came to Florida, then you came to Florida on May 1 of this year?

A. That is right.

Q. Did you have a job at that time?

A. No sir.

Q. In other words, you came to Florida with the intention to remain as a permanent resident with no plans to take the Florida Bar Examination?

A. I didn't say that.

Rosenblatt pursued Nick intensely by asking the same question several different ways. They added up to whether Nick believed he could take the Florida Bar while in contempt of the courts in his own state. Finally, the judge said, "Let's not take time arguing. Move on to something else. Whether he can or can't take the Bar is not determined by this case."

So, Rosenblatt hit upon the job arrangement that Nick had with Colson. Nick confirmed pretty much what I had said previously, but Rosenblatt didn't let loose. He carried Nick back to New York through all the various companies worked for as a beginning adjuster and trial attorney. Having finally exhausted that line, he turned elsewhere.

Q. Would you have essentially the same answer as your wife with respect to why you voluntarily posed with her and with the children for the *New York Daily News* and a variety of newspapers and television stations?

A. It would be similar to hers.

Q. I understand your answer—and correct me if you disagree in any way—she became concerned that the baby might be returned to Miss Scarpetta who would not be an ideal mother. Posing and the cooperation with the press was to get public opinion on your side and to let the public know your side of the story.

A. No, sir. It was not to get public opinion on our side. It was to make the public aware of the problem with adoptions in New York.

Q. Mr. DeMartino, you could make the public aware without emotive pictures obviously designed to create a warm feeling with others toward your family, could you not?

A. Mr. Rosenblatt, that was not the intention. If it's an ancillary, then, yes. Taking a baby from the only home she's know is an emotional subject, I'll grant you.

Q. You knew your wife posed for this picture?

(Once again, Nick moved forward in his seat. His face reddened.)

A. I resent the use of the word *posing*. She held the baby and the picture was taken.

Q. But you knew a photographer was in your apartment?

A. Yes, among the many people working there in our behalf, we thought the guys with the cameras were photographers and wanted pictures.

Q. The same goes for this photograph?

A. And the same goes for every other one who snapped a picture, Mr. Rosenblatt.

Q. Would you let Miss Scarpetta see the baby if she wanted at two or three months after you got it?

A. I can't answer that hypothetical question. The time and opportunity for her asking are long gone.

Q. If Lenore wanted to see her natural mother, would you let her?

A. I would hope she loved us so much that Lenore wouldn't think it necessary, but, if it were, I certainly would, yes. I would do anything for my children, Mr. Rosenblatt.

Q. It's hard to predict what effect that would have on the child.
A. I don't think so. My daughter will know love and seeing her birth mother won't matter one bit. She may be curious just as I was about my grandfather and my great-grandfather.
Q. They were dead, weren't they?
A. No, my grandfather was alive.
Q. Did you meet him?
A. No, he lived in Italy.
Q. What is it about May 1, 1971, that after spending your entire life in New York and your wife spending her entire life in New York, you suddenly decided to dissolve a law practice, sell your home, and come to sunny Florida?

Colson objected, saying that Rosenblatt's questions were repetitious. So, with the court's permission, Rosenblatt rephrased his question.

Q. How about three weeks before May 1 when your wife came down, was there any particular reason?
A. She wanted to see if Florida was as nice as we remembered from our previous visits. She wrote saying she loved Miami with its wide-open spaces, warm sunshine, and outdoor living which in New York is limited to a three-month period in the summer.
Q. When is the last time you were in Florida?
A. Actually there were three occasions when we were here—once on our honeymoon. I remember because we got to the island of Cuba before Castro took over about seven years ago.
Q. But even though you left on May 1, your attorneys in New York advised you of all the legal proceedings which had occurred in New York, had they not?
A. Well, yes, they sure did.
Q. You signed an affidavit on April 8, 1971, where you said in Paragraph 7 that you felt it was likely that if

Miss Scarpetta got the baby, she would take it outside the jurisdiction of the State of New York?
A. That was my opinion.
Q. And it was after—
A. Not outside the State of New York, sir, outside the United States of America. I'm an American citizen and so is my daughter.
Q. Born of Colombian parents.
A. No, sir, she is an American citizen, period.
Q. No, sir, she is born of Colombian parents.
Q. Knowing that the court ordered the surrender of the baby to Miss Scarpetta, you executed that affidavit on April 8, 1971, and your and your wife came to Florida.
A. Not together, separately.
Q. But she came after April 8 and you came shortly after, right?
A. I know of no law, Mr. Rosenblatt, that prevents a person from—
Q. Would you answer my question?
A. That is my answer.
Mr. Rosenblatt: that is all I have.

Nick returned to the seat beside me, and gave my hand that old, familiar squeeze.

Colson took the floor. "Before we rest, we would like to offer one last piece of evidence which is a three and a half minute film."
One of Miss Scarpetta's attorneys objected and wanted to know what was on the film. Colson said the film was of Lenore in our home. The attorney still voiced an objection, but Colson pushed. "It takes three and a half minutes."

Rosenblatt addressed the judge. "The three and a half minutes add up to 5:30 p.m., and my examination took thirty minutes." Colson pushed more, but Rosenblatt held his own and suggested the time would be better used if they each summarized. Colson replied,

"I'll leave it up to the judge."

This back and forth banter didn't mean much at the moment. All I could think of was that the hearing was over and Nick and I would go back to what we had been doing lately, waiting. I wondered how long the judge would take this time. At least, I wouldn't read it in the newspapers or get a call from a radio station. I would at least be given the dignity of receiving the court's ruling in person. My thoughts were interrupted by Rosenblatt who asked for an opportunity to review salient points, ". . . either now or in chambers." Colson waived final arguments for anything the judge desired.

Zalk requested that copies of the New York laws be submitted which led the judge to ask for copies of the record of the original trial resulting in conversations back and forth.

My thoughts turned to Lenore and Linda. I wished to get home to them. I wondered what they were doing, but my attention was brought quickly back to the courtroom when I heard Rosenblatt ask, "Judge, do you intend to rule today?" To everyone's surprise, he said that if the attorneys wanted to give their final argument today, he would rule. A clamor rippled through the courtroom and between attorneys. Colson still pressed to get the film into evidence when Rosenblatt interrupted asked, "Would you waive argument?" Colson quickly answered *yes*.

The courtroom quieted. My heart pounded.
"There is no case the judge has to decide that is any more difficult than one such as we have here," the judge began. "Many eminent jurists have written eloquent opinions involving the same issues I could refer to. I will not. In consideration of all the evidence in the case and the law of this state, I am constrained to the conclusion that after all is said and done, analyzing everything, that the petition should be denied and the

writ discharged."

Noise flooded the room and excitement followed his last sentence. Nick and I stood along with everyone and turned to one another. Above the clamor I shouted, "What did he say? I didn't understand."

"Lenore stays with us," he shouted. "She stays with us, honey." I threw myself into his arms and cried. "Thank you, God."

Our attorneys were jubilant. We all hugged and congratulated one another. Now that it was all over, Nick and I were more anxious than ever to get home. We eventually made our way through the crowd and out. We were giddy with disbelief and relief and joy. A few blocks away from our home, we stopped at a small department store to buy the kids some toys. We literally danced while collecting toys and stuffed animals. We looked strange to the people around but it didn't matter. We both held back admitting later that we felt like shouting, "God is in heaven and all is right with the world."

My mom must have been looking for us by the window because as we approached the house, she flung the front door open, and stood there with both our girls. We ran to them shouting, "Hi, girls! We're home! Mommy and daddy are home. We've come so far to get home," I said kissing the girls.

FOLLOWUP

For the next one and a half years, the case ran through the Florida Courts and finally reached The Supreme Court of the United States.

September 29, 1971, in the *New York Daily News*: Miami Report, the article read, ". . . a situation in which one of two innocent parties must suffer. The 3rd District Court of Appeals in Florida upheld Nick and Jean DeMartino's right to retain custody of their adopted daughter, Lenore."

May 6, 1972, The Miami Herald wrote, "The Florida Supreme Court has added its voice to other decisions in favor of the . . . parents in the Baby Lenore adoption case."

May 31, 1972, BABY LENORE BILL BECOMES LAW.

Joseph R. Pisani's Albany Report in July of 1972, "After more than a year of intensive effort, I can now report, with a great deal of satisfaction, that there will be no more Baby Lenore cases in New York State. On May 31, Governor Rockefeller affixed his signature to my 30-Day Adoption Bill, which, for the first time, clearly defines the point when a natural Mother who has decided to surrender a child for adoption loses all claim to custody of the child. . . . The situation was grossly unfair to adoptive parents, to the child involved and to the natural mother whose conscience was bound to torment her (rightly or wrongly) as long as the possibility of reclaiming her child was left open by legal technicalities."

November 14, 1972, The Miami Herald published,
"Supreme Court Refuses to Hear Case. Couple Will Keep Baby Lenore. The U.S. Supreme Court refused Monday to hear the appeal by the girl's natural mother. 'LENORE BELONGS TO GOD,' the thirty-six-year-old Mrs. DeMartino said Monday, 'and my husband and I are taking care of her for him.'"

Lenore's Epilogue

I am Lenore. Even though I am now forty-one, I have always been and will always be Baby Lenore to the public. I have no real knowledge of life as it might have existed outside this public conflict over my identity. I have no real memory of my birth mother outside of that conflict. Privately, I have absolutely no conflict over my identity, and never have had. I am, simply stated, me.

My parents, Jean and Nick, my sister Linda, my grandparents, aunts, uncles, cousins are all my parents, my sister, my grandparents, my family. To me, the issue of possession has never been to whom I belong as much as who belongs to me. My family belongs to me. I grew up with them. I love them. Though none of this was legal until I was nineteen and I could orchestrate my own adoption by my family, none of the legalities ever really mattered to me anyway. From any given point in my life—before or after my infant adoption, before or after the custody disputes—this was the only family that would ever raise me. I come from this family.

Though God did not have me born to them, I believe He did have me placed with them. Call it Fate if not God. This is the life I've known. This is my life. This is my identity. To tell me otherwise because of conflicting DNA's is to ignore who I am in favor of what I am. To insist that I am someone because of particular knowledge of my body, ignores all particular knowledge of my experience and my person. To use physical criteria to identify a human is called, under any other circumstances, discrimination.

Like any individual, my right of person is infinitely more significant to me than anyone else's right of biology or adoption over me. I am grateful to my birth mother for having me, and I am grateful to my parents for fighting for my right to remain me—their daughter, Linda's sister—Lenore.

Although Linda was always completely and astoundingly disregarded in the legal triangle of myself, my parents, and my birth mother, she is my "big" sister and as such was my most treasured (and possibly most influential) person when I was small. Four years older than I, my earliest memories are filled with her! As a second child, I modeled and related to this other small person much more than any adult. I loved to watch her, follow her, and especially, to be an object of her childish attention and entertainment. From my early infancy, we ate together, slept together, fought together, grew together. She became a great deal of my self, and I of hers.

Though we are both adopted, we are identical to all sisters: completely alike and completely different. Though we don't share physical traits and dress very differently, we do share similar speech and mannerisms. We are both always amused by people who don't know us but insist they can tell we are sisters because of our physical resemblance to each other and our shared resemblance to our mother!

We share similar values and beliefs, but have different interest areas. We are both family oriented, have both married, and both want children but have chosen very different men with whom to have our families. While I am more quiet and even shy by nature, Linda is extremely social and outgoing. She is also more driven and already enjoyed a successful, dynamic career in public relations while I quietly teach elementary school.

In spite of the fact that she has always been quite bold herself and relentlessly cheerleading of me, Linda is not in total agreement with my recent decision to publicly advocate the rights of adoptive children. This is a surprising reversal of our usual roles. Although both of our adoptions were always mentioned in most media coverage, Linda now feels much more private about exposing our family's business through interviews and the publication of this manuscript. She would much prefer to just "let sleeping dogs lie." After all, the last several years of adult lives and married names have afforded us total control over our anonymity for the first time.

Perhaps this difference in our views regarding further public exposure is due to the perpetual public focus on the circumstances of my life and the perpetual interference in Linda's life this has always posed. As a darling little girl and oldest child, she never lacked attention from family and friends, and never seemed to compete with me for more. But the insatiable curiosity of the media and public about the case and about Baby Lenore was a frequent source of interruption for the entire family while we were young.

Though our parents fought tirelessly to shelter us, Linda was affected every bit as much as me by their suppressed anxiety, the extra security needs, and the open verbal attacks in our presence from critics of my parents' fight to keep me. The inescapable attention raised by this type of controversial celebrity rarely felt good to us as children though we knew no other way of life and accepted it blindly as normal.

Even if there had been no publicity and no matter how much more perfectly our parents might have feigned to us safety and ease, Linda and I would still know the scars of insecurity and the long ringing echoes of the total family trauma caused by any child custody battle. Our friends who are children of child custody battles in divorce have felt such trauma even though the warring parties were both biological parents and were both well known to them. Their battles were also catastrophes to the entire extended family whose memory was not erased and whose spirit was not mended immediately after the verdict. Since she is older, Linda has always been even more aware than I. Though she has rarely wavered in her loving and protective role to me, it hasn't been easy for Linda to be the big sister of Baby Lenore.

So, for whatever all her reasons, Linda and I differ in the level of privacy we each now desire about our adoptions and our family's story. We have discussed it and shared our feelings.

Though she disagrees, Linda understands my need to speak up for the sake of other children whose rights are not given priority over the rights of those adults who want them. As close sisters do, she would never want to interfere with something I really need. But also as close sisters do, she will always let me know whenever she doesn't like it.

People are always curious as to whether or not I feel I would have had a good life or been happy had my parents surrendered me to my birth mother after she won custody. This has been a question I have had my whole life to ponder. Olga Scarpetta was, by all accounts, a good woman. She was my birth mother. She obviously loved me. Whatever parts of her decisions were motivated by the complexities of guilt, I accept that both her decision to give me up and her decisions to try to get me back were at least motivated in part by the strength of our natural mother/child bond.

I can only speculate about what my life might have been with my birth mother. The love, nurturing, and security I received from my adoptive parents are the only documented truths and proven life which exist without assumption. Even though my parents' fears for me being placed in this alternate life scenario were well founded, any helpful speculation of that possible life begs me to choose that these fears would not have become realities in the hands of my birth mother and birth family.

Raised by Olga Scarpetta, I would have been brought up as a Colombian either in this country or, most likely, in South America. I would most definitely have been raised speaking Spanish as my primary language and celebrating the mores of my Hispanic heritage. It seems as though there was ample family and means to provide me with similar amounts of love and security that have nurtured me with my adoptive family. I feel that I probably would have lived well and happily.

But to achieve that alternate life with my birth mother, once having been placed in my adoptive parents' home, would have meant the trauma of amputation from my life of my only real home and identity experienced. Mother Jean, Father Nick, Sister Linda, and all of my extended family would have had to be suddenly removed and terminated from my life if I had been made to go with my birth mother. It would have been a form of extended and distorted post term abortion of the existing people in my life and of my existing state of life based solely on the consideration and rights of the birth mother because she did want me. Some children do lose their parents and siblings just as totally to actual physical death. These children survive. They are placed with others, sometimes birth family, sometimes not. They adjust. If they are loved and nurtured, most grow happily and healthfully—some with loving memories of the deceased parents, others too young at the separation to really remember them. The issue is whether it is ever morally fathomable to consciously and purposely place this type of life disaster, separation trauma, and adjustment demand on any child in order to satisfy the rights of any adult.

Who would move to knowingly inflict even the obvious confusion, if not the immeasurable pain, of this type of separation on a child of any age? My birth mother has all my understanding, forgiveness, and even admiration for her initial decision to give me up. However, in spite of this and all her love for me, for her willingness to then attempt to have me experience this adjustment to such total separation of loved ones rather than to continue to endure it herself, I will always hold the courts accountable for giving more than lip service to what is in "the best interests of a child" and to hold full hearings to determine that interest.

Nick's Epilogue

After the honorable Judge Ralph O. Cullen decided our case in Florida, Olga Scarpetta appealed to the court of appeals. They affirmed the lower courts opinion and the Supreme Court in Florida affirmed as well. We were given permanent custody without visitation. When Lenore attained her majority at age eighteen, we began proceedings to adopt her. We had asked her if she wanted us to legally adopt her and she replied "Of course. You are my mom and dad."

We took the next step and had an attorney chosen by Bill Colson to prepare the necessary documents. To all of our shock, we were told that even though she had reached her majority, we still had to get permission from her biological mother. When I say shock, I mean our attorneys and other lawyers that we knew had no idea of this requirement.

We then got in touch with Joseph Zalk, the attorney who represented Olga Scarpetta. He told us that Miss Scarpetta who had married (we never did know the name of her husband) wanted to meet with Lenore. We asked Lenore if she would like to meet her biological mother as we had when she was fourteen years old. She refused then and refused now. She felt sorry for her biological mother but could not get over all of the problems that she had caused us.

Mr. Zalk told us that Olga did not want to pay for his reading over the documents. I agreed to pay, and they were sent to him.

Baby Lenore is now married and living in upstate Florida. She never wanted to see her birth mother even when offered that opportunity as a child and again at age nineteen. Under Florida law, her birth mother had to sign an affidavit consenting to her adoption even though she was no longer a minor. Lenore's only thought was, "Dad, can she stop you from adopting me?" I answered *no*. Later, Olga signed the necessary affidavit, and Lenore was legally adopted.

Olga Scarpetta died two years later of breast cancer. She never saw Lenore except in news photos and on television, but she also never gave us a difficult time after the long court battle. She could have made life unpleasant but did not. She is in my prayers all the time. We never felt anger or animosity toward Olga after the court battle. We believed that she did the right thing in giving up Lenore for Lenore's best interest.

She changed her mind, we believed, out of a sense of guilt and at the urging of her parents who, it appeared, paid for all the legal expenses. We were told so after Olga received her PHD in social science. She told us that we were right in doing what we did.

Linda (no small part of this story) is married and living in South Florida. She owned a successful public relations business and is now a consultant. She is as precocious as ever. At four years old, her uncle described her as the youngest twenty-four-year-old he'd ever met.

I am a commercial real estate broker in Coral Gables, Florida. Jean after miscarrying three children (one in the 7th month), having almost lost Lenore, having life-threatening cancer of the bladder twenty years before her death, breast cancer thirteen years before her death, a hysterectomy, skin cancer, and finally a blood disease which we believe affected her mind, took her own life on April 27, 1994. She left a beautiful note to me, Linda, and Lenore. We know that she is now their guardian angel.

Bill Colson's son, Dean, a brilliant attorney in his own right, became a law clerk for Justice William H. Rehnquist who later became Chief Justice of the

United States Supreme Court. He is the managing partner in the law firm of Colson, Hicks, Eidson. He has two adopted children.

Fifteen years after Jean's death, I married Maria Pilar Huergo. An old-fashioned lady born in Cuba and coming to the United States as a six-year-old. She is a nurturing woman who watches over me. I am lucky to have her. It is a blessing to find love and marriage once. I am twice blessed. Very little substantive changes have been made to the laws of adoption. We now have a Uniform Adoption Act which applies to all states. It prevents adoptive parents from moving out of a state as we did because the laws are essentially the same in all.

The Baby Lenore Bill had been passed in New York giving a biological mother thirty days from the surrender of the baby to rescind her surrender.

NICK'S DEDICATION

I dedicate this book to so many that the list would be too long, too time consuming, and take too many pages. I am compelled to dedicate it to over 100,000 people who signed the petitions to help save baby Lenore, to Joseph Spencer who started our long journey, to Jacob Fuchsberg—a dynamic and conscientious trial lawyer, to Bill Colson who represented us as if Lenore was his own child, to The Committee to Help Save Baby Lenore and, in particular, to John Farro and Barry Tash, to Judge Ralph O. Cullen who let us be persons in a court and who recognized the best interests of a child and did not pay lip service to that very important requirement of the law regarding children. I dedicate this book to Marty McLaughlin of the *New York Daily News* who was dubious and unbelieving but became devoted to our cause, to Owen Fitzgerald—a crime writer for the *New York Daily News*—who referred me to Marty. I must include Bernie Keegan a colleague who referred me to Owen Fitzgerald, to Lenny Chamowitz who got us on all the TV stations, to people who lost their adopted children alone and helpless to react, to The Spence Chapin Adoption Agency who did all they could to ensure that Lenore remained with us, and to our families for the love, devotion and support that they gave us.

    I know that I left out a lot of people. I hope they will forgive me for not including them in this dedication. God bless all of them because I truly believe that goodness is its own reward.

Exhibits

the Adoptive Cradle

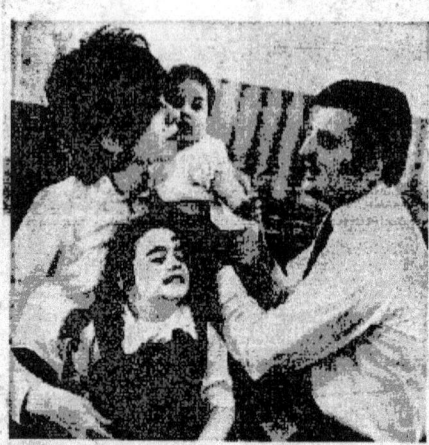

At left, Jane and Nick DeMartino with their older adopted daughter Linda, 4, and baby Lenore, whose natural mother is waging a court battle to regain her.

For thousands of worried couples who have adopted babies in New York—or hope to—the plight of the DeMartinos poses a question of legal custody that only the State Court of Appeals can answer

As legal decisions continued to run against them, public support built up for the DeMartinos, shown above with the Rev. Francis Ridgliane (far left) and Phylis Chernowitz and Bernice Tash (right) at a rally to enlist backing for the adoptive couple.

On June 18, when the infant was a month old, she was placed with the DeMartinos. Not until a few days before the Supreme Court hearing, on Nov. 5, were they informed by Spence-Chapin that Miss Scarpetta was intending to reclaim the baby.

Judge Ascione told THE NEWS that he felt that the agency had used "undue haste" in placing the child and was also at fault for not immediately taking the baby away from the DeMartinos when Miss Scarpetta officially notified the agency that she wanted to revoke her legal surrender.

JANE Edwards, executive director of the Spence-Chapin Adoption Service, explained that it was not uncommon for the natural mother to ask for the child back soon after the birth. However, she explained that in almost all cases, after counseling, the natural mother reverts to her original decision to give up the baby for adoption.

In Miss Scarpetta's case, the usual didn't happen. On June 30, Miss Scarpetta was told by Spence-Chapin the baby had been placed in a fine adoptive home and that she couldn't renege on the legal surrender. She spoke to Jane on a caseworker Gloria Daniels four times during July asking for the child back, without success.

On July 28, she consulted with attorney Joseph Falk of Manhattan and explained her case. On his advice, she sent a letter to Spence-Chapin revoking her consent for adoption and threatening court action if the agency didn't agree.

The letter read: "I regret any inconvenience that my action might cause the adoptive parents of my child but I am sure they will understand that a child should be with her natural mother."

The attorneys for Spence-Chapin—Barrows, Marcus and Bashert of Manhattan—informed Miss Scarpetta's attorney that they were going to contest the action and, after some delay, a hearing was set for Nov. 5.

"The agency contacted me and told me about the legal action only three days before it was scheduled," said DeMartino. "I went out of my mind. I couldn't believe this was happening. How can this mother who gave her baby away want it now four days old suddenly change her mind and take her back?"

After Judge Ascione ruled against them, the DeMartinos were distraught. "My wife was sick and in a terrible emotional state," DeMartino said, "and I just didn't know what to do."

"We were going to lose our baby," he said, "that chubby little Lenore that smiled at us whenever we came into her room. That baby we sat up nights with, that baby that we loved . . . our baby."

Shortly after the decision, the DeMartinos went to see the lawyers for the agency and were assured, DeMartino said, that when the case went to the Appellate Division, the decision would be reversed.

"I'm a real estate lawyer and experienced with this kind of case," said DeMartino, "so I went along with the agency lawyers." On Jan. 19, when the appeal was heard by Appellate Division Judges Louis Capozzoli, Owen McGivern, Arthur Markewich and Emilio Nunez, DeMartino sat in the back and listened.

In an appeal hearing, each lawyer has a specified time to present his arguments to the judges, who have already reviewed all the facts and testimony of the case. The judges then decide to affirm or reverse the decision.

"I couldn't help believing that the judges had already made up their minds," DeMartino said. "As the agency lawyer, Roy Reardon, made his presentation, DeMartino continued, "the judges kept interrupting him and contradicting him as if they weren't interested in what he had to say."

"And when the attorney for Miss Scarpetta started to speak," he said, "one of the judges told him to go back to his office and quit while he was ahead."

"I knew right then and there that they were going to rule against me," said DeMartino.

He was right. On Jan. 28, the Appellate Division upheld Judge Ascione, saying, "In short, the welfare and interests of the child are the primal considerations."

Miss Scarpetta had testified at the original trial that if the baby was returned to her she would hire a 65-year-old nurse from Columbia to care for the infant while she continued full-time in her job as a secretary.

The DeMartino Adoptive Parents Committee has attacked the decision on "moral and humane" grounds and said that they have "grave doubts that the best interests of the infant, Lenore, have been given full consideration."

The committee points out that the decision affecting the child's future should be based on a "methodically authenticated investigation" and not the unsubstantiated statements of the natural mother.

As an example, they cite Miss Scarpetta's plan to bring a 65-year-old nurse for the baby into the country from Colombia. The committee maintains that if the court had checked this, it would have found it not possible.

Edwin Reuling, chief of Immigration Service for the U.S. Labor Department, confirmed the committee's view.

"Right now there is no availability of American nurses to do this type of work," he said, "and if I had an application from a 65-year-old nurse before me right now, it would be denied."

Since the story broke in THE NEWS two weeks ago, there has been a tremendous reaction from the public. Politicians throughout the state have expressed interest in the case and how it will affect future adoptions. In Brooklyn, a Committee to Help Save the DeMartino Baby has been formed, and more than 30,000 people have signed petitions.

are entitled to their day in court under the Bill of Rights and the 14th Amendment....

"The result of legally ignoring the DeMartinos, who have assumed the role of real-life parents from June 18, when the baby was a month old, up to today, is a hearing completely without any testimony at all that deals with the existing emotional and physical state of the child and the ties that now bind Lenore to Mr. and Mrs. DeMartino."

The lawyer's contention is that, essentially, Justice Ascione lacked sufficient information about the welfare of Lenore to make a decision about her future.

Regardless of what happens to the little girl after tomorrow, it would seem that out of the case will come what many consider overdue reform of the state's archaic adoption laws.

Lawyer Jacob Fuchsberg wants the DeMartinos to have a day in court.

 **DAILY NEWS**
NEW YORK'S PICTURE NEWSPAPER

Vol. 52, No. 205　New York, N.Y. 10017, Friday, February 19, 1971　WEATHER: Sunny, breezy and cool

CHILD CUSTODY APPEAL GRANTED

Court to Hear Baby Lenore Case

 DAILY NEWS
NEW YORK'S PICTURE NEWSPAPER

Vol. 52, No. 287　New York, N.Y. 10017, Wednesday, May 26, 1971　WEATHER: Partly cloudy, windy and mild

JUDGE ORDERS: BRING BABY BACK

Exclusive Talk With Nick DeMartino

DAILY NEWS
NEW YORK'S PICTURE NEWSPAPER ®

Vol. 52. No. 246   New York, N.Y. 10017, Thursday, April 8, 1971*   10¢   WEATHER: Sunny, breezy and cool.

COURT RETURNS BABY TO MOM

'Won't Quit,' DeMartinos Vow

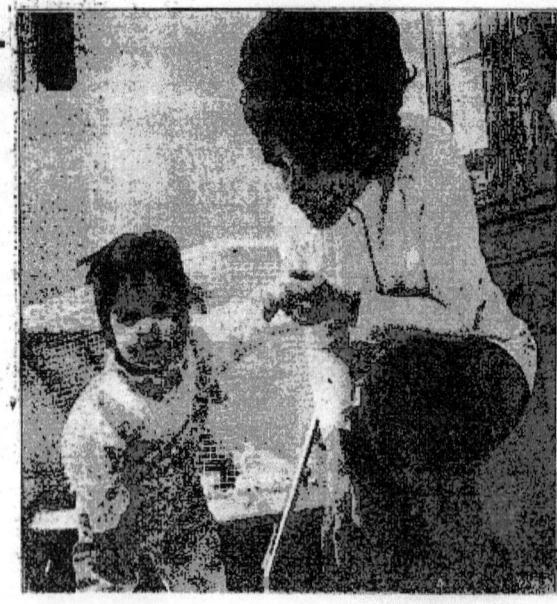

Adoptive Mother: 'This Is Not The End of It'

Struggling to learn how to stand by herself, 10-month-old Lenore clings to her adoptive mother Mrs. Joan DeMartino, at what has been her home in Bay Ridge, Brooklyn. Yesterday, the seven-man State Court of Appeals ruled that she must be returned to her natural mother, Olga Scarpetta, who, after signing infant over for adoption, changed her mind. The angry, grief-ridden adoptive father, who learned of the decision on his 37th birthday, said: "I don't want sympathy, I want justice."

Stories on page 2

DAILY NEWS
NEW YORK'S PICTURE NEWSPAPER

Vol. 52, No. 286   New York, N.Y. 10017, Tuesday, May 25, 1971   WEATHER: Showers, windy and warm.

DeMARTINOS FLEE WITH BABY

> life. I must use every available means to protect my family and at the same time protect those hundreds and maybe thousands to follow. I have not lost my faith in God and maybe we have been chosen as his tool to fight the archaic thinking of our court system. I read where the law

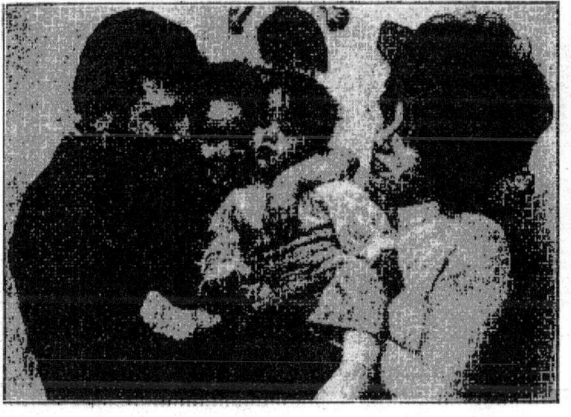

Nick's Letter: 'I Have Faith'

← Nick and Jean DeMartino, shown with daughter Linda, 4, and adoptive baby Lenore, now a year old, during court battles, have left state with the child rather than obey court order to turn the infant over to her unwed mother. Before leaving, DeMartino left letter (see above) for a News reporter, vowing "to fight the archaic thinking of our court system." Jacob Fuchsberg, his attorney, informed Manhattan Supreme Court Justice Charles Lorein of move, calling whereabouts of family "a privileged communication."

Stories on page 3

DeMartinos Facing Contempt Arrest

Judge Orders Them To Return Baby

By MARTIN McLAUGHLIN

State Supreme Court Justice Charles A. Loreto ordered Nick and Jean DeMartino yesterday to surrender their year-old adopted daughter Lenore immediately or face arrest. The couple, who fled the state with the child, face contempt charges if they refuse to surrender the child to her unwed mother.

Loreto two weeks ago suggested that a plan be devised to provide a gradual turnover of the child to the mother, Olga Scarpetta, of Colombia, South America.

There was no move to charge the DeMartinos with kidnaping, however. In response to a request for federal intervention in the case, made by Miss Scarpetta's attorney, Joseph Zalk, U.S. Attorney Edward R. Neaher of Brooklyn declined to authorize an FBI investigation.

Neaher said that federal authorities believe that the DeMartinos had legal custody of the child when they left the state and that Miss Scarpetta still has civil channels through which to seek a remedy.

Loreto ruled that "in view of the fact that the whereabouts of the DeMartinos is presently unknown to the court" the order not be served on their attorney, Jacob D. Fuchsberg.

Noting that the couple might be subject to a charge of abduction for removing the child, Loreto said, "This turn of events is not in the best interest of the child and may prove disastrous to them (the DeMartinos) and harmful to the child."

Calls Talk Ridiculous

Fuchsberg called the talk of abduction "ridiculous." He said that the DeMartinos had never been served with any court order and still have legal custody of the child. "Furthermore," he added, "there was never an order prohibiting their move."

He said that he would move to vacate or appeal the new order, which he described as "tainted with the same lack of consideration that has been prevalent through all the court proceedings which have excluded the DeMartinos from participation."

Noting that all the legal action in the case so far has been strictly between Miss Scarpetta and the Spence-Chapin Adoption Service, the attorney said, "Never in any of these proceedings has anyone ever asked whether the child is alive or dead, sick or well or any other questions concerning what is best for Lenore."

Lenore, who celebrated her first birthday a week ago, was turned over to Spence-Chapin by Miss Scarpetta when she was four days old. The child has been with the DeMartinos since she was 15 days old.

Last week the couple filed an appeal of the State Supreme Court decision with the U.S. Supreme Court, seeking to invalidate the state court's order

Mrs. Doris Burger, baby Lenore's godmother, picks up the child's toys from her crib in the DeMartino home at 16th Ave. in Brooklyn.

awarding custody of Lenore to her mother. The State Supreme Court division, rendered in November, has been upheld by the

(Continued on page 25, col. 2)

Nick Says Family Won't Be Torn Apart

© 1971 by the New York Times Inc.

Nick DeMartino phoned News reporter Martin McLaughlin yesterday. He did not say where the family was. Here is their conversation:

Q. Nick, are you? A. I am fine and so is the whole family. God bless them.

Q. How are you adjusting to your new surroundings? A. Fine, we are living in a very nice apartment and I'm getting set in the business of making a living.

Q. Does that mean that you are establishing a new residence? A. Yes, we have established a new residence and we'll live here where the family won't be torn apart.

Q. What about your job and your business? A. I don't care. If I have to drive a cab or dig ditches to keep my daughter, that's all right with me.

Q. Then you are establishing a new residence, aren't you? A. Yes, we have joined the local Catholic Church, in fact on Sunday I helped to take up the collection. We will be getting a phone tomorrow or the next day.

Q. Do you have any intention of coming back? A. Only as visitors to see our relatives.

Q. How is Lenore? A. She is fine and loves her new home. Linda (the older child) is very happy, too, and Jean is a wonderful mother who doesn't care where she lives as long as she has her children.

Q. How about your getting adjusted? A. Are you kidding? As long as I have my family with me, I can adjust to anything.

Q. What about your legal problems? A. I am leaving them strictly in the hands of Jack Fuchsberg, my lawyer and a friend. I will keep in touch with him.

Q. Generally, how do you feel about the whole thing? A. Marty, believe it or not, I still have my faith in God. I know things don't look good right now, but I also know that Lenore is our daughter and belongs with us.

Q. Do you think a lot of people will lose sympathy with you because you moved? A. I'd hope they wouldn't, but I can't worry about that now. Jean and I are doing what we feel is best. My first duty as a father is to keep my family intact, and I will do whatever I have to.

Q. Then you are all well, aren't you? A. As long as this family is together, we will always be well. I have to hang up now, Marty, but I promise to keep in touch. So long for now.

Words of Hope From Family

By ELLEN FLEYSHER

Downstairs, a small cluster of toys have taken over a corner of the spotless living room while a menagerie of fuzzy and rubbery animals spread by the playpen nestled close to the kitchen.

Upstairs all is in order; the beds are made, the pillows are fluffed and children's drawings share the walls of what is obviously a room shared by two youngsters.

There's only one thing strange about the two-story dwelling at 86th 16th Ave. in Brooklyn's Bay Ridge section. It's empty.

This is Nick and Jean and Linda and Lenore DeMartino's home—at least it was until the other day, when the couple chose to flee New York State rather than turn their adopted "baby Lenore" over to her unwed mother, as ordered by the courts.

They Entertained Regularly

Yesterday a young, attractive woman, her 5-year-old daughter by her side, dropped by to pick up the mail behind the front door, adorned with an American flag decal.

Mrs. Doris Burger, 25, was no stranger to the house—she is Nick DeMartino's elder sister, like him, has two daughters of her own. She is also Lenore's godmother.

"There's been a lot of laughter in this house,"

Lisa Burger feeds doll in baby Lenore's high chair.

she began. "Jesus—I love her like a sister—enjoyed entertaining friends and family.

"Like when neighbors and family came to welcome Lenore. Jean had sandwiches and drinks for everyone."

"And the christening,"—her face beamed. "It was just wonderful. Linda was so excited because my Lisa had a baby sister and family she did too."

Besides the elder daughters were so close in age, Doris and Jean spent much time discussing children.

'A Feeling About Kids'

"She just had a certain feeling about kids, besides being a warm, funny, intelligent person," said Mrs. Burger, who lives in Brooklyn's Bensonhurst section.

"I'm optimistic it will all work out. This just can't happen—it's like if someone wanted to take one of my kids away, well, I would have done the same thing my brother did.

Earlier, Mrs. Burger dropped by the Committee to Help Keep Baby Lenore headquarters at 129 Avenue O, Brooklyn. Volunteers have set up a legal defense fund for the DeMartinos and have asked that contributions be sent to the office. Additional information can be obtained by calling 252-1616.

DAILY NEWS
NEW YORK'S PICTURE NEWSPAPER

Vol. 52, No. 287   New York, N.Y. 10017, Wednesday, May 26, 1971   WEATHER: Partly cloudy, windy and mild.

JUDGE ORDERS: BRING BABY BACK

Exclusive Talk With Nick DeMartino

Stories on Page 3

DAILY NEWS
NEW YORK'S PICTURE NEWSPAPER

Vol. 52, No. 301   New York, N.Y. 10017, Friday, June 11, 1971   WEATHER: Sunny, breezy and warm.

RETURN LENORE, OLGA ASKS FLA.

Story on Page 3

FINAL

DAILY NEWS
NEW YORK'S PICTURE NEWSPAPER

10¢

Vol. 52, No. 289 · New York, N.Y. 10017, Friday, May 28, 1971 · WEATHER: Sunny, breezy and cool

OUR MAN FINDS LENORE IN MIAMI

DeMartinos Tell Their Story

'We Are Not Hiding.' Nicholas DeMartino carried Linda, and his wife, Jean, holds Lenore during walk in Miami. Yesterday the DeMartinos gave an exclusive interview to NEWS reporter Martin McLaughlin in their attorney's office and said: "We are not hiding from the law... We have made Florida our home." —Stories on page 3

DAILY NEWS
NEW YORK'S PICTURE NEWSPAPER

De Martinos Win Lenore in Fla.

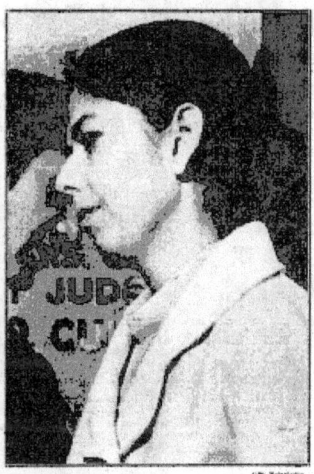

'Thank God! Thank God!'

Olga Scarpetta, Baby Lenore's natural mother, enters Miami court before hearing in which her bid to regain custody of child was denied. Ruling said that Nick and Jean DeMartino (←) should retain custody of the 13-month-old Lenore. After the ruling DeMartino collapsed in his chair and cried out: "Thank God! Thank God!" —*Story on page 5*

DeMARTINOS TO KEEP LENORE

Top Court Spurns Mom's Plea

'God Has Been So Good To Us'

Informed of U. S. Supreme Court's 8-to-1 decision ending the custody battle over their foster baby, Lenore, Nick and Jean DeMartino show their relief in Miami. They fled to Florida from Brooklyn more than a year ago with the baby, now 2½. Supreme Court's ruling upheld Florida court's decision that the DeMartinos, rather than Lenore's mother, Olga Scarpetta, should have custody. "God has been so good to us," said DeMartino.

Story on page 3

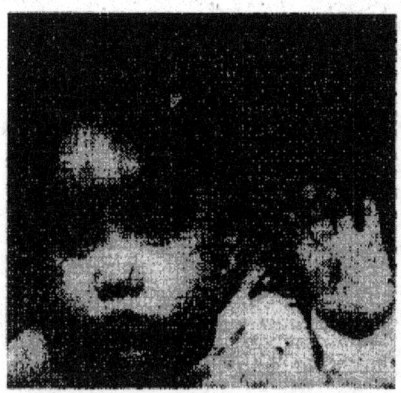

OBJECT OF court action is adopted daughter of Mr. and Mrs. Nicholas DeMartino of New York, Lenore, 1. (UPI)

HOLDING HANDS at press conference, Mr. and Mrs. Nicholas DeMartino discuss move to Miami with adopted daughter Lenore, after New York Supreme Court ordered return of child to its natural mother. At left is their attorney William Colsom. (UPI)

'We Are Not Shopping for Justice'

Adoption Couple in Fla. 'to Stay'

By STRATTON L. DOUTHAT

MIAMI (AP)—Mr. and Mrs. Nicholas DeMartino said yesterday they had moved to Florida to stay and would "respectfully decline" if authorities attempted to force them to return to New York and face a contempt citation for refusing to give up Lenore a baby girl they hope to make their own.

The girl, Lenore, who spent almost all her year-old life with the couple in Brooklyn, became the object of a court fight by her natural mother, who changed her mind about giving the child up before the adoption by the DeMartinos became final.

Both DeMartinos repeatedly denied they had moved to Miami to evade a New York State Supreme Court judge's contempt citation. He sentenced them 30 days in jail each for their failure to surrender Lenore following rulings that terminated adoption proceedings.

Justice Charles Loreto handed down the order Thursday after learning the DeMartinos had left New York. His order stipulated their arrest should they be found in the state.

"We honeymooned in Florida 16 years ago," DeMartino told a news conference in his attorney's downtown Miami office. "We've always liked it and we decided to move down. We are not shopping for justice."

The DeMartinos moved after losing a series of court decisions that followed hearings from which they were banned. New York courts ruled the baby's natural mother, Olga Scarpetta, 32, could have the baby back again.

New York authorities decreed the matter was strictly a legal question between Miss Scarpetta and the adoption agency that had referred Lenore to the DeMartinos.

The agency maintained Miss Scarpetta had not sought the return of her child until after the six-month cutoff period stipulated by New York law. The DeMartinos have appealed to the U.S. Supreme Court.

Neither Lenore nor Linda, the DeMartinos' 4-year-old adopted daughter, was present at the news conference.

Asked to what lengths she would go to keep Lenore, Mrs. DeMartino replied: "Ask any mother to what end she would go in order to keep her child."

Later she was asked if there was any way she would allow her family to be separated. She replied: "There have been cases where mothers fled countries to keep armed men from entering their homes and taking their children away. However, we have moved to Florida to live permanently. We're not running away. The girls love it here in the wide open spaces."

Joseph Zalk, attorney for Miss Scarpetta, said in New York that he had no comment on the DeMartinos' news conference.

"We will have to go to Florida to introduce habeas corpus action," Zalk said, "to regain custody of the child there."

HELP SAVE THE DE MARTINO BABY

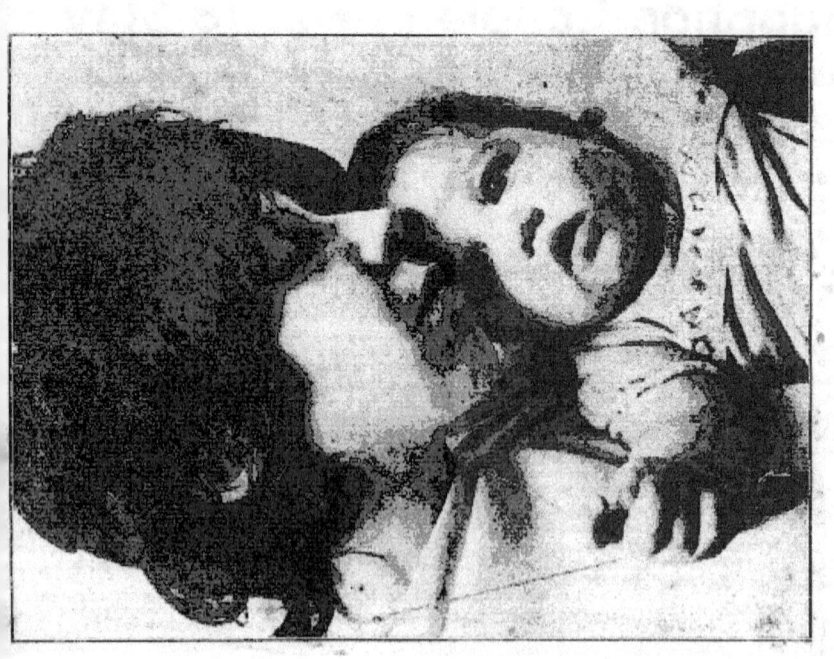

TO WHOM THIS MAY CONCERN

We the undersigned having been informed of the facts involved in the case of Olga Scarpetta against the Spence-Chapin adoption service feel, that the De Martino family should have their day in court as a simple matter of justice. No family should be torn apart and especially in this case where the best interests of a child are at stake. The oral uninvestigated statements of a party should not have been enough in so important a case.

We therefore urge that the De Martino s be allowed to come into this case which so vitally affects them and their baby Lenore.

NAME	ADDRESS	CITY/STATE
1		
2		
3		
4		
5		
6		
7		
8		
9		
10		
11		
12		
13		
14		
15		
16		
17		
18		
19		
20		
21		
22		
23		
24		
25		

Supreme Court of Florida
Office of the State Courts Administrator

Upon the advice of all participating in the Guardian Ad Litem Training Program in the _Eleventh_ Judicial Circuit, _Dade_ County

Jean De Martino

is recognized for dedication in the representation of the best interests of
abused and neglected children, and is commended for service
to the Court and its Agencies in the pursuit of justice;

In witness whereof, we have caused this certificate to be signed by the
Supervising Judge of the Juvenile Division, the chairperson of the
Guardian Ad Litem Advisory Board, and the
Circuit Coordinator of the Guardian Ad Litem Program.

Anna Mae Rose
Chairperson, Advisory Board

Juvenile Judge

Lorie Goodman
Circuit Coordinator, Guardian Ad Litem Program

Jean DeMartino

Thanks For Bringing Our Office System Out of the Dark Ages

STATE OF FLORIDA
GUARDIAN AD LITEM
PROGRAM

December 17, 1987

www.ingramcontent.com/pod-product-compliance
Lightning Source LLC
Chambersburg PA
CBHW061502180526
45171CB00001B/11

9781479321520